ARIANISM AFTER ARIUS

ARIANISM AFTER ARIUS

Essays on the Development of the
Fourth Century Trinitarian Conflicts

Edited by
Michel R. Barnes
and Daniel H. Williams

T&T CLARK
EDINBURGH

T&T Clark Ltd
59 George Street
Edinburgh EH2 2LQ
Scotland

First Published 1993

ISBN 0 567 09641 6

British Library Cataloguing-in-Publication Data
A catalogue record for this book is available from the British Library

Typeset by Buccleuch Printers Ltd, Hawick
Printed and bound in Great Britain by Bookcraft, Avon

CONTENTS

LIST OF CONTRIBUTORS

Dr Michel R. Barnes is Assistant Professor of Patristic History and Theology at Marquette University, Milwaukee, Wisconsin.

Rev. Dr Joseph T. Lienhard, S.J., is Professor of Theology and currently Chair of the Theology Department of Fordham University, The Bronx, New York.

Dr Winrich A. Löhr is Assistent für Kirchengeschichte, Evangelischtheologische Fakultät der Universität Bonn.

Dr Rebecca Lyman is Associate Professor of Early Church History at The Church Divinity School of the Pacific, Berkeley, California.

Dr Frederick Norris is Professor of Christian Doctrine at Emmanuel School of Religion, Johnson City, Tennessee.

Rev. Dr Michael Slusser is Associate Professor of Theology at Duquesne University, Pittsburgh, Pennsylvania.

Dr Kelley McCarthy Spoerl is an Instructor in Humanities at St. Anselm College, Manchester, New Hampshire.

Rev. Dr Richard P. Vaggione, O.H.C., is a monk of the Incarnation Priory, Berkeley, California.

Rev. Dr Maurice Wiles recently retired as the Regius Professor of Divinity in the University of Oxford and Canon of Christ Church.

Rev. Dr Daniel H. Williams is pastor of the First Baptist Church of Crafton, Pittsburgh, Pennsylvania, and a Research Associate with the Department of Religious Studies, University of Pittsburgh.

Rev. Dr Rowan Williams is now the Bishop of Monmouth, Newport, Gwent, having previously served as the Lady Margaret Professor of Divinity at the University of Oxford and as Canon of Christ Church.

PREFACE

This collection of essays was an idea conceived while we were graduate students listening to a lecture on 'Arianism' in the fourth century. It seemed to us then, as it does now, that this topic has been particularly susceptible to misinterpretation through generations of theological biases and historical over-simplifications. Despite the appearance of many publications over the last two decades which have addressed such problems, we are far from achieving a new scholarly consensus about the struggle over 'Arianism' and its significance for intellectual history. This is especially true with regards to the second half of the fourth century to which our work is mainly directed. It is our hope that this volume will contribute to the ongoing dialogue of filtering and reconstructing a new emerging picture of the period.

The study of the fourth century trinitarian controversies is an immensely complicated field, and whatever we have been able to rightly discern in the preparation of this present study is only because – to coin a phrase from Alexander Ross – we have stood on the shoulders of giants. We are indeed indebted to the encouragement and ideas of a number of scholars, some of whom appear in this volume, who helped us at the initial stages of this project. Without their assistance, it is likely that this book would not have become a reality.

We also wish to acknowledge our gratefulness to the American Academy of Religion and to the Centre for Religious Studies, University of Toronto, for the generous grants which funded this project; and to Geoffrey Green of T&T Clark, for his flexibility and cooperation during the long editing process.

M. R. B.
D. H. W.

ABBREVIATIONS

CCSL   *Corpus Christanorum, series latina.* Turnout.

CPG   *Clavis patrum Graecorum,* ed. E. Dekkers. Turnout.

CSCO   *Corpus Scriptorum Christianorum Orientalium.* Louvain.

CSEL   *Corpus Scriptorum Ecclesiasticorum Latinorum.* Vienna.

CSHB   *Corpus Scriptorum Historiae Byzantinae.* Bonn.

CTh   *Theodosiani Libri XVI cum Constitutionibus Simonianis,* eds. T. Mommsen et P. M. Meyer. Berlin.

DTC   *Dictionnaire de théologie catholique.* Paris.

FC   *Fathers of the Church.* New York.

GCS   *Die Griechischen chrislichen Schriftstellar der ersten drei Jahrhunderte.* Leipzig; Berlin.

GNO   *Gregorii Nysseni Opera.* Leiden.

Hanson, *The Search*   R. P. C. Hanson, *The Search for the Christian Doctrine of God.* Edinburgh, 1988.

HE   *Historia ecclesiastica*

JEH   *Journal of Ecclesiastical Studies.* Oxford.

JRS   *Journal of Roman Studies.* London.

JTS   *Journal of Theological Studies.* Oxford.

Kopecek, *Neo-Arianism*   Thomas A. Kopecek *A History of Neo-Arianism.* 2 vols. Philadelphia, 1979.

Mansi   *Sacrorum conciliorum nova et amplissima collectio,* ed. J. D. Mansi. Florence 1759-1798.

NPNF	*Nicene and Post-Nicene Fathers of the Christian Church,* Second series, eds. P. Schaff and H. Wace. Grand Rapids.
Opitz	*Athanasius: Werke,* ed. Hans-Georg Optiz. Berlin.
PG	*Patrologiae cursus completus, series graeca.* Paris.
PL	*Patrologiae cursus completus, series latina.* Paris.
PLS	*Patrologiae cursus completus, series latina, supplementum.* Paris.
PO	*Patrologia Orientalis.* Paris.
PTS	*Patristiche Texte und Studium.* Berlin.
RHE	*Revue d'histoire ecclésiastique.* Louvain
SC	*Sources chrétiennes.* Paris.
TRE	*Theologische Realenzklopädie.* Berlin.
TU	*Texte und Untersuchungen.* Leipzig; Berlin.
Vaggione	Richard P. Vaggione, *Eunomius: The Extant Works.* Oxford: 1987.
VC	*Vigiliae Christianae.* Amsterdam.
Williams, *Arius*	*Arius: Heresy and Tradition.* London, 1987.
ZKG	*Zeitschrift für Kirchengeschichte.* Stuttgart.
ZNW	*Zeitschrift für die Neutestamentliche Wissenschaft und die Kunde der älteren Kirche.* Giessen; Berlin.

INTRODUCTION

The caricature of Arius as arch-heretic and founder of a rival movement to orthodoxy has been a standard feature of scholarship on early trinitarian development that dates back even to the end of the fourth century when Epiphanius published his catalogue of heresies:

> Arius and the Arians who are derived from him . . . [have] stirred up a cloud of dust against the church so that a great fire as well was ignited from him which consumed almost the entire Roman empire.[1]

Not only was Arius the originator of a kind of conspiracy against the church, but this conspiracy possessed a more or less defined body of alien, or heretical, beliefs to which all those associated are called 'Arians'.[2]

One cannot overstate the effect that such a portrayal has had on subsequent writers of Christian doctrinal history unto the present day.[3] Only in the second half of our century was this general view seriously questioned in a number of articles by patristic scholars who disputed the origins of Arius' theology as the product of Antiochene exegesis, or of philosophical rationalism, or as simply unspiritual and insensitive to the time-honoured teachings of the Christian faith.[4]

---

[1] *Panarion haer.* 69. 1.1–2.1, trans. P. R. Amidon, *The Panarion of St. Epiphanius, Bishop of Salamis: Selected Passages* (Oxford: Oxford University Press, 1990), 261.

[2] This kind of argument is of course central to Athanasius' attacks against opponents, e.g., *Orationes contra Arianos* I. 1.2–3.

[3] As R. P. C. Hanson emphasizes in 'The Achievement of Orthodoxy in the Fourth Century AD', in *The Making of Orthodoxy: Essays in Honour of Henry Chadwick*, ed. Rowan Williams (Cambridge: Cambridge University Press, 1989), 142 ff. See M. Slusser's article below for the interpretive history of Arius and 'Arianism' from late antiquity to before Harnack; and the survey of 19th and 20th century scholarship in R. Williams, *Arius: Heresy and Tradition* (London: Darton, Longman, and Todd, 1987), 2–16.

[4] One of the landmark challenges to the traditionally held views about Arius comes from M. Wiles in his response to T. Pollard, 'In Defence of Arius', JTS 13 (1962), 339–347. Furthermore, even these scholarly ideas for the origins of Arius' theology are now questioned, particularly the hypothesis of a 'philosophical rationalism'. See, for example, the recent treatments of the role of philosophical ideas in the doctrinal disputes by Williams, *Arius*, 181–229; and Wiles, 'The Philosophy in Christianity: Arius and Athanasius', in Godfrey Vesey, ed., *The Philosophy in Christianity* (Cambridge: Cambridge University Press, 1989), 41–52.

Instead, Arius has come to be placed firmly within the theological and philosophical traditions of the third century inherited by the church at Alexandria where he was presbyter. What little we know about the views which Arius actually espoused suggest that they were derived from his interpretation of these traditions, enabling him to be no better and no less prepared than his contemporaries to deal with problematic questions about the relations within the godhead.

This more contextual approach eventually touched off what might be called – to use a well-worn phrase – a new quest for the historical Arius; a quest that witnessed a renewed interest in the issues of fourth-century 'Arianism', having produced several book-length treatments by M. Simonetti, *La crisi ariana nel IV secolo* (1975), R. Lorenz, *Arius judaizans?* (1978), R. Gregg and D. Groh, *Early Arianism: A View of Salvation* (1981), R. Williams, *Arius: Heresy and Tradition* (1987) and, most recently, R. P. C. Hanson's *The Search for the Christian Doctrine of God* (1988). A focus on unveiling the historical Arius and re-interpreting subsequent theological debates was also manifest at the 1983 International Patristics Conference at Oxford, from which resulted a volume of select papers edited by R. Gregg. This collection, like most of the monographs just mentioned, was meant to provide answers to the question: 'what is Arianism?',[5] and especially, how it should be viewed through the lens of its own sources rather than through the critical eyes of its opponents.

Perhaps the most central finding in the last fifteen years of renewed research on the subject has been to show how peripheral the person of Arius was to the actual debates which occupied the Church for most of the century. This has been one of the main effects in the 'rehabilitation of Arius' by recognizing the distance between the influence of the unfortunate heresiarch and the theological crisis he is alleged to have provoked.[6] Athanasius and those who came after him may have referred to those who oppose Nicene theology as 'Arians' or 'Ariomaniacs', but it is nevertheless true that the name of Arius appears hardly at all in the literature of the first generation of 'Arians', and the paucity of Arius' own writings seem to argue against his supposed

[5] As stated by Gregg in the introduction, *Arianism: Historical and Theological Reassessments,* Patristic Monograph Series No. 11 (Cambridge, Mass.: Philadelphia Patristic Foundation, 1985), iii.

[6] Thus Rowan Williams' explanation in *Arius,* 166 ff., that it was the Lucianists, not Arius, who were in large part the progenitors of 'Arianism'.

importance. Later on, those accused of being followers of Arius either denied they were 'Arians'[7] or disavowed any formal connection to Arius.[8] Arius himself, therefore had only a minor role in the theological debates which were reputed to be a conflict over his views and which eventually bore his name. It was Athanasius' great polemical success to cast his opponents as 'Arians', yet that success has hidden the character of the debate in the second half of the fourth century.

Given the above conclusions, we believe that there is a continuing need for a modification of language which has been so commonly used to refer to that period of theological turmoil known as the 'Arian Controversy'. With justification did Hanson reject such a phrase as a serious misnomer.[9] For the term 'Arian' obscures rather than clarifies the complexities of differing theological, political and ecclesiastical groups which are found after the deaths of Arius and Constantine (as is true of the well-worn label 'orthodoxy'). The same can be said about the word 'controversy', which assumes a kind of linear evolution of the issues proceeding from Alexandria to the rest of the Roman empire that hardly does justice to a fragmented situation. By the 350s and 360s new alliances and parties make up the theological landscape which favour the definitional position taken at Nicaea (such as the Marcellians, Meletians or Luciferians), or those who articulate their position in opposition to Nicaea (such as the Greek and Latin Homoians or the Eunomians). In some cases classification is altogether inadequate to describe some groups, like the so-called 'Semi-Arians' (a wholly misplaced epithet, also coined by Epiphanius), who rejected the Nicene terminology of the *homoousios* of the Father and the Son, and yet are the most direct precursors of

[7] Palladius' (of Ratiaria) counters Ambrose's charge of Arianism with the argument that he (and his associates) are not Arians (*Scholia Ariana* 337r, 50–51 [SC 367 274]), and the unknown writer of a late fourth century work against pro-Nicenes expresses resentment at being labeled 'Arians' (Frag. 6. V. 277 [CCSL 87 237]).

[8] The disclaimer of the bishops in the so-called 'First Formula of Antioch' (A.D. 341) not to be followers of Arius because they should not be guided by a presbyter is well known (Socrates HE II. 10 [Hahn, 183]). Cf. *Gesta* of the synod of Aquileia (381) where Palladius, who is accused of consenting to Arian doctrines, replies with words to the effect that he does not recognize Arius as an authority (*Gesta* 14 [CSEL 82.3 334]; 25 [82.3. 341]) and does not follow Arius (*Gesta* 12 [82.3 333]). Where the name of Arius is invoked by later anti-Nicene writers, it is not as an ecclesiastical authority figure but as one who bore witness to the same traditional interpretations of faith.

[9] *The Search*, xvii–xviii.

the Cappadocians. One can also point to the instance of a western bishop, Germinius of Sirmium, who publicly and repeatedly espoused creeds which were Homoian (i.e., 'Arian') but refused to ally himself with the political tactics of his anti-Nicene colleagues.

The present challenge for patristic study of the fourth century trinitarian debates, in our judgement, centres on two areas in particular.

First, there is the problem of language due in large part to the new ways in which scholarship is increasingly recognizing the different dialectics that formed the various theologies and parties of the period. As the background and character of distinct ecclesiastical groups become better understood, so a new terminology will have to be created, even though substitutes are just as hard to invent, and the term 'Arianism', despite its obvious distortions, continues to function as a widely recognized label. For these reasons, the opening essays in this volume wrestle with the problem of classification and its implications for reworking historical description.

A second problem that needs to be addressed is how we should link the later conflicts over the doctrine of the Trinity with those earlier events that spawned them. What is our historical justification for thinking that the kind of theologies which characterized a Eunomius, Ufilia or Ambrose are a 'development' from the council of Nicaea and its immediate aftermath? Again, the removal of old classifications creates the need to find new solutions. For example, the reader will find that, compared to the 1983 collection on Arianism, a significant number of papers in the present collection utilize a sense of the 'socio-political' contexts of the debates as well as the doctrinal. Nonetheless, given the multiple permutations of groups and schisms which eventually grew out of the original dissensions of the 320s and 330s, it is difficult to find a common ground of approach for interpreting the particulars. And with the exception of works like M. Meslin, *Les Ariens d'Occident 335–430* (1967), Thomas A. Kopecek, *A History of Neo-Arianism* (1979), H. C. Brennecke, *Studien zur Geschichte der Homöer. Der Osten bis zum Ende der homoischen Reichskirche* (1988),[10]

---

[10] One can also point to a number of critical texts now available which have greatly facilitated studies in later 'Arianism', such as R. Gryson, *Scolies Ariennes sur le concile d'Aquilée,* SC 267; idem, ed. *Scripta Ariana Latina,* CCSL 87, and R. P. Vaggione, *Eunomius: The Extant Works* (Oxford: Clarendon Press, 1987).

much less scholarly attention has been given to the later forms of 'Arianism' and its opponents. The later states of the debate reveal, in fact, the limits of the strategy of reducing non-Nicenes to 'Arians'. Although Athanasius' polemical categories are accepted by Epiphanius and Latin pro-Nicenes such as Marius Victorinus and Ambrose of Milan, few Greek polemicists, even if they are clearly pro-Nicene, bother to refute Arius.[11]

If the last couple of decades have tended to focus on answering the question 'what is "Arianism"?', it is our intent in this volume to turn attention to the inquiry, 'what did "Arianism" become?', and in what ways did the new generation of pro-Nicenes respond? This can be considered the common denominator for the very different articles which appear in this collection. Each contributor deals with a piece (or pieces) of the complex mosaic which make up the dynamics of the period and attempts to reinterpret its historical significance in light of new research. Obviously a multi-authored work will not produce a unified approach to the problems of language or historical method, much less a single solution. Yet each of the authors who appear in this book was invited on the basis of their scholarly knowledge and sensitivity to such issues. At the very least it can be said that the breadth of this collection represents the present status of studies on 'Arianism' in the fourth century and new trends in its research.

[11] Ironically, the western acceptance of Athanasius' rhetoric of *Arius redivivus* has been coupled with the modern scholarly notion that 'Arianism' was primarily an *eastern* problem.

I
HISTORICAL AND
THEOLOGICAL DEFINITION

Chapter 1

TRADITIONAL VIEWS OF LATE ARIANISM[1]

Michael Slusser

Historical sciences . . . recognise the irreducible quirkiness that history entails, and acknowledge the limited power of present circumstances to impose or elicit optimal solutions; the queen among their disciplines is taxonomy, the Cinderella of the sciences.[2]

If scholars have difficulty in agreeing on an account of the later phases of the Arian crisis, part of the reason lies in the centuries of confusion about the taxonomy of the parties and doctrines involved. Terms have been used inconsistently and to a great extent uncritically, and this has infected the terminology with such imprecision that it is hard to imagine how a new normative critical portrayal can arise.[3] The confusion is made more durable by the hundreds of years of virtually unquestioned usage; while particular voices have been raised at various times about one term or another, the whole unsystematic complex needs to be overhauled. The present paper strives to facilitate that overhaul by reviewing the attempts of many writers over fifteen centuries to put into order what their sources told them about the later phases of the Arian crisis. This account is limited in its scope: the reader will not find here a fresh review of the contemporary sources on the Arian controversy themselves, much less an attempt to produce a new and better account of the unfolding of the later phases of Arianism.[4]

---

[1] The research for this article was undertaken with the assistance of a grant from the National Endowment for the Humanities.
[2] Stephen Jay Gould, *The Flamingo's Smile* (New York: W. W. Norton, 1985) 18.
[3] See the comments of Richard P. Vaggione in his review of R. P. C. Hanson, *The Search for the Christian Doctrine of God*, in *Patristics* 19, 2 (January 1991), especially, 'That the problem lies in the categories and not in the skill with which they are applied rapidly becomes obvious . . .'
[4] Thus the works of Theodoret and Augustine on heresies will be examined, but not Theodoret's *HE*, since it can be regarded as more source than evaluation, or Augustine's own controversies with Arians.

Likewise, modern discussions of Arianism starting with Adolph Harnack have been left to the reader's personal researches. Only the older works will be reviewed here, as far as possible in chronological order.

Filastrius of Brescia, who wrote his *Diuersarum hereseon liber* sometime in the 380s,[5] ought to have been well-informed about the vestiges of Arianism in the churches of northern Italy, but his account of the various branches of the Arian movement is terse and betrays no contact with or immediate concern about the heresy. He describes the Arians as those who believed 'that the Son of God was like to God; but saying that this was only in name, and not from believing that he was from the divine substance of the Father himself'. Arians are then distinguished from the *Semiarriani* and *Eunomiani*: the *Semiarriani* diverged from orthodoxy only in their belief that the Holy Spirit was a creature, not from the divine substance; whereas the *Eunomiani* held the more drastic view that the Son was the Father's creature, the Spirit the Son's, so that they were substances as different as gold, silver and bronze.[6]

A somewhat later writer, apparently active in Rome, is known today as Pseudo-Hegemonius.[7] This writer has quite a different description of the original Arian heresy: it said 'there is one God the Father, and his Son our Lord Jesus Christ and the Holy Spirit is [are?] a son by adoption, not by nature, and the Spirit is as remote from the Son as the Son is from the Father.' The Arian movement then split into three. Eunomius and the Eunomians held that where the nature is different things cannot be alike, and applied that to the Father and Son, 'because they were of a different substance'; Macedonius and the Macedonians said that the Son is like the Father in all things; the Arians (apparently not the original ones) say only that the Son is like the Father.[8]

Augustine in his *De haeresibus ad Quodvultdeum* makes large use of Filastrius and Epiphanius – the *Anakephaleiosis*, not the *Panarion*.[9]

---

[5] The estimate is that of F. Heylen. *Filastrius Brixiensis, Diuersarum hereseon liber*, CCSL 9 209.

[6] These are heresies 66, 67, and 68 respectively in Filastrius' catalogue (CCSL 9 244–5).

[7] Ps. Hegemonii, *Aduersus haereses*, (CCSL 9 325–9).

[8] Lines 35–46, (CCSL 9 328).

[9] *Ep.* 222, 2, in Aurelius Augustinus, *De haeresibus ad Quodvultdeum*, ed. R. Vander Plaetse and C. Beukers, (CCSL 5L 46 277). In fact, he tells Quodvultdeus that if someone in Carthage can read Epiphanius' Greek, Quodvultdeus could help Augustine instead of the other way around.

According to Bardy, however, Augustine supplements his sources with the knowledge he gained from his personal contacts with Arians.[10] The Arians' main error is their refusal to say that the Father, Son and Holy Spirit are of 'one and the same nature and substance, or, to put it more expressly, essence (which in Greek is called *ousia*); but that the Son is a creature, the Spirit creature of a creature.'[11] In addition, Augustine recognises Semiarians, Macedonians, and Aetians or Eunomians. His notice on the Semiarians, derived from the *Anakephaleiosis,* says that 'they say that the Son is of like essence to the Father, as if they were not full Arians – as if Arians would not even say "like," though Eunomians are reported to say this.'[12] Eunomians assert that the Son is completely unlike the Father, and the Holy Spirit unlike him.[13] Macedonians 'say the Father and the Son are of one substance or essence, but are unwilling to believe this of the Holy Spirit, saying he is a creature.' Augustine adds that some people call this last group Semiarians, as siding partly with the Arians, partly with the orthodox; and some think that the Holy Spirit is the godhead of the Father and the Son and has no proper substance of its own.[14] Augustine draws a more differentiated picture than either Filastrius or Pseudo-Hegemonius, probably thanks to the *Anakephaleiosis,* but he does not succeed in resolving the perplexing terminology which he finds in his sources. He may have felt no need for more detailed and accurate knowledge; his *De trinitate* shows hardly any sign of relationship to the Arian controversy.

At the other end of the Mediterranean, Theodoret of Cyr produced a *Haereticarum fabularum compendium.*[15] His description of the Arians emphasises their notion that Christ's soul was replaced by the godhead and their forsaking of the apostolic doxology (Matt. 28:19).[16] He has only one other basic category of Arian heretics, the

---

[10] G. Bardy, 'Le "De haeresibus" et ses Sources,' *Miscellanea Agostiniana* II (Roma: Tipografia Poliglotta Vaticana, 1931), 415. On Augustine's late works dealing with the Arians, see Manlio Simonetti, 'S. Agostino e gli Ariani,' *Revue des Études Augustiniennes* 13 (1967) 55–84.

[11] *Haer.* 49 (CCSL 46 320–1).

[12] *Haer.* 51 (CCSL 46 322).

[13] *Haer.* 54 (CCSL 46 324).

[14] *Haer.* 52 (CCSL 46 322–3).

[15] PG 83 339-555.

[16] *Haer. fab. comp.* 5.1 (PG 83 413AB).

Eunomians, about whose founder and views he gives detailed information.[17] He names three minor sects of Arians,[18] but he does not mention Semiarians by that term, speaking instead of Macedonius as an individual who 'blasphemed the Holy Spirit as Arius and Eunomius did,' and said that the Son was like the Father in all things but preferred 'of like essence' to 'of the same essence.'[19]

The authorship and date of Pseudo-Leontius, De sectis, are unclear, but it comes from around 600 C.E.[20] It portrays the trinitarian debates in terms of a contrast between Sabellius, 'who said that the holy Trinity had one nature and one subsistence with many names,' and Arius, who said it had 'three subsistences and three disparate natures. For he said that the Father was first, and [the others were] made for the fashioning of the rest of the things created by him.'[21] A separate notice on Arianism describes it in more conventional terms, as saying that the Son was a creature of God, and likewise the Holy Spirit, and that in the incarnation the body of Christ was devoid of soul.[22] The Macedonians, by calling the Holy Spirit a creature, 'joined halfway in the sin of Arius concerning the godhead';[23] this is as close as De sectis gets to calling anyone a Semiarian. John of Damascus likewise says that the Arians 'say the Son of God is a creature, and the Holy Spirit a creature of a creature,' and portrays the Arian Christ as lacking a soul.[24] Neither the De sectis nor John has a separate notice on Anomoeans or Eunomians; perhaps they are what these writers mean by Arians. John has, however, an unusually detailed notice on Semiarians:

> They call the Son a creature, but in ironic fashion they say he is a creature 'not as one of the creatures. But,' they say, 'we call him Son, but since no passion reaches the Father in his begetting we call him created.'

[17] Haer. fab. comp. 4.3 (PG 83 417A–421B).
[18] The Psathyrians, Cyrtians, and Doulians; Haer. fab. comp. 4.4 (PG 83 421CD), and 4.5 (PG 83 424A).
[19] Haer. fab. comp. 4.5 (PG 83 424A).
[20] PG 86. 1193–268; see B. Altaner and A. Stuiber, Patrologie (Freiburg: Herder, 1978), 510. Maryse Waegeman, 'The Old Testament Canon in the Treatise De Sectis,' L'Antiquité Classique 50 (1981), 813, describes it as 'dating from the sixth or seventh century.'
[21] De sectis 1.4 (PG 86 1197D).
[22] De sectis 3.4 (PG 86 1216CD).
[23] De sectis 4.1 (PG 86 1217D–1220A).
[24] John of Damascus, De haeresibus (PG 94 677–780), at De haer. 69 (PG 94 720B).

The Spirit is clearly a creature for the Semiarians; while some would accept the term 'of like substance,' others reject even that close a tie.[25] Next come Pneumatomachians (Macedonius is not named – nor are any individual Semiarians mentioned by name) who call the Holy Spirit created, 'only a hallowing power.'[26]

Isidore of Seville, who gathered up many of the fragments of the Latin tradition, has little to add to our dossier. In the eighth book of his *Etymologies* he lists Photinians, Aetians, Origenians, Noetians, Sabellians, Arians, Macedonians, Apollinarians.[27] The order in which he lists heresies shows how far the historical progression of the Arian controversy had faded from consciousness. There is also a small work *De haeresibus* assigned to Isidore of Seville by A.C. Vega,[28] which speaks of Fotinians, Arians, Sabellians, Macedonians, Noetians, and Aetians.[29]

The medieval Latin West was not, however, deprived of better historical information on the Arian controversy, for it had the *Historia ecclesiastica tripartita,* a compilation and translation of passages drawn from the histories of Theodoret, Socrates, and Sozomen, with reference also to the work of Theodore Anagnostes.[30] Almost every important monastery in western Europe had a copy in its library,[31] and it was one of the earlier patristic texts to be published after the invention of printing, appearing in five editions by 1500. It

---

[25] *De Haer.* 73 (PG 94 721B).

[26] *De Haer.* 74 (PG 94 724A). John shows an understanding attitude towards Marcellus of Ancyra. Of the writers we have looked at so far, only Theodoret has described Marcellus, saying that like Sabellius he 'denied the triad of hypostases' with his theory of extension from the Father's divinity; John repeats that criticism, but claims that after debate Marcellus came around to a way of thinking acceptable to the orthodox.

[27] *Etymol.* 8.5 (PL 82 301B–2B). Curiously he describes the Donatists as teaching an unequal Trinity; (PL 82 302C).

[28] *S. Isidori Hispalensis Episcopi De Haeresibus liber,* ed. A.C. Vega, Scriptores ecclesiastici Hispano-Latini veteris et medii aevi 5 (Escorial: Typis Augustianianis Monasterii, 1940); R.J.H. Collins, 'Isidor von Sevilla,' *Theologische Realenzyklopädie* 16, 312. I doubt if they can be from the same author, as the *Etymologies* 8.5.55 describes 'Luciferians' in historical terms drawn from the career of Lucifer of Cagliari, while the other work (heresy 46) says, 'Luciferiani dicunt animam de carne et de carnis substantia propagatam.'

[29] Heresies 15, 17, 18, 19, 23 and 27 respectively. The texts are also printed in PLS 4 1815–20.

[30] Edited by W. Jacob and R. Hanslik (CSEL 71). This *Historia tripartita* is often spoken of as the work of Cassiodorus, but one of the members of his community, Epiphanius, really did the work.

[31] Walter Jacob, *Die handschriftliche Überlieferung der sogenannten Historia Tripartita des Epiphanius-Cassiodor,* TU 59: 4.

did not, however, have much influence on the way late Arians were described by medieval theological writers. Peter Abailard, who in his *Sic et Non* presents a more extensive set of quotations relative to the issues involved in Arianism than any other medieval author I have seen, does not quote the *Historia Tripartita*.[32]

The basic theological textbook of the medieval universities, Peter Lombard's *Sententiae,* makes only passing references to Arianism,[33] and while the name of Eunomius appears, no student is likely to have left the study of Lombard with a sense that Arian doctrine went through stages. Thomas Aquinas seems equally innocent of a historical perspective on Arianism. In the sixteenth century, stimulated perhaps by Beatus Rhenanus' very successful edition of the *Historia Tripartita,*[34] theologians became aware once more of some of the complexities of the fourth century debates.

Michael Servetus, who called the standard doctrine of the Trinity into question in his vigorous tracts,[35] is primarily concerned that, if the Word was a divine hypostasis, we do not know our divine savior. Servetus holds that Jesus Christ is God and son of God; he emphasises the contrast between his teaching and that of Arius, who, 'since he most stupidly thought differently of the son than of the father, and couldn't grasp Christ's glory, introduced a new creature above the human level,' a new and separate entity.[36] For Servetus, the

---

[32] Peter Abailard, *Sic et Non. A Critical Edition,* ed. Blanche B. Boyer and Richard McKeon (Chicago: University of Chicago Press, 1976–77). The most relevant *quaestiones* are VI-XXIV, LXVI-LXVII, and LXXI.

[33] Petrus Lombardus, *Sententiae in IV libris distinctae,* 3rd ed., SpicBon 4–5 (Grottaferrata: Editiones Collegii S. Bonaventurae ad Claras Aquas, 1971 & 1981). See book 1, dist. 23, c. 5; dist. 25, c. 3; dist. 28, c. 4, dist. 31, c. 4; dist. 34, c. 5, and for Eunomius, dist. 6, c.un.

[34] Published together with Rufinus' translation of Eusebius, *Historia ecclesiastica,* by Joannes Frobenius in Basel, 1523, and reprinted in 1528, 1535, 1539, 1544; and without the Eusebius in 1548. Martin Luther's 1539 treatise, *Von den Konziliis und Kirchen* (WA 50), depends on it for a sketch of Macedonian doctrine.

[35] *De Trinitatis erroribus libri septem* (1531); *Dialogorum de Trinitate libri duo. De Iusticia Regni Christi, Capitula Quatuor* (1531); *Christianismi restitutio* (1553). None of the books carried identification of the publisher or place of publication.

[36] *De Trinitatis erroribus,* f. 13v (no page numbers were printed in the 1531–2 works, at least in the one-volume edition in the Bodleian Library, Oxford). 'Nam Arrius, quum [quem?] de filio diversum à patre sentiebat stultissime, & Christi gloriae incapacissimus, novam creaturam excellentiorem homine introduxit, cum tamen ea seclusa & seclusa omni distinctione potuisset concedere, Pater me maior est. Sed separatarum rerum pluralitatem philosophari uolens, foedissime lapsus est.'

imagining of trinitarian entities is portrayed as the cause of all the useless discussions of equality or inequality.[37] The Arians separate the second entity from the first, and subordinate it; Macedonius denies that the third entity is God; the Aetians and Eunomians say they are different things; the Origenians rave that the son cannot see the father, nor the spirit the son; Maximinus feared that the father would be a part of God, and each person a third of the Trinity. Servetus also manages to include Nestorius, Eutyches, the Monarchians, Sabellians and Alogi in his catalogue.[38] Eunomius is blamed for identifying the Spirit of God with our created spirit.[39] The 1553 book, directed by its title at the *Institutes* of John Calvin, is a later revised edition of the 1531 volume; in it, Servetus amplifies the catalogue of trinitarian heresies summarised above, and says, 'In this Aetius and Eunomius differ from Arius, in that he says those entities are unequal but like, while they say they are both unequal and unlike.'[40] Calvin's counterattacks did not raise the issue of Arianism.[41]

A new genre of writing began with the remarkable *Ecclesiastica historia* of Matthias Flacius and his associates,[42] better known as the 'Magdeburg Centuriators.' They summarised documentary sources under sixteen different headings, in order to give readers an overview of what had happened in the church in each century up to the late Middle Ages. They seldom give their own views, so their editorial choices in the use of quotations from ancient authors are our main

---

[37] ibid., f. 86v: '. . . et quaerere hic de aequalitate uel inaequalitate naturae, est pascere uentos, quia non est nisi res una, nec scriptura, nec antiquiores [by whom Servetus generally means second-century writers] unquàm in hac re aequalitate uel inaequalitate meminerunt, imò nec cogitarunt, sed primus Eunomius hanc philosophiam adinuenit in Spiritu, sicut Aëtius in Verbo.'

[38] ibid., ff. 38v–39r.

[39] ibid., f. 66v.

[40] *Christianismi restitutio*, 37.

[41] *Defensio Orthodoxae Fidei de Sacra Trinitate contra prodigiosos errores Michaelis Serveti Hispani* (Oliva: Roberti Stephani, 1554) reprinted in G. Baum, E. Cunitz & E. Reuss (ed.), *Ioannis Calvini Opera quae supersunt omnia*, vol. 8 (Brusvigae: C. A. Schwetschke et Filium, 1970).

[42] *Ecclesiastica historia, integram ecclesiae Christi ideam, quantum ad locum, Propagationem, Persecutionem, Tranquillitatem, Doctrinam, Haereses, Caeremonias, Gubernationem, Schismata, Synodos, Personas, Miracula, Martyria, Religiones extra Ecclesiam, & statum Imperii politicum attinet, secundum singulas Centurias, perspicuo ordine complectens* . . . Per aliquot studiosos & pios viros [Matthias Flacius Illyricus, Iohannes Wigandus, Matthaeus Iudex, Basilius Faber] in urbe Magdeburgica (Basiliae: Ioannem Oporinum, 1559–74).

evidence for their views. In the 'Fourth Century,'[43] information on our topic comes up in chapters five *(De haeresibus)*, eight *(De schismatibus)*, ten *(De Episcoporum et Doctorum vitis)* and eleven *(De haereticis)*. They distinguish the heresy of Arius from later heresies, those of Eusebius of Nicomedia, Asterius,[44] and the Semiarians. They notice the way in which some ancient sources treat the Semiarians as orthodox, others as heretical: 'Hence it is obvious that the Semiarians differed from each other in their views.'[45] Then come Macedonians, the heresy of Marcellus and Photinus, and the Luciferians;[46] the heresy of the Aetians or Eunomians, that of the Pneumatomachians, the Acacians, and finally the mysterious heresy of Dorotheus and the Psatyrians or Gothians: 'At Constantinople these heresies sprang up among the Arians, and were the reason why the Arians were divided into separate congregations.'[47] Under the heading of schisms they describe several which are connected with the progress of Arianism. Under the reign of Constantius they list the following: at Alexandria after the death of Arius, and at Constantinople after the death of Alexander; between Acacius of Caesarea and Cyril of Jerusalem; at Antioch, where the onus for the schism is placed on those who refuse to communicate with Meletius; the 'great schism between Easterners and Westerners,' over recognition of Paul of Constantinople and Athanasius; trouble at Rome over Liberius; the monks who withdrew themselves from the communion of Gregory Nazianzen's father; and a schism in Caesarea of Cappadocia.[48] Under Julian, the schism at Antioch reappears, and the Meletians and Eustathians are said to be divided, yet both kept the Nicene faith; Lucifer of Cagliari's nefarious part is noted, as well as the schism between him and Eusebius.[49] Under Valentinian and Valens they list the 'continuation of the schism among the homoousians at Antioch'; a schism among the Arians in Constantinople; and others at Cyzicus, in Rome (over the

---

[43] *Quarta Centuria ecclesiasticae historiae* (Basilium: Ioannem Oporinum, 1560). It takes up all of vol. 2 of the series.

[44] ibid., II:357–62.

[45] ibid., II:362–3.

[46] ibid., II:364–73.

[47] Eunomians: ibid. II:390–395; Pneumatomachians: II:396–7; Acacians: II:399; internal heresies in Constantinople: II:404.

[48] ibid., II:594–7.

[49] ibid., II:598.

election of Damasus), Milan, Caesarea again, and Armenia.[50] The
reigns of Gratian and Theodosius saw five schisms in Antioch and
two in Constantinople.[51] With the exception of the incidents in
Cappadocia and Armenia, the Centuriators take the descriptions of
all these schisms from the histories of Socrates, Sozomen, and
Theodoret.

In their treatment of individuals, the Centuriators list Eusebius of
Caesarea with the 'bishops and doctors,' saying that 'he was *ex professo*
an Arian before the Council of Nicaea, where he thought better of it,
assented to the faith of the orthodox fathers, and professed it in the
public creed.'[52] That enables them not to list him with the Arian
heretics, of whom they list fifty.[53] There are separate lists, without
duplication, of Macedonians,[54] Novatians, Luciferians, Marcellians,[55]
Apollinarians, Aetians,[56] Priscillianists and 'philosophers.' While the
Centuriators sometimes cite Epiphanius, they make virtually no
application to individuals of his category of 'Semiarians.'[57]

About thirty years later there appeared Caesar Baronius' great
compilation, the *Annales Ecclesiastici*.[58] Its title describes his
arrangement of material by years rather than centuries. While its
publication was motivated in part by the desire to outdo the
Centuriators, Baronius based his collection on his thirty years of
providing edifying episodes from church history to the devout people
who met every afternoon at the Oratory in Rome to study and pray.[59]

[50] ibid., II:599–601.
[51] ibid., II:605–8.
[52] ibid., II:913.
[53] ibid., II:1340–76.
[54] Macedonius, Marathonius, Eleusius, Sophronius, Eustathius and Eutropius;
II:1377–8.
[55] Restricted to Marcellus and Photinus; II:1389.
[56] Aetius, Eunomius, Uranius, Theophilus, Asphalius, Aerius; II:1389–95.
[57] They use the term only in II:852, during the discussion of the Council of
Constantinople in 381, and twice in II:967, where it is listed as a name applied to Basil of
Ancyra, and for the Pneumatomachians.
[58] The edition I used was *Annales Ecclesiastici*, Auctore Caesare Baronio Sorano . . .
Tomus Tertius. Editio novissima [i.e. 4th]. Antverpiae, ex officina Plantiniana, 1598; . . .
Tomus Quartus. Antverpiae ex officina Plantiniana, 1594. Baronius' wonderfully
successful work had already been translated into Italian, German, and Polish by 1592.
[59] '. . . Quam ob causam inter alia ex variis diversísque sanctorum Patrum scriptis ad
mores optimos instituendos accepta, Sanctorum vitae, & Ecclesiastica gesta narrantur;
quòd ad virtutis & pietatis studium in auditorum animis excitandum, exempla magnam
vim habeant.' This is from the preface to volume one, which is unpaginated.

His exposition is marked by a desire to edify, particularly with regard to the role of the Roman church,[60] and by detailed information about developments in the Latin West.[61]

Baronius, like the Centuriators, makes extensive use of ancient sources in quotation or summary, but he is much freer than they with his personal comments and evaluations. Only a few examples of his numerous comments can be given from the period which interests us, 343-381 C.E.: he sees the compliance of Hosius at the Council of Sirmium in 357 as worse than any previous fall, even those of Origen and Tertullian; Sozomen was badly informed on the Goths, since he did not know that some of them were Christians as early as Constantine's time; Jerome was wrong to see Lucifer of Cagliari as practically the only orthodox western bishop; the Arian Council of Antioch in 360 first called the Son of God unlike in substance and will "(proh scelus!)" But at that very time "(ô prodigium!)" Constantius lost power.[62]

Unlike the Centuriators, Baronius makes extensive use of Epiphanius' category of 'Semiarians.' In connection with the succession to the see of Jerusalem in 351, those who opposed the Arians joined with Basil of Ancyra and the Semiarians because of the collapse of more orthodox opposition. Basil and his party were also the first to resist the Aetian doctrines of Eudoxius, but Baronius still calls them 'enemies of the Catholic faith.' He describes the Semiarians as those Arians 'who claimed to hate the name of Arius, and at least appeared to confess the divine substance in the Son of God . . . but did not receive the term "consubstantiality". . . .' They called a synod

---

[60] For example, he says the Arians and Constantius so respected the majesty of the Roman church that, when they exiled Liberius, they did not try to replace him with one of their own from outside as they had done in other churches (*anno* 355, LI; III:658); Basil of Caesarea did not condemn Apollinarius, deferring to Rome's historic right to be the first to condemn new heresies (*anno* 372; IV:271).

[61] E.g., how barbarian incursions into Gaul delayed Hilary of Poitier's expulsion from his see (*anno* 355 LXXVII; III:665); that Julian favored the Catholics in Gaul (*anno* 353; III:666); his critical attention to the Goths (*anno* 370; IV:227–9). Louis Ellies Du Pin, *Bibliotheque des Auteurs Ecclesiastiques du Dix-septième Siecle* (Paris, 1708), 5, says that Baronius was much more accurate on the Latins than on the Greeks because his Greek was poor, and for Greek sources which had not been translated he had to depend on the help of Pierre Morin, Metius, and Sirmond.

[62] Hosius: *anno* 357, XVIII; III:704; Sozomen: *anno* 370; IV:228; Jerome: *anno* 371; IV:266; the Arian council: *anno* 360, LIV; III:769.

at Lampsacus, not to attack the Nicene faith but to condemn the monstrous formula which had come out of Constantinople.[63] Baronius is particularly severe in his criticism of Eleusius of Cyzicus' participation in the heresy of Macedonius.[64]

Despite Baronius' Roman bias and the Roman preference for Paulinus in the schism of Antioch, he still gives Meletius a good reputation as leader of the orthodox there, as one who suffered exile for the Catholic faith, and as a man held in the highest veneration by all at his death.[65] He regards the Acacians with scorn, citing Themistius, 'They worshipped not God but the purple.'[66] All in all, despite its weaknesses, Baronius' account of later Arianism is vivid, learned, and more critical than one might have expected.

Dionysius Petavius, or Petau, was a theologian rather than a historian and studied our period not for edifying episodes of church history but for background to his dogmatic treatise on the Trinity.[67] He has separate chapters on Arius, early Arianism, and the 'various and conflicting professions of faith produced by the Arians in a few years.'[68] Then he spends three chapters on the many forms which Arianism took, along with separate chapters on Marcellus and on the Pneumatomachians. Petau's terminology for later Arians includes *Semiariani*, but also dogmatically tinged terms like *Anomoei* and *Homoeusii*.

Petau says that at the Council of Sirmium (357) Liberius of Rome signed, not the 'blasphemy of Hosius,' but a different formula. He expands on the struggle between the Semiarians and the Anomoeans before Ariminum and Seleucia, and contends that at the Council of Seleucia, only the repeated interventions of Count Leonas kept the Acacians and Anomoeans from humiliation at the hands of the Semiarians.[69] Petau's preferred division of the late Arians is into three

---

[63] He credits Epiphanius with the term at *anno* 347, LXVIII; III:579; the Jerusalem succession: *anno* 351, XXVII; III:617; Basil of Ancyra's party: *anno* 356, CXIX; III:697; as enemies of the faith: *anno* 357 XXII; III:706; Semiarians defined: *anno* 358, XV; III:725; synod of Lampsacus: *anno* 365; IV:150.

[64] *Anno* 360, XX; III:761; see also *anno* 381; IV:371.

[65] *Anno* 362; IV:67; *anno* 381; IV:374.

[66] *Anno* 363; IV:141.

[67] Dionysii Petavii, *Theologicorum Dogmatum Tomus Secundus, in quo de Sanctissima Trinitate agitur* (Paris: Sebastianus Cramoisy, 1644). Book I of this volume deals with history, especially heretics.

[68] Book I 7–9; II:35–50.

[69] Book I 9; II:45–9.

groups. The Anomoeans 'openly called the Son a creature, not like
the Father in any way, nor equal.' The Semiarians, while they taught
'that the Son is not at all consubstantial with the Father, that is,
homoousion, yet he is like him in all things, even *ousia* and substance.'
There were some whose views 'made a third group between the other
two, who said the Son was neither consubstantial nor like in
substance, but merely alike *(tantummodo similem)*. . . .'[70] The leader
of the third group was Acacius, whose motivation was not doctrinal
but hatred and jealousy; if one could get beneath the politics to the
real doctrinal preference of this group, one would find them no
different from the Anomoeans.[71]

The Semiarians included some who denied the coeternity of the
Son, and others like Basil of Ancyra who professed it. In Petau's view,
Macedonius himself was a Semiarian only, and did not deny the
divinity of the Holy Spirit.[72] Petau takes issue with Marius
Victorinus' description of the Semiarians as 'secret Arians';
Athanasius, he notes, calls them 'brothers,' though this benign view is
to be attributed to the obscurity of the Semiarian heresy, which
Athanasius did not truly understand.[73] Petau sees Cyril of Jerusalem
and Meletius of Antioch as borderline heretics, and takes an
unusually severe view of Eusebius of Caesarea.[74] Citing Nicephorus'
verdict that he taught 'more and worse things than all the Arians
against the Son of God,' Petau concludes that 'he is no less infamous
and hateful to the Catholic Church than the other Eusebius, of
Nicomedia . . .'[75]

The seventeenth century saw a continuation of the kind of attack
on the doctrine of the Trinity which we have seen with Michael
Servetus, namely, an attack on the notion of three divine hypostases.
The most prominent name is that of Faustus Socinus,[76] whose
theology has many points of contact with that of Servetus. He cannot

[70] Book I 10; II:51.
[71] Book I 10; II:52.
[72] Book I 10; II:53.
[73] Book I 10; II:54–5.
[74] Cyril and Meletius: Book I 11; II:56; and Book I 13; II:76–7. Eusebius of Caesarea:
Book I 11-12; II:57–72.
[75] Book I 12; II:72.
[76] His works, written at various points in his lifetime (1539–1604), were published as
Fausti Socini Senensis, Opera omnia (Irenopoli [= Amsterdam], 1656).

fairly be described as desiring to revive Arianism, and so far as I can see he does not defend it. In speaking against the binding authoritiy of councils he does raise the instance of the Council of Ariminum and Augustine's remark that Catholics should not use the authority of Nicaea against Arians, nor the Arians that of Ariminum against Catholics.[77] Less prominent but more interested in patristic theology was the Englishman, John Biddle, whose first concern was to disprove the divinity of the Holy Spirit. In a distinction which helps us place his position, he concludes that after his arguments

> . . . it will be impossible for thee (especially being thus admonished) to embrace either the opinion of Athanasius, who held the holy Spirit to be a person of supream [sic] Deity, or that of Socinus, who believed him to be the divine power or efficacy, but no Person.[78]

Most of Biddle's patristic researches concerned the ante-Nicene writers, but he pauses to defend Eusebius from the charge of Arianism: true Arians believed that the Son was created out of nothing, while Eusebius believed he was generated out of the Father's substance.[79]

England produced a fine effort in the historical genre with the work of William Cave.[80] Cave wrote history in terms of the biographies of the Fathers, and does not give separate entries to heretics. He treats Eusebius of Caesarea as orthodox.[81] The Council of Seleucia comes up in the context of the life of Hilary, and Cave describes the two main parties, 'the one headed by Acacius, Bishop of Caesarea, the other by George of Laodicea, who were the far greater and more moderate Party.'[82]

[77] This is from his *Tractatus de Ecclesia,* Opera omnia I:330.

[78] John Biddle, *XII Arguments Drawn out of the Scripture: Wherein The commonly-received Opinion touching the Deity of the Holy Spirit is clearly and fully refuted* (n.p., 1647) 51.

[79] *The Testimonies of [Irenaeus, Justin Martyr, Tertullian, Novatianus, Theophilus, Origen, (who lived in the two first Centuries after Christ was born, or thereabouts;) as also of [Arnobius, Lactantius, Eusebius) Hilary and Brightman, concerning That One God, and the Persons of the Holy Trinity* (London, n.d.) 75–6.

[80] William Cave, *Ecclesiastici, or, The History of the Lives, Acts, Death, & Writings, Of the most Eminent Fathers of the Church, That Flourisht in the Fourth Century. . . .* London: Richard Chiswell, 1683.

[81] Amusingly, Cave takes Baronius to task for his criticism of Eusebius, saying that it was because Eusebius' report of Constantine's baptism at Nicomedia just before his death robbed the Church of Rome of the honor of it (33).

[82] *History of the Lives,* 204.

But Cave gives his fullest account of Arianism under the life of Gregory Nazianzen, when he is explaining the anathemas of the Council of Constantinople in 381. Cave singles out chiefly the christological heresies for attention, but he does give a lengthy account of the Eunomian heresy. Eunomius

> corrupted the *Arian dogmata* (poyson it self [*sic*] may be made worse) which he advanc'd to a pitch beyond any other Branch that sprang from that bitter Root, so that at last his Followers refus'd to admit the *Arian* Baptism and Ordination. . . .[83]

In contrast to Petau, Cave blames Macedonius himself for the Macedonian heresy, and even portrays his followers as tending to moderation.[84] Unfortunately for us, Cave's method did not give him occasion to go into the description of late Arianism in greater detail, for he was critical and humorous as well as learned.

The discussions which continued in England in the last decade of the seventeenth century do not delve much deeper into the actual description of late Arianism. Some, like Arthur Bury, Principal of Exeter College, Oxford, take a line related to Socinianism and to English Rationalism, urging that the heart of religion is moral conduct or holiness, and that 'the Mother-error' of the churches over the centuries had been to exalt the importance of correct doctrine.[85] In a later pamphlet he briefly characterised the course of the trinitarian controversy as follows:

> 5. The First most Cruel and most Durable contention was That with Arius, which was not ended when the *Catholicks* fell into a controversie between the *Greeks and Latines,* concerning the title of the *Three.* The *Greeks* would call them *Subsistences:* This the *Latines* thought too much, and would not allow them to be more than PERSONS, And *Greg.Naz.* celebrateth it, as one of *Athanasius's* best performances, that he indulged to both parties the use of their own expressions.

> 6. The *Greeks* therefore kept possession of their *Platonick* word, *Subsistences,* which being not *Classical,* needed to be explained. The most *Authentick* paraphrase was That of *Justinian and his Council,* . . . *triada kata tas idiotetas, egoun hupostaseis, etoi prosopa.* So the *Geeeks* [*sic*] never acknowledged the Trinity to be more than *Three Properties in the Godhead.*[86]

---

[83] ibid., 311.
[84] ibid., 313–315.
[85] *The Naked Gospel* (n.p., 1690), 79.
[86] *A Defence of the Doctrine of the HOLY TRINITY, and Incarnation Placed in their due Light* (n.p., 1694) 4.

But to Bury, the Arian controversy was vague in its posing of the trinitarian issues, compared to the argument in his time between what he called the 'Realists' and the 'Nominals.' He acknowledges that the 'Realist' position was in possession by the late fourth century, but he attributes this to the strength of the party of 'the Fathers who had been against this term [*homoousios*], and yet were not Arians . . .'[87]

An anonymous pamphlet of the time identified the Nominals with the position of the Noetians and Sabellians and likewise with the Homoousians at Nicaea:

> and this is the Party, which after the breaking up of that famous Council, and upon the sudden prevalence of the Arian Faction, were persecuted by the Arians; and were considered by all others as the true Nicene Party, till about the Year of Christ 380, the Realists obtained that it should be said, that God is tres Hypostases, three subsisting Persons. Indeed there are several Comma's in the Nicene Creed, very hardly reconcilable to the Sabellian Doctrine: but as there were three powerful, and almost equal Parties in the Nicene Council, the Arian Party, the Realists, and the Sabellians; the latter thought it enough, if they could procure Homousios (Consubstantial) to be inserted into the Creed.[88]

Unfortunately, the pamphlet's author does not tell us which fourth-century figures belonged to which of his three parties.

The William Sherlock alluded to in the title of Arthur Bury's 1696 pamphlet produced one of the most comprehensive statements of the seventeenth-century controversy.[89] The chapter on the *homoousion* treats an unusually large range of thinkers;[90] Sherlock tends to describe the fourth-century disputants in terms of the seventeenth-century controversy as he sees it, that is, in terms of whether the divine unity is that of a species, or a

[87] *The Judgment of a Disinterested Person Concerning the Controversy about The B. Trinity; Depending between Dr. S**th and Dr. Sherlock.* By a Divine of the Church of England (London: E. Whitlock, 1696), 19. Elsewhere (p. 32) he calls these moderate Arians *Ariani molles.*

[88] *A Discourse Concerning the Nominal and Real Trinitarians* (n.p., 1695) 16–17.

[89] William Sherlock, *The Present State of the Socinian Controversy, and the Doctrine of the Catholick Fathers Concerning A Trinity in Unity* (London: William Rogers, 1698). Dr. Maurice Wiles has kindly shown me papers he has given on the continuing debate in eighteenth-century England; since I expect that they will see publication, I have not tried to describe that debate in the present paper.

[90] ibid., 150–384. Among those quoted and discussed are Theodore Abucara [*sic*], Peter Lombard, Aquinas, and Suarez; some of these Sherlock may know through Petau, whose work he quotes heavily.

singularity, or (Sherlock's own preference) 'One individual Nature common to them all, but subsisting so distinctly in each of them, as to make them Three distinct Persons.'[91] The controversy of his time did not require Sherlock or the others to make finer historical distinctions concerning the stages and *dramatis personae* of late Arianism.

Across in France two remarkable compendia were being written. The *Nouvelle Bibliotheque* of Louis Ellies Du Pin began to appear in 1685.[92] In his treatment of the fourth century he devotes 765 pages to authors, 180 to councils. Du Pin's evaluations are original and direct. 'Socrates, Sozomen, and some other recent authors were wrong to excuse' Eusebius of Caesarea entirely, but on the other hand 'it is a great injustice to call him Arian, and even the chief of the Arians, as St. Jerome did, whom many others followed. . . .'[93] Basil of Ancyra

> was one of the greatest enemies of the Arians or Anomoeans . . . Though they make him the head of the party of those who are called Semi-Arians, it is not certain that he was a heretic; on the contrary, St. Basil speaks of him as a Catholic bishop, and St. Athanasius asserts in his *De synodis* that Basil of Ancyra and those of his party differed only in name from those who professed the consubstantiality. . . .[94]

Acacius of Caesarea is portrayed as joining the Anomoeans out of hatred for Cyril of Jerusalem, then soon repenting and having Meletius and many other Catholic bishops ordained.[95] Du Pin's description of Aetius may reflect his own resentment at the condemnation of the first volume of his *Nouvelle Bibliotheque* by a group of Parisian doctors:

> Be that as it may, it is certain that Aetius knew all the subtleties of

---

[91] ibid., 199. Later, on p. 207, he vigorously attacks Petavius for choosing 'a word to represent the Sense of the Catholick Fathers by, concerning the Unity of the Divine Substance, which they themselves rejected as Sabellianism. . . .'

[92] Mre L. Ellies Du Pin, *Nouvelle Bibliotheque des Auteurs Ecclesiatiques, contenant l'histoire de leur vie, le catalogue, la critique, et la chronologie de leurs ouvrages, le sommaire de ce qu'ils contiennent. Un iugemenт sur leur stile et sur leur doctrine.* 2e ed., T. 2: Des Auteurs du quatrième siècle de i'Église (Paris: Chez André Pralard, 1687).

[93] ibid., II: 20–1.

[94] ibid., II: 216.

[95] ibid., II: 360. Du Pin points out that under Jovian Acacius even signed the Nicene formula.

Aristotelian logic; but he was ignorant in Scripture and in ecclesiastical antiquity. A man of such a spirit would be ready to put forward all kinds of impiety, to defend them brazenly, and even to confound those against whom he disputed.[96]

Du Pin's list of councils and creeds is lengthy, and he is willing to accept creeds as orthodox even where the term 'consubstantial' is missing.[97] Besides the categories already mentioned, he speaks of 'Eusebians' and 'Eudoxians.'[98]

More influential than Du Pin's work, at least on the continent of Europe,[99] was that of an independent and reclusive Parisian scholar, Lenain de Tillemont.[100] His work includes a nearly 400-page 'histoire abregée de l'Arianisme,'[101] perhaps the earliest modern work to try to put all the data together. In contrast to Du Pin, Tillemont embraces strongly the Roman and Athanasian view of late Arianism. At first there were the followers of Arius himself, properly called Arians, and those who protected them, called Eusebians after Eusebius of Nicomedia. This distinction lasted till the Council of Milan in 355, when the Eusebians declared themselves openly for Arius' doctrines and earned the Arian name for themselves.[102] Aetius and his followers are sometimes treated as separate from the Arians, sometimes as the pure form of Arianism.[103] Semiarians for Tillemont are practically indistinguishable from the Macedonians and date from around 358 (when the Semiarians controlled the imperial court) or 360, when Macedonius was deposed, or 362.[104] Tillemont also speaks of the

---

[96] ibid., II: 364.

[97] For example, the third and fourth formulas of Antioch 341 (II: 825 and 827); that of Antioch 345 (II: 832); Sirmium 351 (II: 847); the Council of Antioch under Meletius (II: 867).

[98] ibid., II: 832 and 863.

[99] An English translation of Du Pin's *Nouvelle Bibliotheque* went to several editions, perhaps because of his close association with William Wake.

[100] Lenain de Tillemont, *Memoires pour servir a l'histoire Ecclesiastique des six premiers siecles*, 2nd ed., VI (Paris: Charles Robustel, 1704); VII (1706); VIII (1707).

[101] ibid., VI: 239–633. This section was translated into English by T. Deacon, *The History of the Arians and of the Council of Nice* (London: Geo. James, 1721).

[102] ibid., VI: 247–8. See also VI:354; and Tillemont notes that the original Arians were scarcely mentioned after 341 (VI:411).

[103] The former: VI:408; the latter, VI:411 and 522.

[104] 358: VI: 439; 360: VI:413; 362: VI:527.

Eudoxians or Anomoeans,[105] who are roughly equivalent to the Acacians.[106] He sees the late 350s as a turning point for Arianism, since

> from 357 at least, doctrinal divisions formed among them, which caused great troubles, and ended by separating this tower of Babel into different sects.[107]

In his view, the Semiarians and the orthodox came together because the Semiarians were persecuted by the pure Arians, 'who could not even put up with those who were merely half-hearted heretics.'[108]

As simple as that picture is, Tillemont frequently refers to the fluctuations in communion which defeat even his own attempts to make sense of them. He is puzzled by Pope Julius' cordial correspondence with 'the wickedest Eusebians'. Socrates' claim that communion between East and West was broken at the time of Sardica and Philippopolis faces many difficulties; perhaps 'it was impossible to observe rigorous discipline in the prevailing confusion . . . It is a difficulty which is well worth examining by someone to whom God has given the ability.' Antioch was dominated by the Arian heresy from the time of Eustathius' deposition till 361, but confusingly it seems the orthodox were in the majority. Tillemont seems surprised that Hilary of Poitiers never thought it necessary to break communion with the signers of the decrees of the Council of Ariminum. The Semiarians were simultaneously in communion with Catholic bishops in Asia and separated from the orthodox in the West. Ulphilas the Goth signed the Arian formula of Constantinople (360), but continued in the Catholic communion.[109]

---

[105] VI: 439.

[106] VI: 483 – from about 360 on, Acacius distanced himself from this group. This is not necessarily to his credit, for Tillemont says, 'What made him the horror of the whole world, even of the Arians, is the fact that he seems not to have had any faith, good or bad, and to have known no other God but his passion, his self-interest, and the way the wind was blowing' (VI: 306; cp. VIII: 345). When in 365 Acacius is said to link up with Eudoxius, it is hard to tell 'if this proceeds from his usual shallowness, or if Socrates is misinformed' (VI: 533).

[107] VI: 411.

[108] VI: 522 and 540.

[109] Pope Julius: VI:327; difficulties in Socrates' claim: VI: 337-338; situation at Antioch: compare VI: 428 with VII: 518 and VIII: 342–4; Hilary's mysterious behavior: VI: 462; Semiarians: VI: 540; Ulphilas: VI: 605–6. Tillemont also notes that Augustine and Epiphanius knew only of Catholic Goths. He puts the Arian corruption of the Goths after 377 (VI: 604).

Tillemont offers interesting comments on several comparatively obscure figures. Eusebius of Emesa was solidly Arian, 'because he had always lived with the main partisans of this error.'[110] Marc of Arethusa, while a famous Arian, earned the praise of all the orthodox for his sufferings under Julian.[111] Vincent of Capua may have signed the excommunication of Athanasius in 353, but he received the wholehearted praise of a later council.[112] Tillemont wonders how Parthenius of Lampsacus, described in the *Acta Sanctorum* for February 7, managed to earn such a reputation for sanctity while remaining in communion with condemned bishops of Asia and failing to defend Athanasius.[113] The Semiarians who came as delegates to Liberius from the Council of Lampsacus may have traveled via Illyria and won Germinius of Sirmium away from 'the crudest blasphemies of the Arians' to being 'almost Catholic.'[114] All in all, Tillemont offers a portrait of the Arian controversy whose learning, color, and completeness easily explain its success.

One of the last authors uninfluenced by Tillemont's synthesis was his German contemporary, Gottfried Arnold.[115] The impartiality in Arnold's title comes in part from his conviction that by the fourth century true faith had given way to merely outward expression.[116] He is himself no supporter of Nicaea 325, or of the way in which the churchmen tried to enforce doctrine by imperial power; the praxis of the orthodox was as bad as the doctrine of the Arians.[117]

> In short, both parties and most Christian teachers as well moved away from faith's first contents and had replaced real Christianity with mere opinions, empty propositions, technical terms and pestilential questions.[118]

He does lay out the divisions of the Arians, however. Some 'stayed with the old propositions' – what we now call Arians and

[110] VI: 313.
[111] VI: 326.
[112] VI: 359.
[113] VI: 388–389.
[114] VI: 545.
[115] Gottfrid [*sic*] Arnold, *Unparteyische Kirchen- und Ketzer-Historie, von Anfang des Neuen Testaments biß auff das Jahr Christi 1688* (Franckfurt am Mayn: bey Thomas Fritsch, 1699–1700). The fourth century is covered in part 1, book 4 (I: 129–214).
[116] 'Inmitelst hatte der wahre thätige glaube keine statt mehr . . .' (I: 146).
[117] I: 177–9.
[118] I: 189.

Anomoeans, led first by Aetius and then Eunomius. Others, called Semiarians, partly agreed with the orthodox but preferred *homoiousion* to *homoousion;* their leaders were Basil of Ancyra, Eustathius of Sebaste, Leontius of Cyzicus, George of Laodicea, Sylvanus [of Tarsus] and others. The third party, Acacians after Acacius of Caesarea, were in the middle, and said Christ was like the Father. He passes over further subdivisions among them; 'enough that this makes it clear how intelligence, with all its investigations into divine things, is doomed to catastrophe and produces nothing but disunity and unhappiness amongst its slaves.'[119]

The great *Encyclopédie* of Diderot has brief articles on our subject written (those which are signed) by a certain Abbé Mallet.[120] Only the unsigned article on the Semiarians sketches a division of the Arian movement into categories: those who held for unlikeness, and those who refused the word 'consubstantial,' who nonetheless were 'in the error of the Arians.' Some of the Semiarians said the Son was like the Father in substance, others said it was only in will.

A more specialised dictionary which enjoyed a considerable vogue was that by François-André-Adrien Pluquet.[121] He is much more expansive in the earlier articles, 'Ariens,' 'Antitrinitaires,' 'Arianisme,' 'Eunome,' 'Eunomiens,' than in the later 'Macedonius' and 'Semiariens.' Apart from the titles themselves, the only attempt he makes to describe the categories is to say that 'the Arians were divided into Eusebians, demi-Arians, etc. [*sic*] . . .'[122]

In Germany Johannes Mosheim was placing the field of church history on a more scientific footing. He follows closely the relationship between the emperors and church conflicts, but he also takes a moment to describe the divisions among the Arians:

> The ancients enumerate several sects of Arians, Semiarians, Eusebians, Aetians, Eunomians, Acacians, Psathyrians, and others. But all can fittingly be reduced to three. First are the old, genuine Arians, who against

[119] I: 191.
[120] *Encyclopedie, ou Dictionnaire raisonné des sciences, des arts et des metiers* (Paris: 1751–65). 'Arianisme': I: 649–50; 'Aetiens': I: 156; 'Anoméens': I: 488; 'Consubstantiel': IV: 101; 'Semi-Ariens' (unsigned): IV: 943.
[121] *Mémoires pour servir à l'histoire des égaremens de l'esprit humain par rapport à la religion chrétienne, ou Dictionnaire des hérésies, des erreurs, et des schismes,* 2 vol. [3rd ed.] (Paris: Didot le Jeune, 1776). The first edition was in 1762, the second 1762–4.
[122] ibid., I: 128.

all new formulas and terms simply taught that the Son was not born of the Father, but made out of nothing. From them split, on one hand, the Semi-Arians, on the other, the Eunomians or Anomoeans. . . .[123]

Mosheim describes Macedonius as the 'illustrious teacher of the semi-Arians' who started the Pneumatomachian sect after he was expelled from Constantinople by the Eunomians.[124] He thinks it is a mistake to list Eusebius of Caesarea among the Arians.[125] But late Arianism is not one of Mosheim's major interests.

One of Mosheim's contemporaries, Johann Salomo Semler, makes a greater effort to categorise the late Arians. While Arius and his followers held the Son to be utterly unlike and foreign to the Father's being and properties, Eunomius conceded a likeness *kat' energeian*. That the Son came to be was common doctrine of Arius, the Anomoeans, Acacians, and Eunomians. The Homoeousians, also called Semiarians, made another party, because they thought the Son to be like the Father in substance or in will. Some of this party, led by George of Laodicea and Basil of Ancyra, won out in their efforts to get the others to agree to the use of the word 'substance.' Thus, says Semler, 'It seems undeniable that even the more learned catholics did not defend the *homoousion* as if it were life or death, though one would think otherwise from reading theologians.'[126]

Semler also tries to make sense of the events surrounding Macedonius. When the Acacians enjoyed the imperial favor, they used it to throw out Homoeousians; this pushed Macedonius into the latter camp with Marathonius of Nicomedia and Eustathius of Sebaste. But Macedonius alienated most of them with his views on the Holy Spirit, which came to light at the Synod of Lampsacus in 364 or 365, thanks to Eleusius of Cyzicus. Though the emperor replaced Eleusius with Eunomius, he could not stamp out the Macedonians. Finally the threats of Eudoxius of Constantinople persuaded the Macedonians in 367 to send a deputation to Liberius accepting the Nicene formula, but without elaboration of the clause on the Holy Spirit.[127]

[123] Io. Laur. Moshemii, *Institutionum historiae ecclesiasticae antiquae et recentioris libri quatuor* (Helmstadii: Christianum Fridericum Weygand, 1755), 187.

[124] ibid., 189.

[125] ibid., 159.

[126] Ioh. Sal. Semleri, *Historiae Ecclesiasticae selecta capita* (Halae: Iohannis Godofredi Trampii, 1767–9) I: 156–7.

[127] ibid., I: 167–8.

Another contemporary of Mosheim, C. W. F. Walch, was expressly
a heresiologist.[128] In his first volume he states his aim: to get beyond
the biased judgments of his predecessors and simply lay out what
happened as completely as possible. He also gives a remarkable
annotated catalogue of those predecessors and their now-forgotten
books.[129] Arianism takes up much of Walch's second volume,
published in 1764; he divides late Arianism into two periods, 'from
the death of Arius till the death of Constantius,' and 'from the death
of Constantius to its complete suppression in the Roman Empire.'[130]

In describing the opponents of Nicaea, Walch begins by tracing the
path of the creeds formulated in the East after 340, some of which he
thinks are orthodox (the 2nd and 4th creeds of Antioch 341, the
latter also appended to the letter of the eastern bishops from
Philippopolis in 343), others only half-Arian (the 3rd and 4th
formulas of Sirmium 358).[131] But even Athanasius himself never
distinguished the different parties clearly, and Walch notes that
Socrates makes three parties (Arians, Eunomians, Macedonians),
Epiphanius four (Arians, Semiarians, Macedonians, Anomoeans).[132]
Unlike any previous author, he also categorises the usages of his major
predecessors, Petau, Tillemont, Mosheim and Suicer.[133] The
confusion in terminology he ascribes to 'the fact that the ancients
who fought against Arianism do not observe this distinction.'[134]

As Walch summarises the history of Arianism, the opponents of
the Nicene doctrine had various motives. Some objected to the word
homoousios, others to the underlying concept, but all agreed that their
opponents' great zeal for *homoousios* would frustrate their efforts
against Athanasius. When Constantius came to power they achieved
their objective and then fell out amongst themselves, into parties
which can be conveniently grouped according to whether they were

[128] Christian Wilhelm Franz Walch, *Entwurf einer vollständigen Historie der Ketzereien,
Spaltungen und Religionsstreitigkeiten, bis auf die Zeiten der Reformation* (Leipzig: M. G.
Weidmann, 1762–82).

[129] ibid., I: iii-iv; 49–63.

[130] ibid., II: 511–39, 539–53.

[131] ibid., II: 629–31.

[132] ibid., II: 633, 'Athanasius hat unsers Wissens niemals gnau die verschiedene
Partheien aus einander gesezet [*sic*],' and 634.

[133] ibid., II: 635. [Johann Kaspar] Suicer is cited as distinguishing four positions:
heterousia, anomoiotes, homoiousia and *homoiotes.*

[134] ibid., II: 636.

completely opposed to the doctrine of Nicaea or only objected to the word. Walch thinks it futile to seek theoretical principles for these positions; they merely reflect a variety of views already in use among Athanasius' opponents. Athanasius and Hilary must have been able to see that there was a distinction between the doctrine of Nicaea and the word *homoousios,* since they transmitted to us several formulas which made such a distinction, and even felt compelled to judge some of these formulas leniently; but in their polemics they refused to lay out clearly the doctrinal differences among their opponents. Besides, the second group of their opponents joined the Orthodox under the persecution of Valens. As to the Macedonians, Walch considers them no Arian party.[135]

In the end, Walch sees three types of opponents to Nicaea: (1) those who rejected the doctrine itself along with the word (old Arians, Eunomians, Acacians); (2) the half-Arians, who taught the same doctrine as Nicaea, minus the word *homoousios,* and can be blamed only for maintaining communion with the Arians for so long and showing such severity to Athanasius; (3) various sub-groups which arose after the councils of the 380s.[136]

Edward Gibbon, in his famous work on the end of the Roman Empire, comments on the factions among the Arians, 'who were united only by their common aversion to the Homoousion of the Nicene Synod.' The key question was whether the Son was like the Father. The Arians of Aetius' stripe said 'No'; others said 'Yes,' but denied that he was of the same or a similar substance; and most numerous was the 'sect which asserted the doctrine of a similar substance. . . .' Gibbon doubts '. . . if it were possible to make any real and sensible distinction between the doctrine of the Semi-Arians, as they were improperly styled, and that of the Catholics themselves.'[137] In the West, Arianism died quickly, as the Christians 'happily relapsed into the slumber of orthodoxy,' but 'the strength and numbers of the hostile factions were more equally balanced' in the Eastern provinces, where 'every episcopal vacancy was the

[135] ibid., II: 636–8.
[136] ibid., II: 641–4.
[137] Edward Gibbon, *The History of the Decline and Fall of the Roman Empire* (London: W. Strahan & T. Cadell, 1781) II: 255–7.

occasion of a popular tumult.'[138] But Gibbon does not enter into greater detail concerning the parties themselves.

Wilhelm Münscher, 'the real founder of the new discipline' of the history of dogma,[139] portrays late Arianism in the light of tensions between the Eastern and Western churches.[140] For example, on the Council of Antioch in 341 he says,

> True, its creeds lack the Nicene precisions that the Son is from the Father's essence and that he is *homoousios;* but exactly because these anti-Arian expressions were avoided and the cruder sort of Arianism was still condemned, they could have made a way to the reunion of the contesting parties, if those on the western side had had enough spirit of moderation to desire a reunion.

But the failure to rehabilitate Athanasius doomed this effort; it also frustrated the eastern bishops' repeated attempt to meet western objections with such creeds as the 'Macrostich' or 'Long-Lined' Creed of 343, which Münscher thinks was closer to the ante-Nicene Fathers than Athanasius was, and easily reconciled with Nicaea.[141] Likewise Münscher doubts that the eastern bishops who refused to stay at the Council of Sardica in 343 had any desire to see the doctrines of Arius succeed.[142] The eastern bishops maintained a consistent doctrinal position at Sirmium in 351.[143] At Sirmium in 357, a few bishops took the unprecedented step of attacking the Nicene definitions and trying to foist their own conflicting kind of ideas on the whole church; as a result, both the 'catholics' and a large group of the eastern bishops who preferred the term *homoeousion* found their usages condemned and concluded that full-scale Arianism had been introduced. The easterners held a synod at Ancyra in 358 which so impressed the emperor Constantius that he summoned another meeting in

---

[138] ibid., II: 505–6.

[139] According to Friedrich Loofs, *Leitfaden zum Studium der Dogmengeschichte,* 7 ed. (Tübingen: Max Niemeyer Verlag, 1968) 1.

[140] Wilhelm Münscher, *Handbuch der christlichen Dogmengeschichte,* 4 v. (Marburg: Neue Akademische Buchhandlung, 1797–1808). The first two volumes cover the period to 320; I had access to v. 3 in its second edition (Marburg: Kriegersch Buchhandlung, 1818).

[141] ibid., III: 382; he goes on to say, 'The case of Athanasius, whom the latter condemned and the former [i.e., the West] exonerated, was a total obstacle to any reunion, and it became a matter of honor for both churches not to give in.'

[142] ibid., III: 385.

[143] ibid., III: 387.

Sirmium for 359, where a new formula gave something to each party by throwing out all *ousia*-language but affirming the Son's likeness to the Father in all respects, thus leaving room for likeness of essence.[144]

Münscher opposes the easy general use of the word 'Arian' for all those who were unhappy with the Nicene term *homoousion* or who consented to the deposition of Athanasius. There were some 'pure' Arians who claimed the Son was created in time, and whose doctrine was developed later by Aetius and Eunomius.[145] There were others, however, who accepted the doctrine of Nicaea but found the term *homoousion* dangerously open to misinterpretation, and still others who believed that discussions about the nature of the Son and his relationship to the Father were sophistries which overreached the limited powers of the human mind. Some desired peace in the church and were convinced that total uniformity of thought was impossible. Finally, there were people motivated by personal antagonism to Athanasius. The only trait that all these so-called Arians had in common was jealousy for the honor and prerogatives of their eastern churches.[146]

Ferdinand Christian Baur portrays the period of late Arianism as one in which three different doctrines *(Lehrbegriffe)* sharpened and clarified themselves in controversy.[147] The Arian doctrine is marked by two essential statements, that the Son is created from nothing, and that as a creature he first did not exist, but passed over from nonbeing to being.[148] This implies, for the Arians, a chasm between the world and God, between finite and infinite, and a corresponding realisation that communion with God cannot be had on the level of being; divinisation is possible only through free moral striving. Against the view which sees the divine as objective, as given, so that one can only receive it, Arius upholds a subjective view in which the divine, the absolute, is not just given but must be the law of the person's own

---

[144] ibid., III: 388–90.

[145] On III: 400 Münscher cautions that Eunomius was not strictly speaking an Anomoean, because he did acknowledge that the Son was 'dem Vater ähnlich nach der Schrift.'

[146] ibid., III: 393–5.

[147] Ferdinand Christian Baur, *Die christliche Lehre von der Dreieinigkeit und Menschwerdung Gottes in ihrer geschichtlichen Entwicklung,* 3 v. (Tübingen: C. F. Osiander, 1841–3) I: 342–3.

[148] ibid., I: 343.

activity.[149] But instead of showing the positive worth of this moral freedom, the Arians merely try to chip away at the metaphysical thinking which stood in their way; eventually Eunomius develops Arian ideas in a direction which forsakes entirely the idea of a moral road to divinisation.[150]

The Nicene-Athanasian or orthodox doctrine rests on a Platonic idealist view of 'the incomprehensibility of the divine essence, the incapacity of human nature to touch the absolute, the incongruity between concrete knowledge and the Idea.'[151] Athanasius, according to Baur, juxtaposes the Son as he must necessarily be, as Light from Light, with the free subject which he also is; even in this orthodox doctrine only the Father remains the absolute God.[152] The so-called Semiarian doctrine attempts to choose a middle ground and to speak of Father and Son in terms which are neither Arian nor Athanasian.[153] But under George of Laodicea and Basil of Ancyra the Semiarians rise up against the formulas which would exclude all *ousia*-language; their purpose is to make the essential similarity of Son and Father the real import of trinitarian doctrine.[154] Baur's treatment of late Arianism is less concerned with the specifics of its history than with the great movements of the Christian spirit which the different parties reflected.

Georg Meier also seeks the underlying play of ideas, but in different terms. Here is his description of the eastern majority:

> Overall the eastern view, through all its modifications, keeps following the notion of the essential similarity of the Son to the Father; but sometimes their similarity is stressed, sometimes their distinction. Two ideas carry – or rather divide – the system, since people hold fast to them without seeking to resolve them: the personal distinction of Father and Son, which for them leads to full individuation, severance of essence, since for them 'person' is always the particular, incommunicable conscious essence; and the essential similarity. The former inclines toward the Arians, the latter to the Nicenes.[155]

[149] ibid., I: 353–4.
[150] ibid., I: 360; 380.
[151] ibid., I: 394–5.
[152] ibid., I: 439; 469.
[153] ibid., I: 482.
[154] ibid. I: 482–6.
[155] Georg August Meier, *Die Lehre von der Trinität in ihrer historischen Entwickelung*, 2 v. (Hamburg & Gotha: Friedrich & Andreas Perthes, 1844) 170–1.

Eusebius of Caesarea is the main thinker among what Meier calls the 'old-church party,' who reject the strict consequences of Arianism as well as the Nicene *homoousion,* but lack any positive principle of their own.[156] In Meier's view, the Athanasian vision of stability in salvation gradually won the 'Semiarians' over to the Nicene doctrine.[157]

The last of the authors in this survey is John Henry Newman, whose *The Arians of the Fourth Century*[158] is an ambitious attempt to portray the Arian heresy as part of a much larger conflict between attitudes of mind in the ancient world. His preferred terms for the Arian parties are Eusebians, Semi-Arians, and Anomoeans. The characterisation of the Emperor Constantius as the kind of person who became a Semi-Arian is a good example of Newman's approach:

> . . . resisting, as he did, the orthodox doctrine from oversubtlety, timidity, pride, restlessness, or other weakness of mind, yet paradoxical enough to combat at the same time and condemn all, who ventured to teach anything short of that orthodoxy. Balanced on this imperceptible centre between truth and error, he alternately banished every party in the controversy, not even sparing his own; and had recourse in turn to every creed for relief, except that in which the truth was actually to be found.[159]

Despite the large sale of Newman's book, it had less impact on his contemporaries' and successors' work than did his translation of the writings of Athanasius into English. H. M. Gwatkin seems to be speaking for many when he says,

> Of Newman's *Arians of the Fourth Century* let it suffice to say that his theories have always been scrupulously examined; so that if they have not often been accepted, it is only because there is usually good reason for rejecting them.[160]

Conclusion

At this point this survey must come to an end. Gwatkin and Harnack, who worked quite independently but both depended

---

[156] ibid., 166–7.

[157] ibid., 175.

[158] John Henry Newman, *The Arians of the Fourth Century* (London: J. G. & F. Rivington, 1833). This early work of Newman was reissued in 1854 and appeared in a corrected third edition, at first for private circulation, in 1871. Citations here are from the sixth edition (London: Longmans, Green and Co., 1890).

[159] ibid., 297.

[160] Henry Melvill Gwatkin, *Studies of Arianism* (Cambridge: Deighton, Bell, and Co., 1882) xix.

heavily on a new burgeoning of monographic scholarship on the fourth century, became the points of reference for modern treatments of Arianism, early and late. What can be said about the views of their predecessors, as represented by the selection made in the present survey?

First, the heresiological tradition does not deliver a consistent, canonical picture of the opponents of Nicaea and their doctrines. Rather, because of the inconsistencies among the ancient writers themselves who are the sources of our data, the picture of Arianism seems to vary with the weight accorded to different sources.

Second, the antitrinitarian writers of the sixteenth and seventeenth centuries challenged not the divinity of Jesus but the existence of distinct divine hypostases. Since that challenge resembles the thought of Marcellus of Ancyra or Photinus more than that of any of the Arian parties, neither the antitrinitarians themselves nor their opponents were required to make a serious effort to recover an accurate perception of the Arian controversy.

Third, there are some older writers whose original and careful work can be particularly rewarding for modern scholars to reread. While Petavius and Lenain de Tillemont were the most influential on later scholars, the freshest and most acute analyses are those of William Cave, Louis Ellies Du Pin, and C. W. F. Walch. Some of the most sensitive points of controversy, which may hold out the most prospect for further scholarly progress, are those which concern the Synod of Antioch in 341, the effect of possible power-struggles between Latin and Greek Christianity, the implications of the evidence provided by Hilary of Poitiers, and the coherence of the positions of such enigmatic figures as Acacius of Caesarea, Eleusius of Cyzicus, Meletius of Antioch, and Macedonius.

Chapter 2

ATTITUDES TO ARIUS
IN THE ARIAN CONTROVERSY*

Maurice Wiles

A sixteenth century historian was asked recently: 'What is new in study of the Reformation in England?'. His reply was: 'What Reformation?'. His studies had helped bring to light the religious conservatism of the majority of people in the English countryside and also the importance of social and economic factors for the understanding of the changes in English life in the early sixteenth century; as a result he felt the need to call into question the traditional title 'The Reformation' as a general designation of that period in England. A fourth century historian might be tempted to answer the equivalent question, 'What is new in study of the Arian controversy?' in similar vein with the retort: 'What Arian controversy?'. Recent study of the period has helped to bring out the deeply traditional character of much of the theology, not only of the main body of church leaders at the time, but also of both Arius and Athanasius themselves. Social and political factors resultant on Constantine's changed attitude to the church were highly significant; political pressure for unity, increased potential for interchange between churches, greater opportunities for the exercise of episcopal power, and changed expectations on the part of new converts in the new political climate – all these served to extend and exacerbate ecclesiastical and theological conflicts. It is not unreasonable to look to them, rather than necessarily to the emergence of some newly crucial issue of faith, as the primary reason for increased conflict and controversy in the years around and after Nicaea. That there was religious controversy is no more in doubt than that there was religious

* I am indebted to discussions with Timothy Barnes for the original impetus towards the writing of this article. Rowan Williams and Richard Vaggione made valuable comments on earlier drafts of it. I am grateful for their help.

change in sixteenth century England. The issue in both cases is how dominant and how deep were differences of theological conviction.

In recent years there has been a concentration of study on the figure of Arius and the basic nature of his theological concerns.[1] The debate is far from settled, but important new light has been shed on the issues at stake between Arius and his opponents at the outbreak of the controversy. But much of the most theologically sophisticated public discussion in what we know as the 'Arian controversy' did not get under way until the mid-350s, twenty years after Arius himself was dead. So how significant was Arius himself to the controversy? How was he seen by both sides of the debate in the course of the controversy itself? After all, it has been known by his name ever since. So my question is: in what sense was there an Arian controversy? – with the stress on the adjective 'Arian'.

When Athanasius became Bishop of Alexandria in 328, the Arian controversy, in his eyes, was already over. His own role in relation to it in the earlier days of his diaconate is not easy to determine. His influence at Alexandria at that stage, even if it has been exaggerated by later admirers, must have been considerable enough for him to have secured election as bishop at so young an age only a few years later. And Christopher Stead has recently made out a strong case for seeing him as the author of *Enos somatos,* one of the most significant documents from that early period dealing directly with the substance of Arius' teaching.[2] But, whatever his own role in the controversy leading up to Nicaea, that was all a matter of past history. At the Council Arius' views had been anathematised and Arius himself excommunicated. *Causa finita erat.* All that remained for Athanasius to do was to stand firm against unwarranted attempts to have Arius accepted back by the church in Alexandria, even when those attempts were pressed on him more than once with imperial backing.[3]

That is not to say that the early years of Athanasius' episcopate were free of controversy. But the conflict in which he was involved at that early stage of his career was not a theological one. It concerned his treatment in the area under his episcopal jurisdiction of schismatics

---

[1] See especially R. Lorenz, *Arius Judaizans?* (Göttingen: Vandenhoeck and Ruprecht, 1978) and Rowan Williams, *Arius.*

[2] G. C. Stead, 'Athanasius' Earliest Written Work' JTS ns XXXIX (1988), 76–91.

[3] Socrates, *HE* 1 27; Sozomen *HE* 2 22. See Williams, *Arius,* 76.

who did not accept his leadership, and in particular it concerned his alleged use of violence against them. His behaviour, not his theology, was the weapon his opponents sought to use against him. The schismatics with whom he was in conflict were undoubtedly Melitians. They represented an older and more deep-rooted problem for the Egyptian church than Arius and his supporters. They may well have made common cause with the excommunicated followers of Arius, and they certainly turned to the same outside source of support, Eusebius of Nicomedia. Though Eusebius had more in common with the supporters of Arius, people making complaints against Athanasius while having no difficulty about the theological decisions of Nicaea, were valuable allies politically.[4] However extensive the involvement of the supporters of Arius may have been, there is no evidence of a continuation of the theological argument leading up to and debated at Nicaea. The essential issues were ones of jurisdiction and of behaviour.

A number of the Festal Letters of Athanasius belong to this early period, though the precise dating of the various letters is still a matter of dispute. Nos. 1, 24, 14, 4 and 5 can with some confidence be assigned to the years 329, 330, 331, 332 and 333 respectively.[5] Only in the last of these is there any allusion to heretics. In that letter Athanasius refers to 'heretics and schismatics of the present time' as a third group following reference to 'heathen' and to 'ignorant Jews'. He goes on to spell out why none of the three categories can celebrate a true feast as the Catholic church does. When he comes to the third he speaks of them simply as 'schismatics' who 'keep it in separate places and with vain imagination'.[6] It is the separateness of schismatics not the false teaching of heretics with which he is concerned. If, with Camplani, we assign Nos. 6 and 7 to the immediately succeeding years of 334 and 335, the picture remains much the same.[7] There are similar

---

[4] Sozomen, *HE* 2 21–2. See A. Martin, 'Athanase et les Melitiens' in ed. C. Kannengiesser, *Politique et Theologie chez Athanase d'Alexandrie* (Paris: Editions Beauchesne, 1974), 44–6.

[5] E. Schwartz, ' Zur Kirchengeschichte des Vierten Jahrhunderts' *ZNW* XXXIV (1935), 129 ff. And, for the addition of Letter 24, see R. Lorenz, *Der Zehnte Osterfestbrief des Athanasius von Alexandrien* (Berlin: W. de Gruyter, 1986), 30.

[6] Athanasius, *Festal Letters* 5, 4.

[7] See T. D. Barnes' review of A. Camplani, *Le Lettere Festali di Atanasio di Alessandria* (Rome, 1989) in JTS ns XLI (April 1990), 258–64.

brief references to 'heretics and schismatics', who are 'excluded from glorifying God with the saints'.[8] There is a brief expansion on that underlying theme in the description of heretics as 'those who slay the Word' and schismatics as 'those who rend the coat'.[9]

But the next two surviving letters, Nos. 10 and 11, for the years 338 and 339 respectively, show a marked change. Together with the more ferocious Encyclical Letter, also of 338, they give full vent to Athanasius' indignation at his banishment from Alexandria and the appointment of Gregory in his place. It was less than thirty years since the ending of the great persecution, yet Athanasius can still complain that what he is suffering 'surpasses the bitterness of any persecution'.[10] There is no doubt now about who are the primary enemies in his diocese. In all these documents he rails violently against the *Areiomanitai*.[11] Lorenz points to a number of similarities in both the style and the substance of the polemic of the 10th letter with that of those much earlier anti-Arian letters, the letter of Alexander of Alexandria to Alexander of Thessalonica and the encyclical *Enos somatos*.[12] Arianism as such is not new to Athanasius. He draws on a tradition of argument that he had learnt from Alexander, and perhaps had already developed himself in *Enos somatos*. But it seems as if that tradition had been allowed to lie dormant, at least as far as any exploitation in explicit polemic is concerned, for the first ten years of his episcopate. A number of points about the way in which that tradition of argument reappears at this initial stage in the long drawn out series of his anti-Arian writings merit attention.

1) The designation *Areiomanitai* is a striking one, especially when translated by Robertson as 'Arian madmen' or 'Ariomaniacs'. It seems to fit in well with the fiercely embittered tone of the Encyclical Letter. Yet it is far from clear that it should be heard in quite that emotive way. Its use is not personal to Athanasius. It occurs also in a number of Synodal letters, not only from groups of Egyptian bishops, who might be thought likely to adopt Athanasius' distinctive terminology, but also in the Encyclical letter of Serdica and in the letter of Julius.[13]

---

[8] Athanasius, *Festal Letters* 7, 4.
[9] ibid., 6, 6.
[10] *Encyclical Letter* 1.
[11] ibid., 7; *Festal Letters* 10, 9; 11, 10 and 12.
[12] R. Lorenz, *Der Zehnte Osterfestbrief*, 83–4.
[13] Athanasius, *Apologia Contra Arianos* 44 and 23.

It is used interchangeably in a single chapter with *Areianoi,* as a parallel to other names of heretics such as *Kollouthianoi* and *Melitianoi.*[14] Petavius states that use of the name was enjoined in a letter of Constantine's.[15] Petavius gives no authority for his statement, but it is fully consistent with the way in which the title appears from the outset to be used as a straightforward designation and not only in highly charged contexts.

2) The Arians in these documents, whether designated by the shorter or longer title, are the local Egyptian adherents of Arius, who had been excommunicated and are now excluding the followers of Athanasius from the church. His external opponents who have brought about his exile and enabled the Arians in Egypt to take over authority in the church are not themselves spoken of explicitly as Arians. They are described as *hoi peri Eusebion* and are said to be 'supporters and associates of the *Areiomanitai',* or even as 'belonging to the same heresy'.[16] The distinction is admittedly a fine one, but I think it is significant that at this stage the name itself is not directly applied to them.

3) Pistus, an earlier putative replacement for Athanasius as Bishop of Alexandria, and Gregory, his actual replacement, are each described individually as an Arian. In each case a reason is given for so describing them. Pistus' case is straightforward enough. He had been excommunicated by Alexander and the Council of Nicaea, and then ordained by Secundus, one of the bishops excommunicated at Nicaea for his adherence to Arius.[17] Gregory, on the other hand, was sent from outside to the Arians, and is shown to be an Arian himself, Athanasius says, by his choice of secretary, one Ammon, who had been excommunicated in the days of Alexander.[18] To be an Arian, it would seem, is defined not by a series of beliefs but by belonging to those excommunicated by Alexander along with Arius or by identifying oneself with that group by entering into communion with them. We have no evidence of what Gregory's specific theological views were, but it is perhaps worth recalling that the first choice of the

---

[14] ibid., 77
[15] See ed. A. Robertson, *Select Writings of Athanasius,* NPNF IV: 456 n. 4.
[16] Athanasius, *Encyclical Letter* 2 and 7. Cf. *Apol. Con. Arian.* 17.
[17] *Encyclical Letter* 6; *Apol. Con. Arian.* 24.
[18] *Encyclical Letter* 7.

Eusebian party for the unenviable job of replacing Athanasius as Bishop of Alexandria was Eusebius, later bishop of Emesa.[19] Theologically his position was a long way from that of Arius – as it was also from that of Athanasius. The Eusebians were not concerned to ensure that it would be an 'orthodox Arian' bishop taking over from Athanasius.

4) It would be quite wrong, however, to give the impression that the designation 'Arian' was altogether devoid of theological content for Athanasius at this stage. The Encyclical Letter is too urgent and too angry about the immediate ecclesiastical predicament to spend time on the longer term issues of doctrinal difference. But the 10th Letter, as we have already noted, picks up the anti-Arian argument from the years before Nicaea, and in doing so includes a brief résumé of Arian error. Arians, says Athanasius, deny the Saviour's essential godhead because of his coming down on our behalf, his essential eternity because of his incarnation in time, and his incorruptibility because of his sufferings for us.[20] It is no more than a rhetorical summary, but it is not without significance that in this very early account of Arian teaching Athanasius should lay such stress on the attempt to make sense of the incarnation and the passion as the primary source of Arian error.

In the course of time Athanasius comes to use the term 'Arian' much more widely. But in doing so he is keen to stress the link with the historical Arius. To that end the distinction implicit in his very early use of the term 'Arian' is not lost to sight. It continues to have a function in the pamphlet war of the 350s as he tries to pin the label 'Arian' firmly on his opponents, such as Acacius and his allies. The 'real Arians', Arians in the primary sense of the word, are, he says, those who were originally expelled by Alexander along with Arius-Secundus of Ptolemais foremost among them. Others, though still Arian, are Arian in a secondary sense, judged to be so on the basis of circumstantial evidence.[21] That evidence can take a variety of forms. Acacius and his associates show themselves Arian by joining forces at Seleucia with Arians in the primary sense, people actually ordained by

[19] Socrates, *HE* 2 9.
[20] *Festal Letters* 10, 9. Cf. R. Lorenz, *Der Zehnte Osterfestbrief*, 85–6.
[21] Athanasius, *Hist. Ar.* 71. Cf. also *Ad Episcopos Aegypti* 19 for selective mention of Secundus in this context.

Secundus himself.[22] But it can also show itself doctrinally, by the production of statements of faith which, though not deriving directly from Arius, embody the same essential teaching. By acknowledging the two senses in which someone can be spoken of as Arian, Athanasius is able to argue in the *Epistle to the Bishops of Egypt* that the term as he applies it to his opponents gives expression to a real connexion between them and the historical Arius, which they are anxious to deny.[23] This is important to Athanasius' case, both because the historical Arius was condemned and expelled by the Council of Nicaea and also because the manner of Arius' death was a signal vindication of that expulsion given by God himself.[24] The fact that this latter argument does not appear earlier in the immediate aftermath of the death of Arius but only twenty years later suggests that, whatever its grounding in historical fact, the account of his death has lost nothing in the telling. It had the further advantage for Athanasius of enabling him to conduct the debate in terms of the issues and the slogans that had been familiar to him in his younger days. What has sometimes been ascribed to acute theological vision of what was the unchanging heart of the matter can perhaps also be seen as a symptom of a phenomenon not uncommon in academic life - the older scholar who cannot keep up with the way his younger colleagues are developing the subject and wants to hold the discussion back to the issues that mattered most to him as a young man and with which he feels more at home.[25]

Be that as it may, an identification of the views of latter day Arians with those of the discredited Arius himself is clearly a characteristic of Athanasius' most celebrated work, the *Orations against the Arians*. As Kannengiesser has well emphasised,[26] the Arius of the *Orations* is not the historical Arius accessible to Athanasius, let alone the historical Arius of the modern scholar's reconstruction. His name appears frequently in the opening chapters of the first *Oration,* but exclusively

---

[22] *De Synodis* 12.
[23] *Ad Ep. Aeq.* 5.
[24] ibid., 19. Cf. also *Epp.* 54 and 52, 3.
[25] Cf. J-M. Leroux, 'Athanase et la seconde phase de la crise Arienne' in ed. C. Kannengiesser, *Politique et theologie,* 145–59.
[26] C. Kannengiesser, *Athanase d'Alexandrie, éveque et écrivain* (Paris: Éditions Beauchesne, 1983), 114–20.

in his capacity as author of the *Thalia*. In other, more indefinite, references to his writings, later in the work, his name appears in a secondary position after that of Eusebius,[27] and linked with that of Asterius, who is described in the *De Decretis* as source of Arius' ideas.[28] Important though the figure of Arius is for Athanasius' argument, he hardly emerges consistently as the creative individual originator of the heresy that bears his name, even though it would greatly have strengthened Athanasius' case to present him in that light. Kannengiesser draws attention to a particularly revealing example of the artificial character of the Arius of the *Orations*. In the rhetorical climax to two parallel passages in *Or.* 2:23 and 24, where Athanasius draws out his own orthodox interpretation of some passages of scripture much used by the Arians, he concludes each account with a concessive clause: in the first case it takes the form 'though Arius think otherwise', in the second 'though the Arians burst at the tidings'. Arius, though dead, yet thinketh. The name of Arius is not the historical individual, but a synonym for the Arians. The references to Arius in the *Orations* are surely part of the same strategy we have already seen at work in the *Epistle to the Bishops of Egypt*, namely to identify as closely as possible the latter day, secondary Arians with the individual expelled at Nicaea and struck down by God before that expulsion could be undone. In that Epistle Athanasius describes his opponents' production of new formularies as an attempt to draw attention away from Nicaea and its refutation of Arius. If they really believed that his description of them as Arians was a calumny, their present strategy would be pointless; they would have nothing to fear from the anathemas of Nicaea. Their real objective in putting out new formularies was to prevent that refutation of Arius being used against them. So far from having the effect of distancing themselves from Arius, their actions revealed them as Arius himself fighting on their behalf.[29] Seeing their conduct in that light Athanasius feels justified in identifying the two in his attack on their theology.

So far I have been trying to elucidate Athanasius' view of the significance of Arius himself in the long drawn out theological

---

[27] *Or. Con. Ar.* 1:22; 1:37; 2:24.
[28] ibid., 1:37; 2:24; *De Decretis* 8 and 20.
[29] *Ad Epp. Aeg.* 5.

controversy of the middle years of the fourth century, and the basis on which he justifies the classification of his opponents as Arians. Part of that view, as we have seen, is that his opponents are in reality very close to Arius, virtually *Arius redivivus,* but do all they can to conceal the fact. We need now to ask how those dubbed Arians regarded the one after whom they were being named. Hanson devotes a useful section to this topic in his comprehensive study of the Arian controversy.[30] His overall conclusion is that 'though respected by later Arians' 'he was not usually thought of as a great man by his followers'.[31] Athanasius would no doubt see that as evidence of how effectively the deceitful Arians have succeeded in pulling the wool over Hanson's eyes. But I think Hanson is right in his assessment, and that it could even be strengthened on the basis of the evidence he himself offers.

There is no doubt that in the early years after Nicaea, Eusebius of Nicomedia and his friends made strenuous efforts to get Arius readmitted to communion. How far this was due to collucianist friendship, how far to theological admiration, how far to self-interest (since their own ecclesiastical status was not unrelated to his fate) and how far to its being a good way of getting at their enemy, Athanasius, is hard to judge. Each motive may have had some part to play. But the later account of Philostorgius lends some credence to the suggestion that those who lent him their practical support did not always see eye to eye with Arius theologically.[32] Political considerations were probably uppermost.

It is quite shortly after Arius' death, at the Council of Antioch in 341, that we meet with the first famous statement in which opponents of Athanasius, many of whom had supported Arius against him, clearly seek to distance themselves from Arius. In their letter to Julius (sometimes misleadingly called the first creed of the Council) they say: 'We are not followers of Arius (for how could we who are bishops follow a presbyter?)'.[33] Here they are undoubtedly responding to Athanasius' insistence on describing them as Arians. But there is nothing disingenuous in their reply. Their theological

---

[30] Hanson, *The Search,* 123–8.
[31] ibid., 128.
[32] Philostorgius, *HE* II 3.
[33] Athanasius, *De Synodis* 22.

position is by no means the same as that of Arius. Nor is their activity in setting out an appropriate summary of the faith particularly related to the person of Arius. They would have regarded it as a natural function of Christian leadership. If they had championed Arius against oppression by his tyrannous bishop that did not make them his followers; and if pulling ecclesiastical rank can clinch the argument in the eyes of the Bishop of Rome, so much the better.

But that response, as we have seen, did nothing to deflect Athanasius from his determined strategy to describe them as Arians. The very fact of being called by the name of a human leader, like Marcionites, Valentinians, Manichaeans, Melitians, etc., is evidence, Athanasius says, that those so named are heretics and not Christians.[34] It is a perspective his opponents would have shared. So denial of the description 'Arian' would be a genuinely and strongly felt response, even for people with no particular animus against Arius himself. There is certainly nothing surprising or particularly significant in the explicit disavowal of it by Homoian leaders in the politically complex debates at the Council of Niké in 359.[35]

But all this tells us comparatively little about the actual influence of Arius on the later Eastern opponents of Athanasius or about their attitude to him. More explicit evidence on those questions is forthcoming from the West. Palladius and Secundianus, 'Arian' bishops under cross-examination from Ambrose at the Council of Aquileia in 381, deny all knowledge of Arius and his writings.[36] More surprising is the insistence of Auxentius, Ambrose's Arian predecessor as Bishop of Milan, that he knew neither Arius or his doctrine – more surprising because he had earlier been a presbyter in Alexandria under George, the substitute for Athanasius as bishop there in 357.[37] But we have already seen that those appointed to replace Athanasius were not necessarily chosen for their specifically Arian views. By 357, in any case, the Eastern opponents of Athanasius show little interest in Arius and were particularly anxious to disavow the name of Arian. So while recent studies have tended to give more importance ecclesiastically to Western Arianism than has often been done in the past, they have at

---

[34] *Or. Con. Ar.* 13.
[35] See Jerome, *Adversus Luciferianos* 18.
[36] Ed. R. Gryson, *Scolies Ariennes sur le Concile d' Aquilée* (SC 267 226.28; 376.66).
[37] Hilary, *Contra Auxentium* 14 (PL 10, 617B).

the same time shown it to be almost totally unrelated to Arius himself. Western Arians see themselves as the continuators of a biblically based faith, to which Arius is an irrelevance. They are, as Maximinus puts it, Christians on whom the name Arian has been wrongly imposed.[38]

One other way of approaching the question of the significance of Arius for later Arians is to ask about the influence of his writings. When Ambrose was pressing Palladius and Secundianus about their attitude to Arius' teaching, it is Arius' Letter to Alexander which he quotes to them and which they claim to be unacquainted with.[39] The evidence for use of it by Arians in the East as a doctrinal norm is, as Hanson says, negligible.[40] But Hanson gives some weight to the fact that both Athanasius and Hilary cite it as fulfilling that role, – more weight than seems to be warranted.[41] As Athanasius uses it, it is essentially a historical document with which he is anxious to associate his Homoian opponents. It hardly constitutes evidence that they – or any other Arians of that later period – treated it as a key document for the expression of their own beliefs.

One other case where a later credal formula is said to derive from Arius himself is the brief summary of the faith given by Eunomius at the start of his *Apologia*.[42] But once again our evidence for the link with Arius comes not directly from Eunomius, but from his orthodox opponent, Basil. What Basil says is that the Eunomians claim the formulary to be one that was presented by Arius to Alexander as evidence of his orthodoxy. Basil admits that it had indeed been used by some of the Fathers 'in the simplicity of their hearts' and regards Arius' use of it as a form of dissimulation.[43] It is not clear that we are meant to understand that Arius actually composed it, so that Hanson's description of it as 'the only reference to a specific work of Arius of which we do not have any other knowledge' goes beyond the evidence.[44] In any case the point the Eunomians were apparently trying to make and Basil to deny, has to do with its traditional

[38] Ed. R. Gryson, *Scripta Arriana Latina* I, Fr. 6 (CCSL 87 237).
[39] Ed. R. Gryson, *Scolies* (SC 267 276.90. Cf. also 211.11; 222.21; 224.25; 295.109).
[40] Hanson, *The Search*, 126.
[41] Athanasius, *Or. Con. Ar.* 2:19 (Cf. *De Synodis* 16); Hilary, *De Trinitate* 6:4–5.
[42] Eunomius, *Apologia* 1:5.
[43] Basil, *Adversus Eunomium* 1:4 (p. 29: 509B).
[44] Hanson, *The Search*, 127 n. 149.

character and the range of its acceptability, rather than with its authorship. It thus offers no evidence for any claim that the writings of Arius had authoritative significance for the founder figure of what we choose to call Neo-Arianism.

There is another interesting example of an orthodox assertion of a close link between Eunomius and Arius. Ambrose charges the Arians whom he is attacking with inconsistency for refusing to have anything to do with Eunomius, at the same time as themselves describing him as having produced a fuller version of what Arius had written.[45] It will only be an inconsistency, of course, if the title 'Arian' is one which those he is attacking accept as an appropriate description of their own theology. Those he names are Palladius, Auxentius and Demophilus, and we have already seen how vigorously the first two dissociated themselves from any link with Arius. If Ambrose's report of their view of Eunomius is correct, it seems as if they may have been doing to Eunomius what Athanasius and others had over the years been doing to them - alleging a close link with Arius with respect to someone who may have seen himself in a very different light.

'Arian,' I have argued, as a designation for anyone other than the immediate associates of Arius himself who were excluded from the church in Egypt by Alexander, is a title given by Athanasius to his opponents for a specific polemical purpose of defamation by association. Semi-Arianism, it hardly needs saying, is an even more inappropriate title introduced in the fourth century by Epiphanius to discredit Basil of Ancyra and the Homoiousians, and by Gregory of Nazianzus for use against the Pneumatomachoi.[46] Neo-Arian is a modern name, bestowed by Albertz in 1909 as a replacement for the title Anomaean which he regarded as a misleading title given to them by their opponents.[47] But perhaps even his alternative designation has its roots in the same tradition of early polemical description. All three titles deriving from the name of Arius were or would have been conscientiously disavowed by those on whom they were bestowed. Their primary disadvantage is in suggesting a view of fourth century

---

[45] Ed. R. Gryson, *Scolies* (SC 267 268.83).

[46] Epiphanius, *Panarion Haer.* 73.1.5 (GCS 37 268); Gregory the Presbyter, *Vita S. Gregorii Theologi* (p. 35 276 A).

[47] M. Albertz, 'Zur Geschichte der jung-arianischen Kirchengemeinschaft,' *Theologische Studien und Kritiken* (1909), vol. 2, 209.

theology, where the significant issue is seen as the various schools' relation to the one seminal thinker, Arius. And to approach them with that question in mind can be a dangerous disincentive to any serious study of their theologies in their own right. But the figure of Arius was not perhaps, in fact, very important to any of those known by one of the various expansions of his name. And to Athanasius he was not so much a person to be refuted, as a discredited name with which to undermine others. Tradition (and on this point I confess to having always been very traditional) likes to personalise the controversy in terms of a confrontation between Arius, the arch-heretic, and Athanasius, the embodiment of orthodoxy. But in all probability there was no such confrontation. Arius was dead before Athanasius embarked on any large scale theological debate of the issues that Arius had raised. And then his real quarrel was with the living. The dead Arius was not even a whipping boy, but a whip.

Chapter 3

A TOPOGRAPHY OF HERESY: MAPPING THE RHETORICAL CREATION OF ARIANISM

Rebecca Lyman

Every school child knows from classroom charts that our continent sits squarely in the center of the world. Every theologian knows from church history that Arianism was the tenacious fourth century heresy which denied the divinity of Christ. Yet, as studies over the past decade have shown, historians are less and less certain about the theology of Arius himself or its possible connection to later fourth century authors traditionally labelled 'Arians.'[1] A controversial aspect of these revisions has been the proper use of theological polemic as a historical source; the fragmentation, loss, and distortion of the writings of Arius and of later authors create immense problems in reconstruction. Yet, even within these critical revisions traditional doctrinal categories persist which provide the maps of interpretation and definition: 'high' or 'low' Christology, 'Sabellianism' or 'adoptionism'. These categories may be in some sense inevitable as part of the self-definition of Christian doctrine, yet they must also be recognised as inherited orthodox labels which were invented and used to define and exclude opposing theological thought. The difficulty of reconstructing an ancient religious movement later defined as a heresy is the continuing tendency to put it in contradistinction to its contemporary, if not modern, orthodoxy. The broader historical contours of the controversy are often obscured beneath the implicit oppositions of the interpretative typology.

An essential step in historical reconstruction is therefore understanding the broader context of the polemical constructions as

---

[1] For summaries of recent scholarship, see R. Williams, *Arius*, 1–22, and R. Hanson, *The Search*, 123–8.

a means of recovering the larger intellectual map upon which 'orthodoxy' and 'heresy' were constructed. The purpose of this paper is to explore the techniques of heresiological classification in Cyril of Jerusalem, Athanasius of Alexandria, and Gregory of Nyssa. Following second and third century heresiological models, these authors in part defined their theological conflicts by classifying and defining the opposing opinions and persons in relation to previously condemned positions. Rather than merely polemical artifaces, these labels of 'Sabellian' or 'Samosatene' provide maps of truth and error which reveal as much about the concerns of the authors and their communities as about their perspective on their opponents. By understanding more clearly how the classifications and labels were fixed and used, we may begin to uncover and order the rhetorical creations of an 'Arian heresy' in the fourth century. In selected works we will examine how 'Arianism' appeared to these authors through heretical classification, what polemical associations were currently destructive and used, and what associations or labels they themselves feared.

Heresiological Classifications

In the second century Christian authors gave *hairesis* a technical meaning in order to define a particular theological opinion as unacceptable and dangerous to religious belief. This invention of heresy has long been noted, but the recent work of A. Le Boulluec has allowed us to see more clearly the concrete context and function of the term in the development of Christian theology.[2] In their work against Gnostics, Justin and Irenaeus drew on the contemporary polemics of the philosophical schools to present a contrast of true and false *diadochai*. By creating a separate intellectual genealogy for their opponents, they were able to exclude them as outsiders and individualists. When philosophical succession was further combined with the biblical images of false prophets, heretics could be typed as both intrinsically alien and yet deeply destructive because of their

[2] *La notion d'hérésie dans la littérature grecque IIe-IIIe siècles* (Paris 1985). On the development of the term see M. Simon, 'From Greek *Hairesis* to Christian Heresy', *Early Christian Literature and the Classical Intellectual Tradition,* ed. W. R. Schoedel and R. Wilken (Paris: Éditions Beauchesne, 1979), 101–16 and N. Brox, 'Häresie', *Reallexicon für Antike und Christentum* 12 (1984), 248–97.

seeming membership in the community.[3] Eventually, the characteristics of heresy became a negative norm for orthodoxy by contrasting multiplicity to unity, intellect to spirit or sect to church. Certain theological teachings were therefore classified under labels which were increasingly abstracted and cited as types in contrast to orthodox ideas. Through this intellectualization of theological conflict as *hairesis* the concrete situation of the conflict, the common sacramental life, or the religious coherence of the dissenting position was effectively hidden beneath a label which condemned, excluded, and distanced the idea or person from orthodox life and teaching.[4] An accusation of *hairesis* therefore combined the speculative diversity of the ancient philosophical schools with the demonic succession of false prophets from the Christian tradition.

Classifications and labels therefore were an essential part of the rhetorical strategy in ancient theological conflict. Drawing on pre-Christian methods and labels, theologians regularly fragmented and distorted the views of their opponents; the same charges were often levelled against one another in an attempt of *reductio ad haeresim*.[5] These methods however should not be overlooked as predictable heresiological *topoi*. In general classifications reveal the particular concerns of the institutions and individuals who use them, so that their change and development reveal transitions within the organizing assumptions. Classifications and labels therefore are not abstract or essential categories, but statements of institutional power and control. A label is an effort to stabilise an unfamiliar reality, and fit it into an existing classification; to some extent the label therefore creates a new reality.[6] This new creation however is understood by its relation to older classifications, and indeed these classifications to an extent control the content of the new label.

The growing list of condemned positions in conciliar and secular legal documents, and the production of heresiological handbooks in the fourth century reflected not only theological diversity, but the

---

[3] Le Boulluec, 87.

[4] Le Boulluec, 547–55.

[5] The phrase is from G. C. Stead, 'Rhetorical Method in Athanasius', VC 30 (1976), 131.

[6] Mary Douglas, *How Institutions Think* (Syracuse: Syracuse University Press, 1986), 100–2.

emerging consolidation and complexity of imperial orthodoxy.[7] The
associations of certain theological ideas with previously condemned
groups therefore offer important clues in understanding this process
of theological control and classification. As I have argued elsewhere
the association of Arians with Manichees, for example, should not be
dismissed as abstract polemic, but may reflect significant concerns in
the broader theological context of the fourth century; orthodox and
Arian authors wrote polemics against the Manichees as well as against
one another.[8] The polemical classifications of Arianism by association
with Manichees or Jews therefore offer insights into the broader
theological battlefield which surrounded and shaped the responses of
each author. A clarification of these larger concerns by a study of
heresiological classification may help to locate the Arian controversy
more concretely in the theological landscape of the fourth century.

Cyril of Jerusalem: Heretics in Disguise

In 350 Cyril of Jerusalem was neither clearly allied with those
defending Nicaea or those opposed. Modern studies seem to confirm
him as a traditionalist or moderate, perhaps closest to Eusebius of
Caesarea in his defense of the one begotten Son and condemnation of
Marcellus.[9] Betraying the common expectation of sharp
demarcations between Nicene orthodoxy and Arianism in the fourth
century, W. Telfer described him as 'impervious to contemporary
theological disturbances.'[10] However, Cyril's *Catechetical Lectures* as
standard episcopal teaching for the theological initiation and
protection of the newly baptised offer a helpful perspective on the
definition of heresy for the lay Christian. His lectures therefore were
a secret teaching which should not be repeated outside the

[7] Judith McClure, 'Handbooks against heresy in the West from the late fourth to the
late sixth centuries', JTS n.s. 30 (1979), 190.

[8] 'Arians and Manichees on Christ', JTS n.s. 40 (1989), 493–503. On the activities of
Manichees and Christian fourth century polemics, see S. Lieu, *Manichaeism in the Later
Roman Empire* (Manchester: Manchester University Press, 1985), 95–110.

[9] J. Lebon, 'La position de saint Cyrille de Jérusalem dans les luttes provoquées par
l'arianisme', *Revue d'histoire ecclésiastique* 20 (1924) 181-210; W. Telfer, *Cyril of Jerusalem
and Nemesius of Emesa*. Library of Christian Classics 4 (London: SCM Press, 1955), 19–63;
R. C. Gregg, 'Cyril of Jerusalem and the Arians', *Arianism Historical and Theological
Reassessments*, ed. R. C. Gregg (Philadelphia: Philadelphia Patristic Foundation, 1985),
85–110; Hanson, *The Search*, 398–413.

[10] *Cyril of Jerusalem*, 61.

community (*Procat.* 12); they were essential to protect the new Christians from deadly theological error (4.1–2). On one hand Cyril therefore offered the saving teaching of the church in opposition to error and death, yet at the same time revealed the variety of teaching within it by outlining different theological opinions.

Following the standard outlines of catechesis, Cyril presented an outline of the baptismal creed which assumed the heresiological reality of clear and inherited truth in opposition to the multiplicity and false succession of error. He approached the topic of heresy formally in his sixth lecture after his discussion of monotheism. As reflected both in this lecture and in the fourth, monotheism was crucial for Christian identity over against Graeco-Roman religion, and heresies, forming 'a foundation in your soul' (4.4). The archetypal heretics for Cyril were those 'falsely called Christians who . . . dared to separate God from his creation' (6.12). This blasphemy of the Father makes them enemies of the Son, particularly because they spoke of two godheads, one evil and one good; these two unbegotten sources stand in eternal opposition to one another undercutting God's power and will (6.13). These heretics are of course Manichees, whom Cyril linked to Simon Magus and earlier Gnostics to show the genealogy of error (6.14–19). He concluded, 'Hate all heretics, but especially him who is rightly named after *mania.*' (6.20). Cyril then drew on the contemporary Christian polemic the *Acta Archelai* to expose in detail the absurdity and destructive nature of this heresy by the ridicule of Mani (6.21–30).[11] He concluded with practical advice on the avoidance of Manichees and a warning about the pollution of their sacramental rites as akin to pagans, Jews, or fornicators (6.32–6).

Throughout his lectures Cyril returned to the Manichees as archetypal heretics, although not always by name. 'Heretics' deny almighty God as creator of all (8.3; 9.2; 11.21), divide God into two opposing principles (4.4), deny the goodness of creation (8.3; 8.7), separate Christ and Jesus (10.4), claim Christ is the Sun (11.21; 15.3), the cross is an illusion (13.14;13.37), and resurrection is an illusion (14.21). Although several of these polemical charges could be

---

[11] On the history and use of this document, see S. Lieu, 'Fact and Fiction in the *Acta Archelai*', *Manichaean Studies. Proceedinqs of the First International Conference on Manichaeism*, edited by P. Bryder (Lund, 1988), 69–88.

identified with Marcionite or Gnostic teaching, Cyril tended to focus the venom of his point on the Manichees.[12] Jews, Greeks, and heretics therefore were external opponents to Christian teaching (8.1; 12.27; 13.37), but Manichees were named as the most recent and pernicious.

Given his vehemence, lengthy discussion, and repeated focus on their teaching, Cyril must have known actual Manichaean missionaries. In spite of Diocletian's earlier edict, Manichees continued to flourish in the Eastern empire in the fourth century, perhaps protected by the tolerance for Christians with whom they were usually identified; Constantine did not issue any anti-Manichaean legislation.[13] Since the Christian polemic *Acta Archaelai* may be dated around 340, Cyril's extensive use of them in 350 reflect his attention and concern for this movement as particularly dangerous and heretical. Since they claimed apostolic succession from Jesus through Mani, Manichees may well have been active in Jerusalem.[14]

Cyril also identified certain theological opinions as heretical, but without labelling them by reference to particular individuals or movements:

> For humans have fallen away from the right faith; and some preach the identity of the Son with the Father and others dare to say that Christ was brought into being out of nothing. And formerly the heretics were obvious, but now the Church is filled with heretics in disguise. (15.9)

Since this comment appeared in the lecture on the last days, it perhaps revealed Cyril's pessimistic perspective on the continuing theological controversies after Nicaea. This use of 'heretic' refered to a theological error which cannot be tolerated, yet Cyril does not label the contrasting positions 'Sabellian' or 'Arian.' As he used the opposition several times, these positions indicated the boundaries of acceptable reflection on the Godhead (11.17;11.18;15.9).

---

[12] Two first principles was a pre-Christian polemical charge as discussed in Stead, 'Rhetorical Method', 132. Compare 4.1 to 6.12: the Gnostic charge is not discussed, but the discussion centered on the Manichee doctrine of opposing principles. In 14.21 the Manichees are the most recent representative of the denial of the resurrection.

[13] S. Lieu, *Manichaeism in the Later Roman Empire*, 96.

[14] Epiphanius used the bishop list of Jerusalem to refute claims of apostolic succession by Manichees in *Panarion haer.* 66. 20. 7ff.

Orthodoxy for Cyril therefore lay in a middle way:

> Let the truth be spoken. The Father did not suffer for us, but the Father sent him who suffered. Neither let us say, There was a time when the Son was not; nor let us admit a Son who is a Father. But let us walk in the king's highway; let us neither turn aside on the left hand nor the right. Neither from thinking to honor the Son, let us call him the Father; nor from thinking to honor the Father, imagine the Son to be one of the creatures. (11.17)

Remarkably, perhaps as part of the catechetical pedagogy, he acknowledged certain religious reasons why these errors might be held, i.e. to honor mistakenly the Father or the Son. This acknowledgement however was in stark contrast to the denunciation of Manichaean teaching as polluting or corrupt. Although he understood *hairesis* as destructive and opposed to orthodoxy, Cyril in practice distinguished between overt heretical teachings usually identified with a named individual or school and varied theological errors in reflection.

As studied by R. Gregg, Cyril does not mention 'Arians' by name, but rejected a number of positions which were associated with early Arians such as Arius and Asterius: the Son is by nature, not by adoption (10.4;11.2); only one rather than many (10.3); lord by nature, not by advancement (10.5;11.1); he has no brother, but is alone (11.2), he is begotten, not a disciple (11.12).[15] However, in his two lectures on the nature of the Son, these opinions were not systematised into a movement or labelled according to a teacher such as Arius or Paul of Samosata, but rather contrasted individually to proper understandings of generation and relation:

> And again on hearing of a son, think not of an adopted son but a son by nature, an only begotten son having no brother. For this is the reason why he is called only begotten because in the dignity of the Godhead and his generation from the Father, he has no brother. (11.2)

> Again, I say, on hearing of a son, understand it not merely in an improper sense, but as a son in truth, a son by nature, without beginning; not as having come out of bondage into a higher state of adoption, but a son eternally begotten by an inscrutable and incomprehensible generation. (11.4)

---

[15] R. C. Gregg, 'Cyril of Jerusalem', 85ff.

As seen in these passages Cyril refuted unacceptable positions by offering the correct intepretations rather than by labelling such positions as 'adoptionist' or 'heretical'. The only statement explicitly condemned as 'heretical' was the origin of the Son from nothing, but even this was not identified with Arius by name (11.13; 11.17; 15.9). It was rather one extreme of the heretical positions on either side of the mean of orthodoxy.

Not surprisingly, Cyril also addressed concerns from the opposite side of the contrast: the confusion of the Father and Son. In the context of his concern about monotheism in general, and Marcellus of Ancyra in particular, the distinction of the Father and Son was essential to orthodoxy:

> I know that I have said these things many times, but it is for your safety that they are said so often: neither has he who begat a Father nor he who was begotten a brother; neither was he who begat changed into the Son nor did he who was begotten become the Father. Of one only Father there is one only-begotten Son, neither two unbegotten or two-only begotten, but one Father, unbegotten, for he is unbegotten who has no father, and one Son, eternally begotten of the father, begotten not in time, but before all ages; not increased by advancement, but begotten that which he now is. (11.13)

This accusation of two unbegottens was reportedly raised against Alexander of Alexandria.[16] The implications of assimilation to Manichee teaching were obvious. Cyril's doctrinal oppositions were similar to Eusebius of Caesarea's model argued against Marcellus which placed the teaching of the church between Sabellian ideas and those of Paul of Samosata.[17] Cyril however did not mention Paul of Samosata by name here or elsewhere, but used a mean based on the generation of the Son. Cyril's heresiological contrast reflected not only the controversies of the 330s, but did not go beyond the positions condemned at Nicaea and the Dedication Council of 341.[18]

In Jerusalem therefore heresy was identified with the extreme theological opinions, i.e. identity of the Father and Son or the creation of the Son from nothing as well as Gnostic or Manichean

[16] *Letter to Alexander.* Opitz, *Ur.* 14, 26.

[17] *ET* 1.14; 1.20; 3.6; cf. 1.9; 2.23.

[18] See J. N. D. Kelly, *Early Christian Creeds* (Harlow: Longman, 1981, 3rd ed.) for the anathemas of Nicaea, 216, and Antioch, 269–70. The so-called Third Creed of Antioch contrasted Marcellus, Sabellius, and Paul of Samosata, 267.

teaching. Those resembling the obvious errors of the past were Manichees, whose teaching was condemned repeatedly throughout the work. The contemporary debates regarding the Father and the Son were also important, but Cyril approached them cautiously and in a less polemical way, depending on established norms or perhaps credal norms to contrast the extremes. These positions were held by 'heretics in disguise', those who appeared to be orthodox, yet were in danger of extreme and unacceptable teaching. For Cyril some humility about divine generation would have solved at least part of the theological controversies (11.15), since speculation was fruitless on divine nature. However, he discussed and rejected these theological opinions without fixing them by classification with earlier teachers. Heresy as classically defined was more clearly represented in the co-existent principles and docetic Christology of the Manichees. If nameless, however, the teaching of Arius on the generation of the Son had become one boundary of orthodox speculation.

Athanasius: Demonic Succession

As the episcopal successor of Alexander and one of the main forces in promoting the acceptance of the authority of the Council of Nicaea in the fourth century, Athanasius remains a major and problematic source for theological controversy in the fourth century. His polemical rhetoric has received close study by C. Kannengiesser and G. C. Stead in an effort to uncover his methods in the discussion of Arianism as a heretical movement.[19] In *Contra Arianos,* written in 339/340 and revised in 350, he drew on traditional heresiology to create a theological movement beginning with Arius, and continuing after his death; in his *Letter to the Egyptian Bishops* (356) and *De Decretis* (356) he condensed and continued these themes in an open defense of Nicaea in reaction to his ejection from his see and conflict with Constantius.[20] In this brief section we will focus on two major heresiological themes in these three works: labelling and classification by association with other movements, and the construction of a succession of error.

[19] G. C. Stead, 'Rhetorical Method in Athanasius', 121–37; C. Kannengiesser, *Athanase d'Alexandrie évêque et écrivain* (Paris: Éditions Beauchesne, 1983).

[20] Kannengiesser, *Athanase* 23 f. References in the text use the following abbreviations: *Contra Arianos* = A, *Letter to the Egyptian Bishops* = E, *De Decretis* = D.

In *Contra Arianos* 1.1 Athanasius began his polemic by linking Arius firmly to the devil as the last great heresiarch: '. . . darkness is not light nor falsehood truth nor Arianism good; those who call these people Christians are in great error'. The act of exclusion was completed by the classification of 'Arians' with Manichees: 'For with them for Christ is Arius, as with the Manichees Mani'. (1.2) By establishing a separate movement and demonic succession, Athanasius was able to construct a set of theological opinions and expectations of heresy which might be tied to Arius whatever the actual historical circumstances.[21] 'Arians' were therefore set apart by both their teaching and their succession from Arius; in these works no legitimate theological discussion existed as in Cyril, but a confrontation of truth and falsehood, life and death.

To underscore the separation between Arians and orthodox in these works, Athanasius contrasted the demonic succession of Arius to the Alexandrian episcopal succession from *hagios* Alexander. Bishop Peter for example did not receive the designation of blessed, but the title *hagios* for Alexander, like references to the 'uncorrupt' council (of Nicaea), conveyed the opposition of truth and falsity at stake in the doctrinal debates (E 1–5; 8; 21; D 4; 18; 27; A 2.19)[22] As Kannengiesser pointed out, Athanasius in part defined 'Arianism' by those opposed to the bishop of Alexandria.[23] However, in the context of demonic and holy successions, the original historical conflict between Arius and Alexander was transformed into a mythic and eternal confrontation of error and truth. Those who followed Arius in their teaching therefore shared the rejection and condemnation of the council of Nicaea (E 8). To outline this opposition Athanasius drew on the explosive heresiological themes of false prophets and demonic succession in earlier Christian literature as 'Arians' were portrayed in Satanic roles as seducers, kidnappers, murderers, serpents, and liars (E 3; 7; 11; 19; 21; D 4; A 2.73). By contrast those who uphold the teaching of Nicaea may understand themselves as martyrs or in an apocalyptic sense of fighting with Satan (E 21).

Equally important, the contrast of successions allows Athanasius to

---

[21] Kannengiesser, *Athanase,* 119.

[22] C. Stead discusses a possible early use by Athanasius of Arius as antichrist in *henos somatos* in 'Athanasius' Earliest Work', JTS n.s. 39 (1988), 80.

[23] Kannengiesser, *Athanase,* 120.

personalise truth in himself; as the successor and aide of *hagios* Alexander he may therefore claim personal authority and responsibility to expose Arian theology (E 11). He and his people as Christians stand in contrast to those of the 'Arian' party (A 1.3). On one level this language of course refered to actual factions supporting rival bishops in Alexandria, but it was also a powerful rhetorical move to claim his own doctrinal authority. At the beginning of the *Letter to the Egyptian Bishops* he reminded his readers of Christ's warning about false prophets and gift of discernment; Athanasius, like Christ, then proceeded to warn his followers against the kidnappers and poisoners among them. As this letter in particular reveals, Athanasius linked his episcopal authority to the charismatic exorcisms of the holy man by defining heresy as demonic pollution.

From this stark contrast of holy and profane, Athanasius continued to create a separate movement and exclude it by associating Arians with heretical groups. In *Contra Arianos* the Arians were associated with various heretical groups including Marcionites, Gnostics, and Samosatenes, but primarily Manichees and Jews.[24] Not surprisingly, Sabellius was only mentioned once (3.4), and to clarify his own position. The associations were usually superficial e.g. like Marcionites, they follow their leader not Christ (1.3); like Manichees, Phrygians, and Samosatenes, their baptism is invalid (2.43). The extensive use of Judaism focused on the denial of the divinity of Christ, and misplaced defense of monotheism. The polemical purpose was of course to label the created groups of Arian thinkers as heretical by their association with other condemned movements. The repetition of these associations encouraged the reader to push Arian theology out from the center of the tradition into the fringes of extreme and false beliefs which surround the orthodox center. However, these associations form no clear pattern of heresiological definition as in Cyril, i.e. Sabellianism in contrast to Arianism. Athanasius did not see orthodoxy as a mean between extremes, but

---

[24] Kannengiesser lists the groups in *Athanase,* 124. For the three works discussed here the named groups are as follows. E: Marcion (4); Paul of Samosata (4); Mani (4;16); Jews (9; 13; 17). D: Jews (1; 2; 9; 27); Paul of Samosata (9). A: Marcion (1.3); Paul of Samosata (1.38; 2.43; 3.26); Gnostics (1.56; 2.21; 2.71; 3.60); Phrygians (2.43); Mani (1.8; 1.23; 2.40–1; 2.43; 3.25); Jews (1.8; 1.10; 1.38; 1.39; 1.55; 2.1; 2.17; 2.40; 3.2; 3.8; 3.16; 3.27; 3.28; 3.67).

rather an inviolate and static body of teaching ringed by falsity, which as demonic was multiple, changing, and corrupting. Thus, Arians were both Jews in their monotheism and Gnostic in their polytheism. If doctrinally incoherent, these contradictory labels only served in Athanasius' polemic to show the multiplicity and shifting nature of Arian falsity. As defined as the final demonic attack on orthodoxy, Arianism became a mirror image of falsity to any true doctrine, establishing the norm of Nicaea by its relentless opposition.

After Judaism, an important heresiological association for Athanasius was between Arians and Manichees. Given the long activity of Manichaean missionaries in Egypt, and the earlier polemics of Egyptian Christians against Manichees, such a rhetorical strategy was not surprising.[25] First, the Manichees were listed as a heretical group along with others (E 4; A 2.43). They were also cited in tendentious parallels to label and therefore reject Arian exegesis: can the Manichees receive the gospel if they reject the law (E 4; A 1.8)? Thus, by analogy the partial scriptural exegesis of the Arians must also be heretical. Second, a subtler form of association is Athanasius' continual reference to the madness of the Arians (*mania*), which verbally was reminiscent of the founder of the Manichees, Mani, and often used polemically. Thus, the Arians like the Manichees denied creation, but were *manikoteron* because they deny the Word (E 17). His repetition of the term *ariomaniac* therefore conveyed not only the non-rational and wild sense of heretical thought, which Athanasius used to link Arians to other groups such as Jews and Valentinians (A 2.17; 2.71; 2.41), but also linked them to the highly competitive and foreign group, the Manichees.

More important was Athanasius' use of Manichees in his discussion of Arian teaching about creation. Because the Arians denied the creative power of the Word, they 'have joined themselves to the Manichees. For they also confess the existence of a good god, so far as the mere name goes, but they are unable to point out any of his works either visible or invisible' (E 16). Athanasius used this label concerning creation several times, not claiming that they teach the same thing, but showing an inevitable similarity: 'and so denying him as the creator, and end up grovelling with the Manichees (A 1.23;

---

[25] See Lyman, 'Arians and Manichees', 497f.

3.25).' Such a point gained polemical power from the current Christian defense against the Manichees on precisely this point.

Athanasius also attacked the Arians on grounds of polytheism, which again he linked to the Manichees (A2.40–2.41). The Arian separation of the Son resulted in a co-existent wisdom which he claimed created two ingenerate principles:

> And they battle with us for saying that the word of God is eternal, yet forget their own doctrines, and say themselves that Wisdom coexists with God unoriginately. So dizzied are they . . . as the Manichees who make to themselves another God, after denying Him who is. But let the other heresies and the Manichees also know that the Father of the Christ is one . . . and let the Ariomaniacs know in particular that the Word of God is one . . . .

This charge is particularly interesting since the Nicene position was closer to being suspect as Manichaean as having two eternal beings; Arius had defined *homoousios* as Manichaean in his letter to Alexander.[26] This may well be an example of the rhetorical move when the author accuses the opponent of the very charge which was levelled against him, i.e. an eternal wisdom created two ingenerates.[27] Elsewhere Athanasius noted that he has been accused of this: 'We say not two ingenerates' (3.16); 'They reproach us with two eternals' (3.28). However, in these passages his immediate defence, perhaps of being labelled as a Manichee, was to accuse the Arians of being Jews, and denying the divinity of the Son for the sake of a perverse monotheism.

Another charge associated with the Manichees was the denial of the reality of the Incarnation. If the Arians denied the eternal origin of the Son, they were like Manichees in making the Incarnation an illusion (2.43). If they denied the reality of his body, so they were Manichees (3.35); if they thought Christ was ignorant, they were already Manichees (3.50). In these instances the conclusions do not follow theologically from the premise presented as Arian, i.e. the Son was a only creature, but underline the unity of heresy over against orthodoxy. The description of a created Son was therefore equivalent to a docetic understanding. Equally important, as in the passage discussed above concerning co-existent wisdom, these charges seem

[26] Opitz, *Ur.* 6, 12.
[27] Stead, 'Rhetorical Method', 134–5.

to be the exact opposite of what 'Arian' authors taught about the reality of the Incarnation.[28] The rhetorical labelling therefore was doctrinally incoherent, but polemically effective by associating Arians with acknowledged heretics.

In his heresiological rhetoric about succession and association, Athanasius revealed the fierce local conflict within the Alexandrian church which gave rise to the fourth century controversy. Arians were heretics *par excellence* in exegetical duplicity, demonic teaching, and seductive intentions. For Athanasius the controversy of the fourth century lay between truth and falsehood, eternally embodied in Arius and Alexander, and now passed to their successors. The personalisation of the confrontation between holy and demonic was an intensification of traditional heresiology which supported Athanasius' own institutional power and integrity. Equally important, the association of Arian teaching with a variety of condemned groups hid any theological coherence, and reduced it to a distorted mirror of orthodoxy. The association of Arianism with the Manichees functioned to define it as intrinsically alien and secretly destructive of orthodoxy. However, the rhetoric of this association together with his avoidance of Sabellianism may reveal the strategies of his opponents to label him as a Manichee or a Sabellian.

Gregory of Nyssa: Ungrateful Patients

A third case of labelling and classification in fourth century heresiology may be found in Gregory of Nyssa's *Contra Eunomium*. Basil had written a highly rhetorical attack on Eunomius, teaching and character in 372/3; Eunomius had responded with his *Apologia Apologiae* in 378. Written in 380 during a period of missionary activity and ascendency by Eunomius and his followers, Gregory's treatise was yet another extensive attack on Eunomius' character and teachings.[29] Gregory admitted in a letter to his brother, Peter, that he was angry at Eunomius' abuse of Basil, so that his writing contained both insults and doctrine. Yet, the contrast between Gregory's measured admission of his intention to abuse Eunomius and the

---

[28] For a summary of texts which suggest 'Arians' defended the reality of the human experiences in the Incarnation, see Hanson, *The Search,* 109 ff.

[29] Kopecek, *Neo-Arianism,* 366–494.

violent response of his brother Peter is instructive: Peter encouraged Gregory to expose Eunomius as a pupil of the devil, a murderer, to stab the serpents, and reveal the pollution of heresy. Like Athanasius, Peter reflected a monastic perspective where heresy was linked to demonic pollution in contrast to the bitter, but more philosophical polemics of Basil and Gregory.[30] Gregory approached heresy as a matter of sickness or poor education rather than pollution, depending on theological argument rather than extensive classification or a demonic succession.

Echoing his letter to his brother, Gregory focused on Eunomius' teaching and background rather than a traditional typology of heresy. Eunomius was linked to Arius in only one passage in a quite general sense about wheat and tares in the church (1.6). On one hand Eunomius was a well-known theological opponent, but Basil in his earlier polemic had also made only one link between Eunomius and Arius (1.4). Eunomius was thus characterised as a devious theologian in his own right, but not linked to any separate theological or ecclesiastical succession. Thus, exclusion rested on rhetorical and theological argument, yet even this presupposed a closer relation to real theological issues at stake on each side than the stark opposition of Athanasius' polemics.

As done by Basil, Gregory tended to treat Aetius, Eunomius, and his followers as unenlightened and socially inferior philosophical opponents.[31] They were weak (1.2), fanciful (2.3; 2.4), contagious (1.24), and schismatic (1.2). References to their self-education were important to type them as unphilosophical (1.15), labored (1.3), or cheaters (1.6). On the whole they were ungrateful patients, who have refused correction from their theological betters (1.1).

Polemically, Gregory primarily used Jews and Manichees in classification. Eunomius' passionate defense of monotheism therefore was as alien and opposed to the true faith as was Judaism (1.15; 2.4; 4.4; 4.9). The heretical parameters were therefore extreme monotheism or an unacceptable cosmic dualism. Like Cyril, Gregory defined orthodoxy as the mean between the two extremes of the confusion of the Father and Son or the creation of the Son, but these

---

[30] *Ep.* 29 and 30 in *Grégorie de Nysse. Lettres*, ed. P. Maraval, SC 363.

[31] On the sociological aspects of Cappodocian polemic, see Kopecek, *Neo-Arianism*, 505–8.

extremes were now labelled 'Sabellianism' and 'Arianism' in his account (1.34). Reflecting the controversies of the 360s and 370s, Gregory also admitted the difficulty of finding a mean which would not ultimately veer too closely to one side rather than the other (1.41). As in Athanasius it appears that Sabellianism has been used of the orthodox, for Gregory denied the charge (1.19).

In the first book Gregory discussed at some length the charge by Eunomius that he taught two ingenerate beings. Gregory turned the charge on Eunomius by insisting that he himself has taught two first principles, if the Son was not generated from the Father (1.34). Indeed, if the nature was not identical between the Father and the Son, then 'the mischief of the Manichees is brought into the church' (1.35). Again, the rhetorical device was used to turn the original accusation upon the opponent.[32] The Manichaean label was also underlined by Gregory's insistence that any other position would be heretical.

Gregory's discussion then focused on the diminution of being as leading to opposition between the two gods. Just as uncreated and created nature were deeply opposed, so two divine natures will result in two wills which will be opposed. To his credit, Gregory admits that this was a forced argument, and many will dismiss it as foolish, but he goes on anyway to note how 'Manichaean teaching' creeps in with a wrong understanding of generation (1.35). This pre-Christian argument of opposing powers was a common accusation, and here was a direct attack on the unity of will proposed by some theologians as appropriate to the relation of the Father and the Son. However, the context of this accusation after his denial of two ingenerate principles seems to link it specfically to Manichaean teaching. Indeed, according to Gregory the Manichees were better for they try to shield God from evil by proposing two principles, whereas the Arians give personal existence to a nature opposed to the Good, even though from the Good. The astonishing conclusion to this lengthy argument was that one therefore cannot use the notion of ingenerate deity because it may lead one into heresy, clearly Manicheanism.

This backdrop of Manichaean teaching was implicit elsewhere where Gregory claimed that he was a true monotheist in opposition

---

[32] Stead, 'Rhetorical Method', 134–5.

to the Jewish teaching of the Arians. If the Son were distinct, he would be in opposition to the Father (2.10). In these cases the Eunomian doctrine of two gods was being interpreted according to a synthesis of Marcion's teaching of a higher and lower deities in conflict together with the co-existent principles of the Manichees. The power of the heresiological label however now came from the association with the contemporary rivals, the Manichees. Equally important, Gregory's discussion seems to reveal that this association with the Manichees was an attempt by the author to distance himself from the label as applied to his own teaching.

Gregory therefore argued for a middle position between Sabellius and Arius, yet used the labels of Jew and Manichee in order to push Eunomius from the center. Given the strength of Eunomius at the time of Gregory's work and the legislation against the Manichees in the 370s, this was an important polemical move.[33] Yet, the use of the heresiological labels was less important than the theological arguments which tried to refute the charge of Manichaean teaching and associate it with the opponent.

Conclusion

In his defense to Alexander, Arius outlined his own position by the rejection of opinions associated with heretical groups. After forty years of theological polemics, his own name would be attached to a heretical position, and used to define the boundaries of orthodox thought. As seen in these three authors the creation of an Arian heresy was done on a map which included other active groups and revealed certain sensitive areas of concern: Sabellianism, Manichaeanism, and Judaism were the main named categories of classification. Contrary to the early letter of Alexander concerning Arius, Paul of Samosata and other 'adoptionists' were little used. Instead, the classification focused on appropriate relations between Father and Son or creation. Given those concerns, both sides appeared to use Manichee as an excluding label.

Equally important, the variety of concerns and style of rebuttal should caution us against sweeping definitions about orthodoxy in the fourth century. In Jerusalem, Cyril approached heresy with

---

[33] Lieu, *Manchaeism*, 110.

caution, reserving his polemics for those clearly outside the community, the Manichees. In Alexandria, Athanasius understood the conflict in sharply apocalyptic and monastic terms of the opposition of good and evil or purity and pollution. In Constantinople, Gregory approached the debate with bitter philosophical rhetoric, but with little traditional heresiological succession and labelling. 'Arians' therefore inhabited different theological and rhetorical spaces according to the perspective of the author in the shifting imperial orthodoxy of the fourth century.

II
POLITICAL AND
ECCLESIASTICAL DIVISIONS

Chapter 4

DID ATHANASIUS REJECT MARCELLUS?

Joseph T. Lienhard, S.J.

It may seem perverse to consider, in a volume on Arianism after Arius, two fourth-century bishops who are remembered principally for their rejection of Arianism, and who suffered deposition and exile for – as they believed, at least – their opposition to the errors of the Arians. But the relationship – personal and doctrinal – between Athanasius of Alexandria and Marcellus of Ancyra is one part of the larger question of theological alignments in the fourth century. *Athanasius contra mundum* is too simplistic, as simplistic as Jerome's cry, 'The whole world groaned and marveled that it was Arian.'[1] And Marcellus is like a dark and burnt-out star, itself invisible but deflecting the orbit of anything that comes near it. Understanding Athanasius' allegiances can sharpen the focus on much of fourth-century controversy.

As long as the *Fourth Oration Against the Arians* was accepted as a genuine work of Athanasius, it was generally held that Athanasius, at some point, definitively and publicly rejected Marcellus' teaching. John Henry Newman, for example, wrote: 'If Athanasius' account of the tenets against which he himself writes in his fourth *Oration,* answers to what Eusebius tells us of those of Marcellus, as in fact they do, the coincidence confirms Eusebius as well as explains Athanasius.'[2] Henry Gwatkin, too, in the most influential book on Arianism ever published in English, accepted the *Fourth Oration* as authentic and hence assumed that Athanasius had refuted Marcellus just as Eusebius had. He wrote:

> The gleanings of Athanasius are better than the vintage even of Eusebius. Both parties, he says, are equally inconsistent. The conservatives who

---

[1] *Altercatio Luciferiani et orthodoxi* 19 (PL 23 [1883] 181B).
[2] *Select Treatises of St. Athanasius in Controversy with the Arians,* tr. by John Henry Newman, vol. 2 (London: Longmans, Green, 1920), 200.

refuse eternal being to the Son of God will not endure to hear that his kingdom is other than eternal, while the Marcellians who deny his personality outright are equally shocked at the Arian limitation of it to the sphere of time. One party rests on the Sonship, the other on the doctrine of the Logos; so that while each accepts one half of the truth, neither can attack the other without having to confess the other half also. Athanasius then goes on to shew that the Marcellian system is involved in much the same difficulties as Arianism.[3]

Seeberg wrote: 'Athanasius also attacked the views of Marcellus without naming him, and, after reviewing them, had only ridicule for the oddities of the "old man".'[4] And more than a few modern scholars, often enough in *obiter dicta* assume the same: that Athanasius, at some point, definitively rejected Marcellus and his ideas.

But once the *Fourth Oration* is recognised as spurious, the evidence for saying that Athanasius rejected Marcellus, except for one difficult passage in Hilary's writings, all but vanishes, and the possibility emerges that Athanasius was more closely aligned with Marcellus than is usually granted.

Marcellus in Athanasius' Writings

The first place to look for evidence of Athanasius' and Marcellus' relationship is their writings. Marcellus never mentions Athanasius in his extant writings,[5] but the deacon Eugenius, who was the spokesman for Marcellus and all who had remained faithful to him, addressed a letter to Athanasius in 371. (The letter is considered below.)

Marcellus' name is found in Athanasius' writings twenty times, mostly in documents that Athanasius cites. In the *Apology against the Arians* (ca. 357) Athanasius reproduces Julius of Rome's letter to the Eusebians (written in 341) and the encyclical letter of the (western) synod of Sardica (343). Both of these letters are favorable to Marcellus, and each uses Marcellus' name eight times. In the work

[3] Henry Melvill Gwatkin, *Studies of Arianism* (2nd ed.; Cambridge: Deighton Bell, 1900), 86–7.

[4] Reinhold Seeberg, *Text-Book of the History of Doctrines,* tr. by Charles H. Hay (repr. Grand Rapids: Baker, 1977), I, 221.

[5] I consider only works that are surely authentic: the fragments of the *Contra Asterium* and Marcellus' letter to Julius of Rome (critical edition by E. Klostermann and G. C. Hansen in GCS Eusebius 4, 185–215).

On the Synods of Seleucia and Rimini (finished ca. 361) Athanasius quotes the creeds of Theophronius of Tyana, put forth at the Dedication Council of 341, and the *Ekthesis makrostichos* of 344. Both condemn Marcellus by name.

Only twice, therefore, in his own writings, does Athanasius himself name Marcellus. In the *Apology for His Flight* (ca. 357) Athanasius lists Marcellus among other deposed bishops, in a sort of living martyrology: many bishops, he writes, had been exiled, Marcellus among them; some, himself included, had been condemned to death; and one – Paul of Constantinople – had actually been executed.[6] And in the *History of the Arians,* written ca. 357 (fifteen to twenty years after the events), Athanasius gives his own, favorable judgment of Marcellus' case: the Eusebians had accused Marcellus of heresy and had him banished, but Marcellus was vindicated at Sardica and the Eusebians could offer no defence:

> Of Marcellus, the bishop of Galatia, it is perhaps superfluous for me to speak; for all men have heard how Eusebius and his fellows, who had been first accused by him of impiety, brought a counter-accusation against him, and caused the old man to be banished. He went up to Rome, and there made his defence, and being required by them, he offered a written declaration of his faith, of which the Council of Sardica approved. But Eusebius and his fellows made no defense, nor, when they were convicted of impiety out of their writings, were they put to shame, but rather assumed greater boldness against all. For they had an introduction to the Emperor from the women, and were formidable to all men.[7]

Hence, ca. 357, Athanasius can praise Marcellus as a living martyr and write that the Eusebians had no case against him.

A History of the Relations between Athanasius and Marcellus

Ancient historians and other sources report at least seven instances of contact between Athanasius and Marcellus.

1. The Synod of Tyre (335)

The first time Athanasius and Marcellus might have met was at the Synod of Tyre in 335. A synod was called in 334 for Caesarea in Palestine to investigate Athanasius' conduct, but Athanasius refused

---

[6] *Apologia de fuga sua* 3.

[7] *Historia Arianorum* 6 (tr. NPNF IV: 271–2). Other translations, unless a source is noted, are the author's.

to attend. In the summer of 335, a synod met in Tyre, and Constantine forced Athanasius to attend. Before the synod ended, Athanasius withdrew to Constantinople. The synod's judgement went against Athanasius and he was deposed. The bishops, about sixty in number, then moved to Jerusalem to dedicate the new church of the Anastasis.

Whether Athanasius met Marcellus at Tyre depends on the date of Marcellus' deposition. Older historians, following Socrates and Sozomen, have Marcellus the subject of debate at Tyre, and place Marcellus' deposition in 336, at a synod in Constantinople.[8] Wilhelm Schneemelcher wrote,[9] without explanation, that Socrates is wrong to assert the deposition of Marcellus at the synods of Tyre and Jerusalem. He wants to date Marcellus' deposition either in 330/31 (when the Eusebians began to move against Athanasius, as he writes) or around 334, just as Arius was again condemned. But Schneemelcher has to invent a synod in Constantinople to do this. Hanson returns to the date 336, probably correctly.[10]

If Marcellus was deposed only in 336, then he was present at Tyre, and Sozomen's account can be accepted: Marcellus refused to assent to the definitions of the Synod of Tyre. The most significant of these definitions was the deposition of Athanasius. It is probable, therefore, that Athanasius and Marcellus became allies at Tyre.[11]

---

[8] Socrates (*HE* 1. 36) has this sequence: the bishops assembled at Jerusalem required Marcellus to retract his views, which they found to be like Paul of Samosata's. Marcellus promised to burn his book, but did not do so. The emperor then summoned the bishops to Constantinople. Once at Constantinople, they deposed Marcellus and replaced him with Basil. The Synod of Sardica later reinstated Marcellus. Sozomen (*HE* 2. 33) reports that the Eusebians were angry with Marcellus for three reasons: he did not consent to the definitions of the synod in Phoenicia (that is, Tyre), or to the decision in favour of Arius made at Jerusalem, and he refused to attend the consecration of the church of the Holy Sepulcher. Like Socrates, Sozomen has Marcellus deposed at Constantinople.

[9] 'Zur Chronologie des arianischen Streites', *Theologische Literaturzeitung* 79 (1954), 393–400.

[10] Hanson, *The Search*, 217–8.

[11] In his summary of the decree of Philippopolis (*The Search*, 297), Hanson writes: 'Athanasius had assented to the deposition of Asclepas and Marcellus.' But he may misinterpret a passage in the decree. It reads: 'Etenim adhuc cum esset episcopus Athanasius, Asclepam depositum sua sententia ipse damnauit. sed et Marcellus similiter illi nunquam communicauit' (*Decree of Philippopolis* 13 [CSEL 65 57]). This passage does not say that Athanasius assented to Marcellus' deposition. Grammatically, *illi* should refer to Athanasius, who is mentioned first in the preceding sentence, 'the former'. But the sense is that just as Athanasius acceded to the deposition of Asclepas, Marcellus, in his turn, never

2. The Synod of Rome (340)

If Athanasius and Marcellus did not meet in Tyre, then their first meeting was in Rome. The year or so that they spent together may have been their most important contact. There they were forged – whether they wanted it or not – into a 'party', and there they probably influenced each other's ideas. It is more than likely that two exiled, eastern bishops, both of whom had been at Nicaea, would have talked at length with each other. And some evidence supports this probability.

In 338, during the manoeuvring that preceded Athanasius' second exile, a synod at Alexandria addressed a long encyclical letter to all bishops, but particularly to Julius of Rome.[12] Eusebius and his partisans also wrote to Julius, and seemed to suggest a synod.[13] Julius of Rome jumped at the chance to hold a synod and sent two presbyters to Eusebius to propose the synod formally. In March of 339 Athanasius left Alexandria for exile and set out for Rome, where he hoped for redress from Julius' synod. He spent eighteen months there. Marcellus also, hoping for reinstatement, went to Rome. So did Asclepas of Gaza and other bishops. Eusebius and his followers – if they had ever wanted a synod in the West, which is far from certain – abruptly lost any taste for it. They retained Julius' presbyters for a year, partly to prevent the assembly of a synod at Rome that would retry the case of Athanasius, since they maintained that his deposition at Tyre was valid.

Julius held the synod, and its outcome was inevitable: it vindicated both Athanasius and Marcellus. The letter that Julius of Rome addressed to the Eusebians in 341, after the synod, is crucial to the history – as distinct from the theology – of Arianism.[14] It is probably this letter, more than any other document, that led to the formation and solidification of parties. The letter regularly links the names of

---

entered into communion with Asclepas, either. Theodor Zahn (*Marcellus von Ancyra. Ein Beitrag zur Geschichte der Theologie* [Gotha: Andreas Perthes, 1867], 44) writes simply that Marcellus resisted Athanasius' deposition. K. J. Hefele and H. Leclercq (*Histoire des conciles* I, 2 [Paris: Letouzey et Ané, 1907], 667) write: 'Marcellus had protested against the deposition of St. Athanasius, and his refusal to take part in the Council of Jerusalem had exasperated the Eusebians.'

[12] Text in Athanasius, *Apologia contra Arianos* 2–19.

[13] Implied in Julius' response; ibid. 21.

[14] Athanasius preserves it in *Apologia contra Arianos* 20–35.

Athanasius and Marcellus,[15] implying that they represent a common cause and, further, that they are members of a larger party. Julius writes, for example: 'The bishops Athanasius and Marcellus have many supporters who speak and write in their behalf' (23), or: 'For not only the bishops Athanasius and Marcellus and their fellows came hither and complained of the injustice that had been done them, but many other bishops also . . .' (33). The Roman synod accepted all of them as orthodox. The letter also urges the Eastern bishops to avoid the heresy of Arianism (32), and darkly mentions dreadful charges brought against the Easterners (33).

Athanasius and Marcellus were together in Rome in 339 and 340, perhaps for as long as a year or more. It may have been Marcellus who encouraged Athanasius to take up the pen against the Arians.[16] Athanasius probably wrote *Orations against the Arians* I and II in Rome, around 340 and 341 – that is, when he and Marcellus were together there. As early as Zahn[17] it was noted that Marcellus influenced Athanasius' exegesis of Prov 8:22.[18]

Another point might be added. Not much is known of the structure of Marcellus' fateful work, the *Contra Asterium*. But a little-noted fragment of Acacius of Caesarea's *Contra Marcellum* suggests that it dealt at length with the exegesis of controverted biblical texts.[19] If this is the case, then Athanasius may have learned from Marcellus not only some exegesis, but also the literary form of the *Orations against the Arians*.

Conversely, Athanasius may well have influenced – and moderated – Marcellus' theological thought. Apart from the *Contra Asterium*, which he wrote in the decade immediately after Nicaea, Marcellus' only other certainly authentic work is the profession of faith he made

[15] Four times in that order (23, 27, 33, 35), and once in the reverse order, but in a quotation from the Eusebians' letter (34). Translations that follow are from NPNF IV:112 and 117.

[16] So Martin Tetz, 'Athanasius von Alexandrien', *Theologische Realenzyklopädie* 4 (1979), 337–8.

[17] *Marcellus*, 118.

[18] In *Orationes contra Arianos* 2, 18–82. Luise Abramowski ('Dionys von Rom [268] und Dionys von Alexandrien [264/5] in den arianischen Streitigkeiten des 4. Jahrhunderts', ZKG 93 [1982], 240–72) detects Marcellan influence on Athanasius' sources in the *De sententia Dionysii*.

[19] See J. T. Lienhard, 'Acacius of Caesarea: *Contra Marcellum*. Historical and Theological Considerations', *Cristianesimo nella storia* 10 (1989), 1–22.

to Julius of Rome in 340.[20] Marcellus' letter to Julius has four parts: an exposition of the Eusebians' errors, a short treatise on the preincarnate Son, a copy of the Roman creed, and a specifically theological account of why the Godhead is indivisible. In this letter Marcellus taught one God in one *hupostasis,* the eternal existence of the Son-Word, and the importance of the title *Logos.* He gave up insisting that the Preincarnate may be called only *Logos* and saying that the reign of Christ will end, but firmly adhered to the confession of one *hupostasis.* Many authors assume that Marcellus' profession to Julius was deceptive, and that his mature and definitive thought is to be found in the *Contra Asterium.* But the Eusebians refined and moderated their language after Nicaea (no longer writing, for example, of more than one *ousia* in the Godhead). It would hardly be surprising if Marcellus did the same. It is more reasonable, and more probable, to assume that Marcellus' confession of 340 is sincere, and represents an advance on his part toward a less idiosyncratic theology, while reinforcing his insistence on the phrase 'one *hupostasis*.'

3. The Synod of Sardica (343)

The second sure contact between Athanasius and Marcellus is that at the (western) Synod of Sardica (343 or 342). The circumstances are well known. The western Emperor Constans intended the synod to effect a reconciliation between East and West. But the synod never met as a body. The Westerners wanted Athanasius and Marcellus seated, a move the Easterners could not agree to, since they held that both of them had been validly deposed; so the Easterners withdrew to Philippopolis. The western synod acquitted Athanasius of all the charges against him, and vindicated Marcellus' orthodoxy. The bishops there concluded: 'We have therefore pronounced our dearly beloved brethren and fellow-ministers Athanasius, Marcellus, and Asclepas, and those who minister to the Lord with them, to be innocent and clear of offence, and have written to the diocese of each, that the people of each church may know the innocence of their own bishop, and may esteem him as their bishop and expect his coming.'[21]

---

[20] Text in GCS Eusebius 4, 214–15.
[21] Cited in *Apologia contra Arianos* 44–50, here 49 (tr. from NPNF IV:126).

This encyclical regularly links the names Athanasius and Marcellus: six times in all, and always in that order.[22] It calls those who opposed Athanasius and Marcellus 'Arian madmen,' and attacks them repeatedly as heretics and violent criminals.[23] Sardica clearly strengthened the sense of party unity and hardened the spirit of opposition.

Another question needs to be asked, about the theology of the so-called profession of faith of Sardica.[24] Tetz points out that the theology of the Creed of Sardica is that of the West, and of Asia Minor. He is convinced that Athanasius had nothing to do with its composition and, right from the start, had distanced himself from it.[25] The creed would, of course, delight Marcellus: 'There is one *hupostasis* (which the heretics themselves call *ousia*) of the Father, the Son and the Holy Spirit'.[26]

It is no surprise that the eastern bishops, who regrouped at Philippopolis, saw things very differently. Their synodical letter is at pains to show that the Easterners who had gone to Rome in 339/40 were not in fact a party.[27] They recount examples of disloyalty and fickleness, and add some lurid details, to portray the 'party' gathered around Athanasius and Marcellus as nothing more than thoroughly unsavory opportunists. They give the following examples. Protogenes of Sardica and Cyriacus of Naissus (Nisch), who in 343 were Marcellus' allies, had signed a *liber sententiarum* against Marcellus at the time he was condemned, and the book is extant (3). Athanasius had signed Asclepas' deposition (13). Paul of Constantinople was present at Athanasius' *expositio* and signed his condemnation (13). Protogenes had anathematised Marcellus and Paul, but later received them into communion (20). Thus the eastern bishops at Philippopolis betray their fear: that their enemies are gaining support. Not only have all the western bishops, collectively, stood behind

---

[22] In 44 (thrice), 45 (twice), and 49; in five of the six instances Asclepas' name is added.
[23] Ibid., 44, 49, and *passim*.
[24] Extant in a Greek translation in Theodoret, *HE* 2. 8, 37–52 (GCS Theodoret 112–18).
[25] Martin Tetz, 'Über nikäische Orthodoxie. Der sog. Tomus ad Antiochenos des Athanasios von Alexandrien', ZNW 66 (1975), 194–222, here 204.
[26] Creed of Sardica, 4 (GCS Theodoret 113).
[27] Extant in a Latin translation in Hilary, *Fragmenta Historica* A. IV. 1 (CSEL 65 48–67).

Marcellus and Athanasius, but some eastern bishops are joining them. They try to show that these eastern defectors are united only in crime.

But the true object of the synod's hatred is the pair Athanasius and Marcellus. They write, for example: 'Others, who in the past were exposed on account of their crimes, are now joined with Marcellus and Athanasius' (11); 'Marcellus and Athanasius and the rest of those who have been defiled' (21); 'Athanasius and Marcellus, through whom the name of the Lord is blasphemed among the nations' (22); 'Athanasius and Marcellus, who blasphemed impiously against the Lord and lived as men defiled' (23).

The western bishops, assembled at Sardica, sacrificed the unity of the Church to defend their vindication of Athanasius, Marcellus, and other eastern bishops, and thereby reinforced the Athanasian-Marcellan party. The decree of the eastern synod of Sardica-Philippopolis shows how clearly perceived this faction was. The synods at Sardica and Philippopolis are the high-water mark of the East's and the West's mutual anger and rejection in the fourth century, and the principal point of controversy at those synods was the status of Athanasius and Marcellus.

4. The Condemnation of Photinus (345)

The next point of contact is described by Hilary.[28] The passage is obscure, and not easy to interpret. Its main points are these:

Athanasius realised that Marcellus was putting forth new ideas, similar to the doctrines of Photinus. So Athanasius cut Marcellus off from communion, before Photinus was convicted. Marcellus had read his book at Sardica, and was restored to his see. Athanasius did not condemn him for this book, but for his leanings toward Photinus. In fact, no synod had ever been convoked against Marcellus, except that in Sardica. Not even the western condemnation of Photinus included a judgement on Marcellus. But enemies of Athanasius in the East wrote back to the Westerners and mentioned Marcellus as one who taught what Photinus did. They wanted to raise doubts about Athanasius, and about Marcellus as well. But Hilary is clear: Athanasius did not deny Marcellus communion because of his book. And when Athanasius denied Marcellus communion, Marcellus

---

[28] Hilary of Poitiers, *Fragmenta Historica* B. II. 9, 1–3 (CSEL 65 146–7).

voluntarily refrained from entering a church.

Brennecke, in his book on Hilary of Poitiers,[29] provides a thorough analysis of this passage. Early in 345, some eastern bishops wrote to the West, pointing out that Marcellus was Photinus' teacher and that Athanasius was in communion with Marcellus. After Gregory of Alexandria died (26 June 345), Constans wanted Athanasius restored to his see. Constantius laid down two conditions for the restoration: the condemnation of Photinus, and Athanasius' separation from Marcellus. Athanasius broke off communion with Marcellus, and returned to Alexandria. Thus Brennecke interprets the passage in Hilary politically, as one moment in the East's efforts to divide and conquer. East and West had agreed in rejecting Photinus. Marcellus was sympathetic to Photinus. The Easterners saw an opportunity to get the West to reject Marcellus, *haereticorum omnium execrabilior pestis*, as the bishops at Philippopolis had said. According to Brennecke's theory, the East could swallow Athanasius if he could be detached from Marcellus.

But it is clearly possible that Athanasius broke off communion with Marcellus for theological, rather than political, reasons. This possibility raises a larger, and much-vexed question – whether Athanasius was a gangster and a thug, or a pastor and a theologian. Athanasius' action in 345 may not have been as purely political as Brennecke thinks it was. If Athanasius wrote the *Third Oration against the Arians* around 345,[30] and if it is directed (in part, at least) against Photinus, then the split may well have been over theological issues. Marcellus' repentance is also noteworthy: he voluntarily withdrew from the church, at least temporarily. This is not the action of the founder of a dissident sect. If Marcellus came to see the errors he had made in the *Contra Asterium* (as he undoubtedly did), then he may also have seen the errors he made in agreeing with Photinus.

---

[29] Hanns Christof Brennecke, *Hilarius von Poitiers und die Bischofsopposition gegen Konstantius II. Untersuchungen zur dritten Phase des arianischen Streites (337–361)*, PTS 26 (Berlin: de Gruyter, 1984), 57–62.

[30] As Tetz ('Athanasius von Alexandrien' 339, 344), for example believes. See also Hanson, *The Search*, 419, who is vaguer. Charles Kannengiesser (*Athanase d' Alexandrie, évêque et écrivain. Une lecture des traités Contre les Ariens*, Théologie Historique 70 [Paris: Beauchesne, 1983]) tries to show that the *Third Oration* is unauthentic and may be the work of Apollinaris of Laodicea. But his thesis has found little acceptance.

5. The Schism at Antioch (362)

The next contact between Athanasius and Marcellus was also indirect, mediated by the Eustathians at Antioch.

Athanasius was the moving force behind, and surely the author of, the *Tome to the Antiochenes* sent from Alexandria to Antioch in mid-362. He used the *Tome* to try to reconcile two parties: the Eustathians, led by the presbyter Paulinus, and the Meletians. Athanasius tried, quite precisely, to reconcile the Meletians to the Eustathians: that is, Athanasius has always been in communion with the party of Paulinus, and representatives from Paulinus came to Alexandria and asked Athanasius to effect a larger reconciliation.

It is generally assumed that Marcellus and his followers had maintained communion with the Eustathians at Antioch. Hanson, however, in a recent article,[31] studied the *Fourth Oration against the Arians* and concluded that it comes from Eustathian circles in Antioch and was written between 350 and 360. Hanson thus has to suppose that, at the time, the Eustathians were hostile to Marcellus, and is then forced to say that they must have been reconciled by 370 or so. But Hanson's thesis is rather improbable.

Tetz, on the other hand, in his thorough analysis of the *Tome to the Antiochenes* assumes that Marcellus was consistently in communion with the Eustathians.[32] Paulinus, who added an explanation to the *Tome* (11, 2) clarifies his position by confessing the Trinity in one *theotes* and anathematising two heretics: Sabellius and Photinus. By the fourth century, rejecting Sabellius' teaching represented no commitment at all; Marcellus himself had done it in the *Contra Asterium*. But Paulinus' anathema against Photinus is more interesting. If he is in communion with Marcellus at the time he wrote the *Tome* then Marcellus must have abandoned any loyalty to his erstwhile disciple, too. When he did so is unclear; nothing is known of Marcellus or his actions between Athanasius' break with him in 345 and the time around 362.

It is often said that Athanasius, in the *Tome,* simply accepted the terms 'one *hupostasis*' and 'three *hupostaseis*' as equally orthodox ways

---

[31] R. P. C. Hanson, 'The Source and Significance of the Fourth *Oratio contra Arianos* Attributed to Athanasius', VC 42 (1988), 257–66.

[32] 'Über nikäische Orthodoxie', 207. Tetz writes of an 'enge Gemeinschaft' between Marcellus and his community, and the Eustathians.

of expressing the Christian faith in the Godhead. But the situation is a little more differentiated. His old friends, the Eustathians, are asked to give up their adherence to the Creed of Sardica. Then the *Tome* broaches the question of three *hupostaseis*. 'Three *hupostaseis*' does not mean three separated and dissimilar subsistences, or three *ousiai,* or three *archai,* or three gods. The expression simply affirms the subsistence of the Three in the Godhead.[33] There is still one *theotes,* and one *arche.* Thus the Eustathians are encouraged to accept the Meletians, who confess three *hupostaseis,* as orthodox.

The Meletians are then asked what they mean by 'one *hupostasis.*' They equate *hupostasis* with *ousia* and *phusis,* yet reject Sabellianism. 'One *hupostasis*' means 'one person,' 'one center of consciousness,' Marcellus' *hen prosopon.* In the rest of the *Tome,* however, the Meletians' position is characterised with the phrase 'three *hupostaseis*' while the phrase 'one *ousia*' characterises the Eustathians. 'One *hupostasis*' is never mentioned again.

Theologically, the *Tome* explicitly rejects the doctrinal authority of the western Creed of Sardica. Hanson takes this as a simple lie on Athanasius' part; in fact, it is his clearest proof of Athanasius' dishonesty.[34] Tetz's interpretation is subtler. He points out that the theology of the Creed of Sardica is that of the West, and of Marcellus.[35] Athanasius had nothing to do with its composition and, right from the start, distanced himself from it.

6. Basil of Caesarea and Eugenius the Deacon (371)

The next contact between Athanasius and Marcellus is also indirect; it is mediated by Basil of Caesarea.[36] Soon after his election in 370, Basil began to try to win three groups over to his side: the western church, the Egyptian church under Athanasius' leadership, and some parties in Asia Minor who opposed him. And he suspected all three groups of sympathy with Marcellus.

In epistle 69, written in 371, Basil asked Athanasius to write to the Westerners and win them over. Specifically, he is to persuade them to

[33] Tetz (ibid., 206) writes that the Meletians are still permitted a sort of subordinationism.

[34] Hanson, *The Search,* 244–6, 640.

[35] 'Über nikäische Orthodoxie', 204.

[36] See J. T. Lienhard, 'Basil of Caesarea, Marcellus of Ancyra, and "Sabellius"', *Church History* 58 (1989), 157–67.

condemn Marcellus' teaching. Athanasius never did so, and left Basil's letters unanswered. But Basil was not the only party who appealed to Athanasius. His plan to resolve the schism in Antioch in favour of Meletius did not escape the attention of the clergy in Ancyra who had remained faithful to Marcellus. In 371, probably because they knew of, or suspected, Basil's plans, the Marcellians consulted their leader Marcellus. A deacon of the group, Eugenius, wrote an exposition of their faith and carried it to Athanasius in Alexandria.[37] The *Expositio* shows that Marcellus was in communion with at least some bishops in Greece and Macedonia. A synod of bishops in Alexandria examined the draft. They may have asked Eugenius to add a few sentences about Christology, and he did so.[38] The bishops, including Athanasius, then signed it, thereby accepting the Marcellian profession of faith and remaining in communion with Marcellus. In 372, Basil complained to Meletius (*ep.* 89) that his letters to Athanasius had accomplished nothing.

In other words, in 371, Basil tried to drive a wedge between Athanasius and Marcellus. In Basil's mind, one thing would unite Athanasius and the Westerners with himself and the Meletians at Antioch: the condemnation of Marcellus.

How should this event be evaluated historically? Marcellus, it is clear, is no isolated or deserted epiphenomenon in 371. He is in communion with the Eustathians at Antioch under Paulinus, with Athanasius, and with bishops in Greece and Macedonia. The group has enough strength to stand up to Basil. Marcellus still evokes a great deal of loyalty from Athanasius. Whatever disagreement they had had over Photinus is long forgotten, and Athanasius is willing to defy the new bishop Basil to stand by Marcellus.

What is the theological position of the *Expositio*?[39] The *Expositio* rejects as heretical Arius, the Pneumatomachi, Sabellius, Paul of Samosata, Photinus, and the Anomoeans. All but the last had already been rejected in the *Tome to the Antiochenes* or Paulinus of Antioch's coda to it. The repeated rejection of Photinus is noteworthy.

---

[37] Tetz has published a critical edition and a thorough analysis of this *Expositio*: 'Markellianer und Athanasios von Alexandrien. Die markellianische Expositio fidei ad Athanasium des Diakons Eugenios von Ankyra', ZNW 64 (1973), 75–121.

[38] Ibid., 113.

[39] Ibid., 113–15.

Positively, the *Expositio* again appeals, explicitly, to the Creed of Nicaea but implicitly, and probably more forcefully and clearly, to the *Tome to the Antiochenes,* as authoritative.[40] Nevertheless, in Trinitarian doctrine, the Marcellians remain in line with the western Creed of Sardica. Thus, as late as 371, a theological tradition lives on, one that I have elsewhere called 'miahypostatic' theology.[41]

7. Epiphanius of Salamis and Athanasius' Smile (ca. 372)

The last passage on Athanasius and Marcellus is a famous story that Epiphanius of Salamis reports. He writes: 'I myself once asked the blessed pope Athanasius about this Marcellus, what his opinion of him was. He neither defended him nor expressed hostility towards him. He only smiled, and indicated that he was not far from error, but he considered him excused.'[42] Epiphanius listed Marcellus in his catalogue of heretics, but had a hard time saying just what his heresy was.

Conclusion

Marcellus' and Athanasius' known relationship falls into two blocks, each about a decade long: from the synod of Tyre to the condemnation of Photinus (335 to 345), and from the Synod of Alexandria to Eugenius' letter and Athanasius' smile (362 to 372).

In the first period, Athanasius and Marcellus are joined as enemies and victims of the Eusebians, and as exiles. They discovered their common ground at Tyre. At Rome in 339–340 Marcellus, who was at least ten years older than Athanasius, may have been Athanasius' theological mentor. But Athanasius soon outstripped Marcellus, both in his productivity and in the development of his thought. The *Contra Asterium* was Marcellus' one original work. Athanasius' and Marcellus' personal solidarity was probably strongest at Sardica. A year or so later Athanasius broke off communion with Marcellus over Photinus – perhaps to force him to correct his errors, but

---

[40] According to Tetz (ibid., 103), Sardica put Marcellus' theology 'in den Mittelpunkt'. And further, the *Expositio* refutes the *Fourth Oration,* which may be of Apollinarian provenance. The Marcellians' opponents come from an Apollinarian direction.

[41] See J. T. Lienhard, 'The "Arian" Controversy: Some Categories Reconsidered', TS 48 (1987), 415–37.

[42] Epiphanius, *Panarion haer.* 72, 4 (GCS Epiphanius 3, 259).

opportunism on Athanasius' part cannot be excluded. Marcellus then disappears from sight for seventeen years. Sometime during those years Athanasius and Marcellus were reconciled, perhaps earlier rather than later.

In the second period, Athanasius is at the center of attention and the aged Marcellus and his followers are more passive, part of a large but scattered group eager, because of their doctrinal and theological convictions, to remain in communion with Athanasius and with each other. Some of the clergy and laity of Ancyra had remained faithful to Marcellus for thirty-five years, and Marcellus was far from isolated: he was in communion with the Eustathians at Antioch, and bishops in Greece and Macedonia. Basil of Caesarea saw Marcellus and his circle as a serious obstacle to unity in the Church, which meant unity on Basil's terms. Eugenius the Deacon frustrated Basil's efforts to heal the schism at Antioch and secured Athanasius' approval for the Marcellians' confession of faith. Formally, the basis for agreement was the Creed of Nicaea. But in fact, it was Nicaea as interpreted by the pro-Paulinian *Tome to the Antiochenes*. Yet the Marcellians continued, in spite of Athanasius, to revere the Creed of Sardica. The theology of 'one *hupostasis*,' even in the early 370s, unites this group.

By the 370s, Marcellus and Athanasius may have differed theologically on what document validly interpreted the teaching of Nicaea: the Creed of Sardica or the *Tome to the Antiochenes*. If the data presented here are correct, then the Creed of Sardica best represents the views of Marcellus. It does not represent Athanasius' theology, and he never had much enthusiasm for it. With the *Tome to the Antiochenes,* Athanasius tried to wean the Eustathians (and by extension Marcellus) away from the Creed of Sardica and toward a position closer to his own. Eugenius the Deacon's *Expositio* appealed to Athanasius for his recognition and acceptance, and hence echoes the *Tome to the Antiochenes*. But it does not abandon the theology of the Creed of Sardica. This analysis suggests one important difference between Marcellus and Athanasius, even granting that Marcellus had long since moved away from much of what he had written in the *Contra Asterium*. Marcellus and his followers, even in 371, preferred the rigidly miahypostatic language of the Creed of Sardica. Athanasius, whose thought had continued to develop, rejected the Creed of Sardica as outmoded, and tried to make the *Tome to the*

Antiochenes a rallying point – without, however, showing any personal enthusiasm for the expression 'three *hupostaseis*.' The acceptance of the Cappadocian settlement was not as easy as is often assumed.

Chapter 5

A SENSE OF TRADITION:
THE HOMOIOUSIAN CHURCH PARTY

*Winrich A. Löhr**

Introduction

The historian who wants to give an account of the second phase of
the Arian struggle cannot fail to notice the key role different church
parties seem to play in this context. The fourth or fifth century
sources describe the great doctrinal debates of the fourth century as a
contest between warring factions, full of deceit and intrigue and more
often than not with a powerful emperor as the final arbiter. But what
exactly is a church party? How can this historical phenomenon be
adequately described, its impact and importance be assessed? We
want to study some aspects of this phenomenon, using the
Homoiousian church party as an example. But before we start some
preliminary remarks might be appropriate.

There is an increasing awareness in recent scholarship that the
traditional designations for church parties – i.e., Nicenes, Homoians,
Homoiousians, Anomoians (or Heterousians) – can be very
misleading indeed.[1] Such designations are often derived from ancient
sources that themselves tend to be biased, sometimes even unreliable.
The historical reality is certainly more varied and fluid than these
labels allow. On the other hand, the existence of definite theological
alignments, centered around and named after credal documents
cannot and need not be doubted. In the beginning their structure was
rather loose, their 'edges' were blurred and their different traditions
not yet sharply defined. Nevertheless, these informal factions or
parties existed among the clergy and (especially near the end of the

---

* I wish to thank Mrs Brenda Kirton for her critical comments upon the English style
in this essay.

[1] See Jeffrey N. Steenson, 'Basil of Ancyra and the Course of Nicene Orthodoxy'
(unpublished diss., Oxford, 1983), 22–32. I am grateful to Dr. Steenson for permission to
quote from his dissertation.

century) some of them developed into real 'churches', rivalling the
then 'orthodox', i.e. Nicene church.

It should be pointed out that church parties as such were an
entirely novel historical phenomenon. They had no real parallel in
the second or third century church. Their very existence was closely
tied to what one may call the institutional framework of the 4th
century church: the whole cumbersome mechanism of the various
provincial and ecumenical synods and councils. This institutional
framework had developed procedures to decide about the truth in
intricate theological matters and to try to impose a certain kind of
doctrinal unity on the church. The new empire of Constantine and
his successors (created by a revolution from above) was more
centralised, more bureaucratic and more uniform than the old empire
of Augustus, the Flavii and Antonines.[2] It is therefore not surprising
that the church, which had become an important yet ultimately
incalculable element in the empire's precarious edifice, reflected to a
certain degree this general tendency towards 'unity from above'.

The fact that the policy of the more ambitious emperors such as
Constantius or Theodosius aimed at doctrinal unity and the
eradication of party-spirit cannot conceal the intrinsic ambivalence of
the phenomenon of fourth century church parties: They were as
much the result as the agents of a doctrinal debate that was firmly
embedded in a certain institutional and political context. Therefore,
the protest against the emperor's intervention in church affairs that
was sometimes voiced by the protagonists of one party or another
seemed to be neither consistent nor fundamental: only those that
were temporarily or permanently defeated in the great doctrinal
struggles of the age indulged in the anachronistic luxury of imagining
a church free from the influence of the emperor and his
administration.

In the following pages we do not want to discuss anew the
doctrinal profile of Homoiousian theology.[3] We rather want to direct

---

[2] See Karl Christ, *Geschichte der römischen Kaiserzeit* (München: C. H. Beck 1988), 712
ff; 782 ff; Elisabeth Herrmann, *Ecclesia in re publica. Die Entwicklung der Kirche von
pseudostaatlicher zu staatlich inkorporierter Existenz* (*Europäisches Forum* 2) (Frankfurt;
1980).

[3] For the profile of Homoiousian theology, compare Jaako Gummerus, *Die
homöusianische Partei bis zum Tode des Konstantius* (Leipzig; 1900); Manlio Simonetti,
'Sulla dottrina dei Semiariani', in *Studi sull'arianesimo* (*Verba Seniorum* n.s. 5) (Roma:

our attention to some less studied aspects of the Homoiousians which are nevertheless important to get a clearer view of their self definition as a church party. In order to do this we must first give an outline of the career of the Homoiousian church party. After that we will describe the formation of the Homoiousian theological tradition and then proceed to an analysis of Homoiousian hereseology. A further paragraph will deal with Homoiousian strategy. Then – in a final paragraph – we try to draw some further, more general conclusions from our observations.

1. The Career of the Homoiousian Church Party – An Outline

Although the second Sirmian council of 357 had already rejected 'homoiousios' (together with 'homoousios') as an adequate element of theological terminology, the 'birth' of the Homoiousian church party is conveniently assigned to the easter council of Ancyra in 358. According to the rather sparse hints in the extant sources it was the conflict about the succession of the Antiochene bishop Leontius that furnished the occasion for the Ancyran synod. The ambitious bishop of Germanicia, Eudoxius, had apparently captured the see of Antioch by feigning imperial support. Moreover, at that time he obviously commanded the allegiance of Aetius, a theologian and pupil of the deceased Leontius. Eudoxius quickly tried to promote Aetius' pupils (among them the able Eunomius) to the ranks of the Antiochene clergy. But the bishops of some neighbouring sees must have taken offense. One of them, George of Laodicea, wrote a letter to his eastern colleagues, in which he urged them to remove Eudoxius from his new appointment.[4] Meanwhile Eudoxius had tried to confirm his new position by convening a synod at which he and some fellow

Editrice Studium, 1965), 160–86; Adolf Martin Ritter, 'Dogma und Lehre in der Alten Kirche', in ed., Carl Andresen, Die Lehrentwicklung im Rahmen der Katholizität (Handbuch der Dogmen-und Theologiegeschichte I) (Göttingen: Vandenhoeck & Ruprecht, 1982), 185–98; Steenson 'Basil of Ancyra', passim. Let us also mention once and for all: Winrich A. Löhr, Die Entstehung der homöischen und homöusianischen Kirchenparteien – Studien zur Synodalgeschichte des 4. Jahrhunderts (Bonn: Wehle, 1986). The question as to whether and how far the Homoiousians were influenced by Athanasius merits further attention. For our present purpose, suffice it to point out that the Homoiousians did not define themselves as adherents of Athanasius. Cf. also Adolf Martin Ritter, 'Arius redivivus? Ein Jahrzwölft Arianismusforschung' Theologische Rundschau 55 (1990):153–87.
4 Sozomen, HE 4. 13.2–3 (GCS 50, 155:21–156:4); Epiphanius, Panarion haer. 73.2.8 (GCS III, 270:8–10). Cf. Gummerus, 63 f.

bishops approved the second Sirmian formula of 357.[5] George of
Laodicea and his friends had some reason to consider themselves
outflanked by their adversaries. Apparently the new bishop of
Antioch tried to become the protagonist of Constantius' attempt to
impose doctrinal unity on the church.

This seems to have been the political context in which Basil of
Ancyra and some of his fellow bishops drafted the synodical letter of
Ancyra, a kind of founding-manifesto of the Homoiousian church
party.[6] The prooemium of the synodical letter is an important source
for the Homoiousians' view of their own tradition. Its main body is a
thoroughgoing theological critique of Aetian theology. It proposes to
describe the exclusive relation of the Son to the Father as *'homoios
kata ten ousian'*. The Nicene terminology is rejected, several appended
anathemas condemn in turn the 'Sabellianism' of Marcellus and the
doctrine of Aetius' circle.

Soon after the Ancyran synod an Homoiousian delegation headed
by Basil of Ancyra went to the emperor's court at Sirmium in order to
protest against Eudoxius' seizure of the Antiochene see.[7] They had
considerable success: in an angry letter to the Antiochene clergy
Constantius made it abundantly clear that Eudoxius' bold initiative
lacked imperial support. Moreover, the emperor seemed to endorse
the Homoiousian doctrinal position.[8] For the time being, the
Homoiousians had won the emperor's confidence.

Constantius, however, was confronted with an uncomfortable
situation: since the second Sirmian formula of 357 had failed to end
the East-West schism that had broken up at Serdica, a new basis for
doctrinal unity had to be found. Therefore, Constantius decided to
convene another synod at Sirmium (summer 358) in order to effect a
reconciliation between the Illyrian bishops (Ursacius, Valens and
Germinius – the protagonists of the imperial church policy in the
West) and the Homoiousians around Basil of Ancyra. Four African
bishops also attended.[9] On request of the Illyrians the Homoiousians

---

[5] Sozomen, *HE* 4.12.5–7 (GCS 50, 155:1–14). Cf., Gummerus, 62–63.

[6] Epiphanius, *Panarion haer.* 73.2–11 (GCS Epiphanius III, 268:30–284:10).

[7] Sozomen, *HE* 4.13.5–6 (GCS 50, 156:10–18). Consult also Manlio Simonetti, *La crisi ariana nel IV secolo (Studi ephemiridis Augustinianum* 11) (Roma: 1975), 241 f.

[8] Sozomen, *HE* 4.14.1–7 (GCS 50 156:19–157:12). See Gummerus, 91–2.

[9] Sozomen, *HE* 4.15.2 (GCS 50 158:11–14). For the date, compare Brennecke, *Hilarius von Poitiers,* 339.

had to explain the difference between *homoiousios* and *homoousios*.[10]
Basil and his friends seemed to have convinced the emperor and the
Illyrians of the orthodoxy of their position. As a result of its
deliberations the synod issued a dossier of credal documents that
confirmed the Eastern synodical tradition since 341. The emperor
had laid the groundwork for the new doctrinal unity of the church in
East and West. He seemed to aim at a broad theological consensus
based on the Eastern synodical tradition. The 'extreme' positions of
both Nicaea and Aetian theology, however, were not embraced by this
consensus.

Meanwhile, the preparations for the great synod that should heal
the Serdican schism and confirm the doctrinal unity of the church
were already under way. After much delay – occasioned by a
catastrophic earthquake in and around Nicomedia and prolonged
consultations of the bishops by the emperor – it was decided that
there were to be two synods in 359: one in the West, at Rimini and
one in the East at Seleucia. After concluding their deliberations both
synods should send a delegation to the court at Constantinople,
where the newly established unity should receive the final, imperial
touch.[11]

On May the 22nd, 359, some leading Eastern bishops – among
them Basil and the three Illyrians – assembled at the emperor's court
in Sirmium in order to work out a credal formula that could serve as
a model for the two synods at Rimini and Seleucia. As a result of this
fourth Sirmian synod the so called 'Fourth Sirmian formula' was
issued. Although this creed clearly rejected Aetian theology, it had a
flaw from the Homoiousian point of view: it contained a clear
injunction against *ousia* terminology.[12]

As the summer of 359 passed, Constantius' cleverly devised
strategy of doctrinal reconciliation between East and West ran into
new difficulties. At the first session of the Western synod at Rimini a
majority of the bishops insisted on their allegiance to the creed of
Nicaea. Autumn came, and the Eastern bishops assembled at

[10] Hilary, *De synodis* 81 (PL X 534A–B)
[11] For the synod of Rimini and Seleucia, see now Hanns Christof Brennecke, *Studien
zur Geschichte der Homöer* (Beiträge zur historischen Theologie 73) (Tübingen: J. C. B.
Mohr, 1988), 5–86.
[12] See Athanasius, *De synodis* 8.3–7 (Opitz, 11, 1), 235:21–236:15).

Seleucia, but again only a minority approved a creed based on the 'Fourth Sirmian formula'. Even prominent Homoiousian bishops such as George of Laodicea or Silvanus of Tarsus deserted their leader Basil and refused the compromise of Sirmium.[13] By the month of October, the emperor's policy seemed to have failed.

The nadir, however, became the turning point: At Niké, a small town in Thracia, on October 10th, 359, both the 'Nicene' and the 'Homoian' delegation from the Western synod at Rimini signed a creed which closely resembled the fourth Sirmian formula. The delegates returned to Rimini and by and by the whole synod confirmed (with some important additions) the compromise that the two delegations had reached.

Whereas the West had accepted an Homoian creed, the Eastern synod at Seleucia ended in open schism with both parties excommunicating each other and sending delegations to the emperor at Constantinople. Constantius, however, was determined to make the final act a success. First, after a short examination, he banned Aetius and his adherents and thereby robbed the Homoiousian party of any pretext to suspect and sabotage the Homoian orthodoxy he was about to establish. Then, as a second step, Constantius convened a gathering of the Western and Eastern delegates in the last days of December 359. In the presence of the emperor the bishops (among them the protagonists of the Homoiousian party) seemed to have no difficulties in reaching an agreement on the basis of the decrees of Niké – Rimini. On January 1st, 360, Constantius celebrated his 10th consulate conscious of being an efficient defender of Christian orthodoxy and a worthy successor to his great father.[14]

For the Homoiousians, however, the complete downfall followed quickly. In January 360 a Constantinopolitan synod chaired by Maris of Chalcedon deposed the whole phalanx of leading Homoiousian bishops (mostly on charges of malpractice) and replaced them by bishops of Homoian allegiance.[15] This was the end of the Homoiousian church party as an important factor of fourth century church politics. What followed were years of a frustrating and ultimately unsuccessful agitation against the decrees of the synods at

[13] See especially Gummerus, 137 ff; Brennecke, *Studien zur Geschichte,* 40–8.
[14] Brennecke, ibid., 48–56.
[15] Steenson, 280 ff; Brennecke, *Studien zur Geschichte,* 54 f.

Constantinople. In their predicament, some Homoiousians were in favour of a rapprochement with the anti-Homoian western bishops. Therefore, in 366, a Homoiousian delegation went to Liberius of Rome. They carried with them a letter in which they confirmed the decrees of the Nicene council.[16] Another wing of the Homoiousians, however, continued to adhere (as far as we can see) to the Second Antiochene formula and their anti-Nicene tradition.

2. Orthodoxy Defined: The Homoiousian Tradition

As we have already indicated, the synodical letter of the Eastern synod at Ancyra is justly regarded as the founding manifesto of the Homoiousian church party. The rather unusual prooemium of this letter is a rich mine of information about the context of tradition in which the Homoiousians defined their own peculiar point of view.[17] The prooemium provides the reader with a kind of brief synodical history since the Diocletian persecution from a Homoiousian perspective: the synod at Constantinople that deposed Marcellus of Ancyra (336), the Antiochene synod *in encaeniis* (341), the Eastern synod of Serdica (342), the so called *Ekthesis makrostichos* (345) and the first Sirmian synod of 351 that deposed Photinus are mentioned or alluded to. Two points are striking in this brief synodical history: 1. The omission of the synod of Nicaea; and 2. the anti-Marcellan/anti-Photinian bias of the emerging Homoiousian tradition.

Furthermore, the prooemium points out that after all these synods one should have expected to live forever in peace and unity under the reign of the pious Constantius. But the devil himself instigated a new heresy, at Antioch, at Alexandria, in Lydia, Asia minor and Illyricum. To put up a firm resistance against these heretics the bishops assembled at Ancyra. It was their task to defend the true sonship of the Only-Begotten according to the faith handed down from the fathers.

The synodical letter of Ancyra was not only directed against the supporters of Aetius or Marcellus and their disciples. As the allusion

---

[16] Sozomen, HE 6.11.1–3 (GCS 50 250:12–251:9). See Brennecke, *Studien zur Geschichte*, 216 f.

[17] Epiphanius, *Panarion haer.* 73.2 (GCS Epiphanius III, 268:30–271:6). Consult also Steenson, 32ff, 130ff. For a translation of the synodical letter, see Steenson, 339–55.

to heresy in Illyricum indicates, the three Illyrians were also under indirect attack. Keeping this in mind, the brief synodical history at the beginning of the letter assumes still another, more special significance: it makes clear that the Homoiousians as one wing of the former Eusebian middle party were now claiming exclusively for themselves that common synodical tradition that they had hitherto shared with the Illyrian protagonists of the second Sirmian formula. With this bold move the Homoiousians made an important step towards establishing their own peculiar doctrinal point of view as the orthodox mainstream tradition.

At Sirmium, in summer 358, another element was incorporated into the Homoiousian tradition: the anti-Nicene bias. The Ancyran synodical letter had already indicated that the Homoiousians refused the 'homoousios' for the same reasons as Arius and Eusebius of Nicomedia had done: according to them *homoousios* and *ek tes ousias* had materialist implications, they belonged to a terminology fit for corporal entities but not subtle enough to describe adequately the relations between spiritual substances.[18]

Now, in Sirmium, on request of the Illyrians, further reasons were added:

1. *Homoousios* suggests a 'substantia prior' of which Father and Son are participants.

2. *Homoousios* had already been condemned by the Antiochene synod against Paul of Samosata in 268.

3. *Homoousios* is unscriptural. The fathers of Nicaea were forced to use it because of the heretics' allegation that the Son is the Father's creature.[19]

The second reason is especially interesting for us. For, whereas the synodical tradition put forward in the Ancyran letter started with the Constantinoplitanean council of 336, now the Homoiousians cited a synod of the late third century in support of their doctrinal position. Since the fathers at Antioch preceded the fathers at Nicaea by more

[18] See also Sozomen, *HE* 3.18. See Steenson, 195–208. Steenson justly points out that the Homoiousians rejected the *homoousios* and preferred the *homoiousios* instead mainly because they suspected the *homoousios* of materialising implications. Nevertheless, as their Antiochene argument (see below) shows, the Homoiousians could also associate the *homoousios* with the Sabellianism of Paul of Samosata and Marcellus of Ancyra.

[19] See note 10.

than fifty years (so the argument seemed to run) their decrees must command greater loyalty than those of the Nicene council.[20]

It is interesting to observe that the Homoiousians could use the reference to the Antiochene synod of 268 for quite different polemical purposes. In the second Homoiousian document that has been transmitted by Epiphanius (hypothetical date: summer 359) the fathers of Antioch are cited in support of the Homoiousian use of *ousia* terminology that had been prohibited by the fourth Sirmian formula. Allegedly, the bishops at Antioch had called the Son an *ousia* in order to stress his independent, hypostatic existence.[21] Thus in this Homoiousian document which was perhaps directed to a Western audience the anti-Nicene bias had been silently dropped. For the time being, the task of defending the *ousia* terminology against the Homoian creed seemed to be more urgent.

In her seminal study, 'Dionys von Rom (+268) und Dionys von Alexandrien (+264/5) in den arianischen Streitigkeiten des 4. Jahrhunderts' Luise Abramowski has demonstrated how Athanasius referred to the interpolated and forged letters of the two Dionyses in order to counter the 'Antiochene argument' of the Homoiousians.[22] The Homoiousian argument had at last found its peer – a Nicene argument from tradition. Both turned out to be historical fictions of remarkable longevity.

But, unless we are mistaken, the Homoiousian tradition acquired yet another important element. Already at the synod of Seleucia (359) a majority of the bishops had declared the sufficiency of the creed of the Dedication Council at Antioch in 341 (Antioch II).[23] As we already mentioned, in the years after 360 a substantial part of the Homoiousian party refused to deviate in any way from Antioch II. Therefore we consider it to be likely that the story of the Lucianic

[20] See Hanns Christof Brennecke, 'Zum Prozess gegen Paul von Samosata: Die Frage nach der Verurtei lung des Homoousios', *ZNW* 75 (1984), 270–90.

[21] Epiphanius, *Panarion haer.* 73.12.1–8 (GCS Epiphanius III, 284:1 2– 285:28). For a translation of this document, see Steenson, 356–368. Cf. Manlio Simonetti, 'Per la rivalutazione di alcune testimonianze su Paolo di Samosata', *Rivista di Storia e Letteratura religiosa* 24 (1988), 184 f. Simonetti seems to consider the Homoiousian claim as authentic.

[22] *ZKG* 93 (1982) 240–72.

[23] Socrates, *HE* 2.39.19; Sozomen, *HE* 4.22.6. See also Brennecke, *Studien zur Geschichte*, 45.

origin of Antioch II arose at that time in an Homoiousian
ecclesiastical milieu. The fifth century church historian Sozomen
seems to have read about the Lucianic origin of Antioch II in his
sources, but he himself was apparently in doubt about that particular
piece of information.[24] Wolf-Dieter Hauschild has pointed out that
Sozomen might have derived it from the lost synodical history of
Sabinus of Heraclea. As far as we can reconstruct the work of the
latter from the sparse hints in Socrates and Sozomen, Sabinus'
synodical history was written from a decidedly Homoiousian point of
view.[25] It is not improbable that Sabinus himself suggested the
Lucianic origin of Antioch II.

If the legend of the Lucianic origin of Antioch II arose in an
Homoiousian milieu, different interpretations as to the reason for this
historical fiction might be contemplated. First of all the Homoiousians
could claim the authority of a venerated Eastern martyr for their creed.
Since Lucian had died around 312, a Lucianic creed would obviously
be older and could hence claim a greater authority than its nearest rival,
the Nicene creed. And finally, since we have clear indications that the
followers of Aetius and perhaps also the Homoians laid claim to the
authority of Lucian, the Homoiousian legend of the Lucianic origin of
Antioch II could also be interpreted as a further attempt to appropriate
exclusively a common Eastern tradition.[26]

Besides, it is quite remarkable to observe how the hard core of the
defeated Homoiousian party seems to have emphasised the validity
and sufficiency of one single creed, namely Antioch II. This is in
contrast to the earlier attitude as expressed in the prooemium of the
Ancyran synodical letter according to which the Homoiousians
defined their doctrinal position by referring to several creeds and
councils. The new, more exclusive emphasis upon Antioch II also

---

[24] Sozomen, *HE* 3.5.9 (GCS Epiphanius III, 106:30ff).

[25] Wolf-Dieter Hauschild, 'Die antinizänische Synodalaktensammlung des Sabinus von
Heraklea, VC 24 (1970), 1 5–26. See also Winrich A. Löhr, 'Beobachtungen zu Sabinos
von Herakleia', ZKG 98 (1987), 386–91.

[26] Compare Philostorgius *HE* 2.13–15 (GCS 21 25:1–27). Cf. also the fragments of an
anonymous Homoian historian: Anhang VII,4 (GCS 50 205:1 f). We also gratefully
acknowledge that Prof. N. C. Brennecke (Erlangen) made available to us both his
unpublished inaugural lecture, 'Heiliger und Ketzer? Lukian von Antiochien in der
Geschichte des Arianischen Streites', and his new TRE article about Lucian. Both papers
contain many new and interesting observations and conclusions.

reflects the general trend of the age towards a single creed as the explicit basis of church unity.[27]

Although the Homoiousians tried to introduce 'pre-Nicene' elements into their tradition, it was the fourth century with its interdependence of church and state which really shaped their outlook. When in 358/59 Constantius was preparing the great synod of Rimini and Seleucia, a fierce debate arose as to where the bishops should assemble. According to Sozomen, first Basil and his friends refused to go to Nicaea and preferred Nicomedia instead. Later on, however, Basil apparently recommended Nicaea as a suitable place, because – as he wrote – the theological problems should be solved in the same place where they had first been raised.[28] Basil's remark clearly indicates that the Homoiousians had an intense awareness of the continuity of problems and arguments that linked their debate with Homoians and Aetians to the earlier debate before and around the council of Nicaea. To put it briefly, for the Homoiousians Nicaea was not the solution to but the starting point for a doctrinal debate. Since the fathers at Nicea had used inappropriate terminology to defend the true sonship of the Only-Begotten, the Homoiousians had to rectify their theological clumsiness. In doing so they could draw support from a venerable tradition that reached back to the legendary fathers of Antioch or to the no less legendary martyr Lucian. So the Homoiousians were not only prepared to engage Marcellus, Homoians and Aetians alike in a debate about theological terminology, they likewise forged new weapons in the ongoing debate about heresy and tradition.

3. Heresy Defined: The Homoiousians' Picture of Their Adversaries

Every theological tradition has its corresponding hereseological perspective, a way to define and denounce the 'other,' the outsider, the deviation from the path of orthodoxy.[29] The Homoiousians are no exception to this rule.

[27] Cf. Wilhelm Schneemelcher 'Serdika 342. Ein Beitrag zum Problem Ost und West in der Alten Kirche', in *Gesammelte Aufsätze zum Neuen Testament und zur Patristik,* ed. W. Bienert y K. Schäferdiek (*Analecta Vlatadon* 22) (Thessaloniki; 1974), 339f.

[28] Sozomen, HE 4. 1 6. 1–2. 15 (GCS 50 158:32 ff. and 161:10 ff.)

[29] For the origin and development of hereseology, compare: Alain Le Boulluec, *La notion d'heresie dans la litterature grecque IIᵉ -IIIᵉ siecles,* Tome I: *De Justin à Irenee,* Tome II: *Clement d'Alexandrie et Origene* (Paris: Études Augustiniennes, 1985); Norbert Brox, 'Haresie', in: *Reallexikon für Antike und Christentum* 13 (1986), 248–97. A comprehensive study of the hereseology of the post-Constantinian church is still lacking.

One part of Homoiousian hereseology was inherited from the Eusebian past of the Homoiousians: The attack on Marcellus and his Sabellian heresy. In this context, two accusations were levelled against Marcellus: i) His doctrine of the Godhead does not recognise an independent hypostasis of the Son; ii) his christology borders on psilanthropism and thus repeats the error of Paul of Samosata. Apparently the Homoiousians perceived a close theological link between Sabellianism and psilanthropism. If – according to their logic – the unity between Father and Son receives too much emphasis, then the christological unity suffers accordingly: the Logos adopts a mere man.

Now, it is interesting to see that the hereseological association of Marcellus' theology with the Samosatene heresy provided the theological rationale for the 'Antiochene' argument. The *homoousios* could be seen as Marcellan theological terminology; Marcellus, in turn, was denounced as a 'pupil' of Paul of Samosata; hence – so the argument ran – the fathers of Antioch rejected the *homoousios* by rejecting Paul of Samosata.[30] The Antiochene argument provides us with a good example of the pitiless logic of ancient hereseology.

But Marcellus was in fact only the lesser enemy. The Homoiousians' main attack was focussed on Aetius and his pupil Eunomius. As we have already indicated, in the prooemium of the Ancyran letter of 358 the Homoiousians tried to define the heretical essence of Aetian theology: it is directed against the true sonship of the Only Begotten. As such it is an invention of the devil, devised in order to disturb the peace that the church had so far enjoyed under the rule of the pious Constantius.[31] Theological argument and deft political propaganda are blended here without apparent strain.

The second Sirmian formula of 357 introduced a new type of argument into the theological debate: from then on, the adversary's theological terminology could be denounced as 'unscriptural'.[32] The precise meaning and historical impact of this kind of argument merits an extensive treatment. Here, however, we must limit ourselves to the rather general remark that it is symptomatic for the second phase of

---

[30] Cf., Brennecke 'Paul von Samosata', 284, and Abramowski, 263.

[31] See note 17.

[32] For the Second Sirmian formula, see A. Hahn, *Bibliothek der Symbole und Glaubensregeln der Alten Kirche,* 3rd ed. (Breslau: Von E. Morgenstem, 1897), 161.

the 'Arian' debate. During this debate a kind of technical terminology was created, and the 'Arian' struggle dealt not only with the theological problem of the Father-Son relation, but also with the hermeneutical problem of the uses, abuses and limits of theological terminology.[33]

Now, the Homoiousians adapted this new kind of argument quickly for their own peculiar aims: with explicit reference to Matthew 28:19 they rejected the Aetian terminology of *agennetos – gennetos* in favour of their own, scriptural Father – Son language. The heretics were branded as using unscriptural terminology.[34] Furthermore, with recourse to a well known cliché of hereseology, they are pictured as sophists, trying to reason about the mystery of the Father-Son relation, a mystery as deep as the mystery of the cross.[35] Moreover, in denying the likeness according to the *ousia,* they strip themselves of eternal life contained in the *gnosis* of the Father and the Son.[36]

In a second Homoiousian document (summer 359) one can observe a marked change in the Homoiousian attitude towards their adversaries. Now not only Aetius and his circle were under attack, but likewise the Illyrian trio. The letter which was perhaps also directed to a Western audience[37] basically attempted to defend the Homoiusian *ousia* terminology and to interpret the fourth Sirmian formula in an Homoiousian sense. In their edifying version of recent synodical history the Homoiousians presented themselves as the protagonists against a concerted Homoian-Aetian intrigue to abolish the *ousia* terminology. According to them, this intrigue reached a climax in the second Sirmian formula of 357. But at the two following Sirmian councils this attempt was successfully foiled – not least by Constantius himself who was the orthodox mouthpiece of the Son himself.[38] So, according to this rather unconvincing piece of

---

[33] Compare Kopecek, *Neo-Arianism.*

[34] Epiphanius, *Panarion haer.* 73.3.1 ff; 73.19.1 ff; 73.20.2–7 (GCS Epiphanius III, 271:7 ff; 291:26 f; 292:21 ff.). See also Steenson, 238 f. As mentioned before, the Homoiousians also rejected the *homoousios* as unscriptural.

[35] Epiphanius, *Panarion haer.* 73.6.1 ff (GCS Epiphanius III, 275:14 ff).

[36] Epiphanius, *Panarion haer.* 73.11.2 (GCS Epiphanius III, 282:17– 24).

[37] Steenson, 211, thinks that it was directed to both an Eastern and a Western audience. Compare also Gummerus, 121 f.

[38] Epiphanius, *Panarion haer.* 73.14.6–15.5 (GCS Epiphanius III, 287:2– 288:12).

Homoiousian hereseology the attempt to abolish the *ousia* terminology was only a plot to establish the Aetian terminology of *agennetos – gennetos* and *anhomoios kat ousian.*

It is remarkable how the Homoiousians here use an hereseological device that was already known to the hereseologists of the second and third century: the fabrication of an amalgam out of two different adversaries.[39] The narration of the plot, the unveiling of the political intrigue – definitely a fourth century element of hereseology – was meant to confirm the plausibility of the amalgam.[40] But in the context of fourth century church politics the hereseological amalgam was not only used to reduce the heresies under attack to an easily recognisable pattern. Rather, the amalgam pointed the way to new theological alignments: in their letter of summer 359 the Homoiousians apparently wanted to effect a coalition with those Western bishops which opposed the Homoianism of the Illyrians.

This central piece of Homoiousian hereseology – the idea that Homoians and Aetians are plotting together for the abolition of *ousia* terminology in order to establish the Aetian terminology as orthodox – might also have influenced the 'historian' of the Homoiousian church party, Sabinus of Heraclea. When Sozomen, whose account perhaps here depends on Sabinus, tells his readers about the division of the great synod of 359 into two synods, he blames it on the Homoians who allegedly wanted to preclude a joint condemnation of Aetius in this way.[41] Our picture of the elements of Homoiousian hereseology is complete: on the one hand, the Homoiousians rejected

---

[39] Le Boulluec, 344 f. It is interesting to observe that at this stage of the controversy the Homoiousians were not yet prepared to link their Aetian adversaries to the earlier Arians around Arius and Eusebius of Nicomedia. This is in marked contrast to, e.g. Athanasius' hereseology.

[40] The suspicion of a political 'intrigue' or conspiracy plays an important part in the polemical literature of the fourth/fifth century, compare e.g., Hilary of Poitiers, *Collectanea antiariana Parisina,* B 1,4 f. (CSEL 65, 101:3 ff.). Cf. the analysis of Brennecke, *Hilarius von Poitiers,* 325–34; Yves–Marie Duval, 'La "manoeuvre frauduleuse" de Rimini. A la recherche du Liber adversus Ursacium et Valentem', in *Hilaire et son temps. Actes du Colloque de Poitiers 29 septembre – 3 octobre 1968 à l'occasion du XVIe Centenaire de la mort de Saint Hilaire* (Paris: Études Augustiniennes, 1969), 51–103; Athanasius, *De synodis* 1.1 ff (Opitz 11,1) 231:1 ff. The subject would merit an extensive, monographical treatment which could throw much light on the political context of doctrinal debates in the fourth century.

[41] Sozomen, *HE* 4.16.21–22 (GCS 50, 162:12 ff). See Löhr, Beobachtungen zu Sabinos', 388 f. But compare Brennecke, *Studien zur Geschichte,* 10 f.

Sabellianism in its different guises. On the other hand, Aetius and his circle were denounced as devilish sophists, prone to syllogisms and unscriptural terminology, evacuating the mystery of the true sonship of the Only-Begotten, trying to reduce the Son to a mere creature, intent on disrupting the politico-religious peace of the Roman empire. The Western and Eastern Homoians were pictured as the devious accomplices of Aetius and his circle. And surely, between the Scylla of Sabellianism and the Charybdis of Aetian theology – could not Homoiousian theology be seen as the golden via media?

4. A Strategy That Failed: Homoiousian Church Policy

Why did the Homoiousian church policy fail? In order to answer this question, we have to deal with two preliminary questions:

   i) What were the aims of Homoiousian church policy?

   ii) How did the Homoiousians want to realise their aims?

   ad i) As mentioned before, the Homoiousian party came into existence in order to counter the influence of Aetian theology. Therefore, the aim of Homoiousian church policy was clear and simple: the Homoiousians wanted to see the Aetian doctrinal terminology condemned. At the same time, they tried to impose as orthodoxy their own brand of moderate subordinationism with a strong emphasis on the exclusive Father-Son relation.

   In the early phase of their struggle the Homoiousians' attention was almost exclusively preoccupied with the Eastern scene.[42] As Constantius involved their leaders in the preparations of the great synod and as they began to fear the influence of the Western Homoians, they tried to find allies in the West. A few hints in the sources point to some kind of Homoiousian propaganda in 358/9, directed to a Western audience.[43] Again Basil of Ancyra seems to have been the mastermind. But these activities never amounted to a comprehensive strategy which could have elicited the emperor's support. The Homoiousians remained essentially dedicated to a tradition of creeds and councils that was centered around the Serdican schism and hence deeply compromised in the eyes of the

---

[42] See Steenson, 211.

[43] Apart from the letter of 359 (cf. note 37), see, e.g., Sozomen, HE 4.24.5–6 (GCS 50, 179:11–22); Marius Victorinus, Adversus Arium 1.28.9–29.6 (SC 68 266–70).

majority of the Western bishops. Therefore, as the emperor had to learn, the Homoiousian type of orthodoxy was not a possible choice for someone who was intent on establishing explicit doctrinal unity between the Eastern and Western churches.

ad ii) Until 360, the close symbiosis of church and state that Constantine the Great had inaugurated and that had been developed by his son Constantius was never seriously called into question by Basil and other leading Homoiousians. It is interesting to observe how the Homoiousians established their close relationship with the emperor: Basil and his friends appealed to Constantius to remove Eudoxius from his Antiochene appointment. The emperor decided in their favour, Basil had secured a position of privileged access to Constantius. The downfall of the party followed the same pattern: complaints about Basil's ruthless methods in dealing with his adversaries reached the emperor.[44] Moreover, at Constantinople in winter 359 Eudoxius managed to win the confidence of the emperor when his case was examined. From then on, Eudoxius and the Homoians enjoyed a privileged position at the emperor's court.

This pattern was symptomatic for the relations between the emperor and the church in the fourth century. Since the emperor exercised his power to a considerable extent by delivering his judgement in cases presented to him by his subjects, it was imperative for the protagonists of the different church parties to have their case heard by him. Only those bishops that managed to win free access to the emperor could use their *parrhesia* to secure a position of power and influence for themselves and their friends.[45]

For someone who wanted free access to the emperor, the court was a factor not to be neglected: some of the leading Homoiousians were 'court bishops' par excellence, they apparently had close and effective relations with some of the men around Constantius.[46] Furthermore, Basil himself seemed to have been on close terms with the provincial

---

[44] See Philostorgius, *HE* 4.10 (GCS 21 63:1–16).

[45] Our – far from exhaustive – observations on this point are indebted to Fergus Millar, *The Emperor in the Roman World (31BC – AD337)*, (London: Duckworth, 1977), 551–607. Millar's analysis of the emperor's role vis a vis the church deserves to be followed up for the whole period from the sons of Constantine to Justinian. See also the review of Millar's study by K. R. Bradley in *Gnomon* 51 (1979) 258–63.

[46] See Steenson, 67. Steenson, however, thinks that the Homoiousians position at the emperor's court was comparatively weak.

administration in the East. In the summer and autumn of 358 he did not shun from using his power in order to persecute his theological adversaries.[47] And from late 358 well into the spring of 359 Basil played an important part in the different stages of the preparation of the great synod.

Thus Homoiousian church policy presents the picture of a strategy of simple 'realpolitik' taking into consideration the dominant role of the emperor for the fourth century church. Drawing on the support of the political power the Homoiousians wanted to rebut the influence of Aetius and his friends.

An interesting question, however, remains: did the Homoiousians want to establish an Homoiousian creed? The question is rather difficult to answer. Difficult, because it seems to be precisely one of those controversial questions that caused a split in the Homoiousian party. Basil of Ancyra, on the one hand, took part in the synod that issued the fourth Sirmian formula (May 359). For him, then, a new formal creed was a legitimate way to establish church unity. But at Seleucia in September 359, a substantial group of Homoiousian bishops seems to have refused to follow Basil's lead. They rejected the Homoian compromise worked out at Sirmium.

With these last observations we have already touched on the answer to our central question: why did Homoiousian church policy fail? For, as far as we can conclude from the extant sources, the downfall of the Homoiousian church party began around summer 359 and was completed at the synod of January 360 in Constantinople. Basil's ruthless and brutal methods in dealing with his adversaries may have incurred the emperor's wrath, court intrigue and tactical mistakes might have contributed. But these are only part of the explanation. Another important cause for the Homoiousians' demise lay deeper and we think that it was precisely at the synod of Seleucia in September 359 that it was laid bare.[48] Why did the Homoiousian majority reject the Homoian formula of May 359?

At least two reasons can be indicated. Firstly, in Seleucia the doctrinal position of the fourth Sirmian formula was openly supported by the Homoian and Aetian adversaries of the

[47] See Steenson, 68.
[48] For the synod of Seleucia, cf. Sozomen, *HE* 4.22 (GCS 50 172:8–176:13); Gummerus, 137 ff; Brennecke, *Studien zur Geschichte,* 40–8.

Homoiousians under the lead of Acacius of Caesarea. This caused great suspicion among the ranks of the Homoiousians. According to a traditional understanding, credal statements were meant to make the truth stand out over against heresy, to define doctrinal error and to exclude the heretic. Therefore, a credal document that had won the support of those that one had come to denounce as heretics could easily be suspected as not being able to fulfill its proper function.

Now, it was difficult to reconcile this understanding of the use and function of creeds with the exigencies and constraints of Constantius' church policy: for the emperor, credal documents were essentially a compromise that served to describe and define the unity of the church.

The second reason for the Homoiousians' rejection of the Homoian compromise is intimately linked with the first one: most of the Homoiousian bishops assembled at Seleucia did not see the need for new credal statements. According to them, doctrinal truth was something old and venerable and stable. Essentially, it could only be defended, at best restated, but never be improved upon. Moreover, doctrinal truth was embodied in and expressed by the tradition the bishops were claiming as their own. The Homoians' insistance on putting forward a new credal document in order to reach a compromise with the West was interpreted as an implicit attack upon this cherished view of the completeness and sufficiency of traditional doctrine. As the conflict between Homoians and Homoiousians wore on, the position of the latter group had apparently hardened. From then on, the Homoiousians regarded Antioch II as the explicit and binding expression of their faith, sufficient to ward off all heresy.

From this perspective, the synod of Seleucia revealed the internal constraints and contradictions of the Homoiousians as a church party. On the one hand, their leaders wanted to be the agents and protagonists of imperial church policy. On the other hand, they had to pay respect to the sensibilities of the Homoiousian ranks. Those sensiblities favoured a view of tradition, truth and heresy that could not easily be brought into agreement with the goals of a ruthless and determined imperial policy.

Now we want to draw some further – admittedly rather tentative – conclusions from our preceding observations.

i) The conflict between the claims of tradition, the exigencies of an ongoing doctrinal debate and the constraints of church politics seems to be a characteristic trait of the post-Constantinian church. If one studies the fourth or fifth century sources of synodical history, one gains the impression that the theologians involved in the great doctrinal debates were – at least to a certain degree – theologians with a bad conscience. On the one hand, they acknowledged the claims of a venerable tradition that had come to be seen as perfect, complete and sufficient to ward off all possible heresy. On the other hand, they felt the pressing need for new and more precise doctrinal formulas.

ii) In their predicament, some theologians were tempted to manipulate the tradition in order to square it with the exigencies of their situation. Thus the Homoiousians ascribed the rejection of the *homoousios* to the Antiochene fathers and claimed a Lucianic origin for their favourite creed. Here we can see the germs of a development that produced, e.g., the florileges or the sophisticated hermeneutics of the Chalcedonian dossier.[49]

Manipulated tradition found its counterpart in flawed and imprecise hereseology. For example, the finer distinctions between Sabellius, Paul of Samosata, Marcellus and Photinus became blurred. A curiously ambivalent view of heresy developed. On the one hand, heresy was 'new', compared with 'old', orthodox tradition. On the other hand, since the 'old' tradition was deemed sufficient to ward off all possible heresy, the 'newness' of heresy had to be reduced to 'old' and well-known patterns. Thus the logic of hereseology was based on the constant camouflage of the fact that every new heresy rejected meant in effect a new (corresponding) orthodoxy established.

As the contest between different church parties wore on, the demand for tradition threatened to exceed the supply of it. Therefore some theologians applied themselves to fabricate the necessary documents. These forgeries dramatically highlighted the impasse into which the argument from tradition could lead.

iii) The Homoiousian view of tradition, heresy and the role and

---

[49] See Henry Chadwick, 'Florilegium' in: *Reallexikon für Antike und Christentum* 7 (1969), 1131–60, esp. 1157. Cf. also Andre de Halleux, 'La definition christologique a Chalcédoine', *Revue théologique de Louvain* 7 (1976), 3–23; 155–70. For the wider ideological background, consult Peter Pilhofer, *Presbyteron Kreitton. Der Altersbeweis der jüdischen und christlichen Apologeten und seine Vorgeschichte* (WUNT 2. Reiyhe 39) (Tübingen: J. C. B. Mohr, 1990).

function of theological creeds already foreshadows problems and developments of the following centuries. In the same way, the pattern of their relations to the source of political power, the emperor, tells us something about the political constraints of doctrinal debates in the post-Constantinian church. Those doctrinal debates were by no means academic affairs in which a given theological problem was followed through to its logical conclusions. They were rather subjected to sudden reversals and forceful interventions by emperors who were challenged by one party or another to exercise their power of arbitration. If an emperor refused to play his role as arbiter of ecclesiastical conflicts or if his judgement did not suit one of the parties concerned, there were other authorities one could try to win. In 366, when the Homoiousians failed to attain from Valens the repeal of the decrees of Constantinople, they sent a delegation to the West that should meet Valentinian and – significantly enough – the bishop of Rome, Liberius. In the fifth century the constant rivalry between the great sees of Rome, Alexandria, Constantinople and Antioch assumed an increasing importance for the formation of theological alignments and church parties.

If we study closely the emergence, rise and fall of the Homoiousian church party, we can observe in a nutshell various circumstances and constraints that contributed to shape of the making of early Christian doctrine. This study is rewarding because it can help us to put the results of the doctrinal debates of the post-Constantinian church into a proper hermeneutical perspective.

Chapter 6

THE SCHISM AT ANTIOCH SINCE CAVALLERA

Kelley McCarthy Spoerl

The schism at Antioch began after the deposition of Eustathius in the late 320s or early 330s.[1] It intensified after the election and deposition of Meletius in 361, and was not definitively resolved until late in the fifth century. The schism is of interest to historians of the 'Arian' controversy because it is almost completely contemporaneous with that controversy and involves many of the same ecclesiastical figures who appear in the theological and political struggles that the preaching of Arius unleashed.

At the heart of the schism stands Meletius, bishop of Antioch from 360 to 381, a figure who simultaneously aroused in his contemporaries reactions of extreme disapproval and reverence. It is his rivalry with Paulinus, chief of the original followers of Eustathius, for recognition as the legitimate bishop of Antioch that provides the crux of the schism and all attempts to resolve it. Ancient sources reflect the extreme biases for and against Meletius that seem to have been held by Meletius' contemporaries. While Theodoret of Cyrus and Basil of Caesarea praise Meletius' orthodoxy, both Jerome and the anti-Nicene historian Philostorgius baldly state that Meletius endorsed Arian teachings and had 'polluted himself with the communion of heretics'.[2]

---

[1] The date of Eustathius' deposition is uncertain. Henry Chadwick, 'The Fall of Eustathius of Antioch', *JTS* 49 (1948), 27–35 places it in 326. R. P. C. Hanson, 'The Fate of Eustathius of Antioch', ZKG 95 (1984), 171–9 places it in 328/329. R. V. Sellars, *Eustathius of Antioch* (Cambridge: Cambridge University Press, 1928) dates it circa 330–1. All these sources discuss the varying accounts in the church histories by Socrates (*HE* 1.24), Sozomen (*HE* 2.19) and Theodoret (*HE* 1.21).

[2] Jerome, *Eusebii Pamphili Chronicorum Liber Secundus, anno 1 Juliani* (PL 27: 503–4). The statement actually refers to Paulinus, who Jerome said never polluted himself with the communion of heretics. Nevertheless, the pointed reference to Paulinus' rival for the Antiochene episcopacy is patent in this remark.

The biases of these ancient sources continue into modern commentators, most importantly in Ferdinand Cavallera's monumental study, *Le schisme d'Antioche*.[3] This study, first published in 1905, remains the largest and most comprehensive study of the schism, and continues to be cited in scholarly treatments of the period. Cavallera adopts self-consciously from Theodoret and Basil their extremely positive evaluation of Meletius' life and career, and his book ends up constituting almost an apologia for Meletius' status as legitimate bishop of Antioch and the Nicene orthodoxy that he inherited, along with Basil and the Cappadocians, from Athanasius. This bias is never more obvious than in the conclusion to *Le schisme,* where Cavallera makes it clear that he argues for the orthodoxy of Meletius over against the thesis of Theodore Zahn (later adopted by Harnack) that Meletius and the other 'Neo-Nicenes' of his generation, including the Cappadocians, were not true adherents of the Nicene *homoousion,* but closer in theology to the 'semi-Arians,' the Homoiousians, so-called because they held that Father and Son were *homoiousia.*[4]

The influence of Cavallera's book in scholarly treatments of the church history of the fourth century, combined with his overt bias in favor of Meletius' theological orthodoxy and canonical legitimacy, has obscured important doctrinal dimensions of the schism as well as our understanding of certain events that occurred during the period of the schism. Two examples come to mind. First, although Cavallera recognises a certain difference of approach in trinitarian doctrine distinguishing the Eustathians and the Meletians[5] (i.e., a preference for asserting one or three *hupostaseis* in the Trinity), he ultimately discounts the importance of both doctrinal and political issues as motivating factors contributing to the schism, and asserts that the conflict rested entirely on disciplinary grounds.[6] It now seems wholly inadequate to dismiss so quickly the question of the doctrinal issues

---

[3] Ferdinand Cavallera, *Le Schisme d'Antioche (IVe–Ve siècle)* (Paris: Alphonse Picard et Fils, 1905).

[4] ibid., 299–323. [See 'A Sense of Tradition: The Homoiousian Church Party' by W. Löhr on the theology of the Homoiousians, and 'Traditional Views of Late Arianism' by M. Slusser for an account of the scholarly habit of describing their theology as 'semi-Arian' – eds.]

[5] ibid., 168, 228.

[6] ibid., 323.

separating the two parties.[7] Secondly, because of his bias Cavallera must posit *a priori* good relations between Meletius and Athanasius of Alexandria.[8] But this presumption of goodwill between the two bishops makes it very difficult for Cavallera to explain satisfactorily subsequent events in the history of their relationship, such as Athanasius' granting of episcopal recognition to Paulinus during his sojourn in Antioch in 363 after Meletius deferred his offer of communion, or Athanasius' failure to make an aggressive attempt to seek Western recognition for Meletius despite Basil's repeated entreaties in the early 370s.[9]

In this article I can offer only a first step in beginning the necesssary project of reassessing Cavallera's work. My own reassessment will focus on the figure of Meletius, the linchpin of the Antiochene schism. My strategy is to return to the foundational evidence for the evaluation of Meletius by examining in detail the historical accounts of Meletius' early career and initial ascent to the Antiochene see, and particularly his sermon on Prov. 8:22[10] for which, according to some sources, he incurred the first of his three exiles. While some scholars have not hesitated to apply various labels to Meletius' theology, none (and this includes Simonetti, who makes the best attempt of all) have done so on the basis of any detailed analysis of either two of the extant statements we have from Meletius, the sermon on Prov. 8:22, or the synodal statement of 363. I will try to rectify this oversight by treating the sermon on Prov. 8:22 in detail. I have chosen to focus on the latter document exclusively because the Proverbs sermon belongs to a distinct period in Meletius' career, one

---

[7] Particularly in light of Lienhard's re-evaluation of the deep differences, not just in trinitarian theology but also in soteriology and Christology, that distinguish the tradition that recognised one *hupostasis* (which he calls the 'miahypostatic' tradition) from the one that recognises a plurality (the 'dyohypostatic' tradition). See 'The "Arian" Controversy: Some Categories Reconsidered', *Theological Studies* 48 (1987), 415–37; and 'Basil of Caesarea, Marcellus of Ancyra and 'Sabellius', *Church History* 58 (1989), 157–67.

[8] Cavallera, 23, 228.

[9] On Basil's letters to Athanasius regarding the Antiochene schism, see David Amand de Mendieta, 'Damase, Athanase, Pierre, Mélèce et Basil' in *L'Eglise et les Eglises 1054–1954* (Chevtogne, 1954), I:261–77, and A. Pekar, 'St. Basil's Correspondence with Saint Athanasius of Alexandria', *Analecta ordinis S. Basilii Magni* 10 (1979), 25–38. I have written on Athanasius' meeting with Meletius in Antioch in 363 in an unpublished paper, 'Athanasius and Meletius in Antioch: Autumn 363', (Paper presented at the North American Patristics Society meeting, May 1989).

[10] Preserved in Epiphanius, *Panarion haer.* 73.29–32.

dating from his first emergence as bishop of Sebaste circa 358 to his first exile in early 361. This period seems to have been one of confusion and/or reticence for Meletius, a time in which many of what were later viewed as contradictory aspects of his thought and activity were operating simultaneously, thus giving rise to the varying estimations of him that were to continue in ancient and modern scholarship. However, with his 363 statment, in which he gives his qualified endorsement of the Nicene creed and of *homoousios*, Meletius appears already to have moved on to another stage in his life, in which he perhaps sought to transcend the confusions of previous years in favor of a more clearly and openly defined doctrinal stance. Since the years between 358 and 361 were the critical ones in determining later evaluations of Meletius, it seems reasonable to confine the purview of this study to this period.

Accordingly, I will preface my analysis of Meletius' sermon on Prov. 8:22 with a review of Meletius' early career that considers the circumstances, first, of his election initially as bishop of Sebaste and then of Antioch and, second, the delivery of his sermon on the Proverbs passage. The analysis of the sermon will then seek to identify the sources of the theological ideas expressed in this statement and any parallels in literature contemporary with it. My conclusion will discuss whether this information can offer any support for the previous characterisations of the theology expressed in this sermon as Homoousian, Homoiousian, or Homoian. Through these efforts we can begin to get a more accurate understanding of the political, doctrinal and canonical realities that caused the intractable alienation between the Eustathian and Meletian communities at Antioch, and so begin to move beyond Cavallera's bias.

1. Meletius' Early Career

A native of Meletine in Armenia,[11] Meletius first appears about 358, when he was elected bishop of Sebaste, capital of the imperial province of Armenia Prima, to replace the city's former bishop, Eustathius.[12] The exact chronology and relationship between these two events (Eustathius' deposition and Meletius' election) is

[11] Philostorgius, *HE* 5.5.
[12] Socrates *HE* 2.44, Sozomen *HE* 4.28, Philostorgius *HE* 5.1. Theodoret, *HE* 2.31.2 speaks of 'a certain city of Armenia'.

unclear.[13] Socrates and Theodoret seem to place these events in a period prior to 360 and do not mention under whose auspices Meletius came to Sebaste; Sozomen, however, suggests that Meletius was elected to Sebaste after Eustathius' 360 deposition and thus through the offices of Acacius of Caesarea. In any case, Meletius' stay in the city seems to have been a brief one; Theodoret says that the insubordination of the people compelled Meletius to abandon the see, and he continues to relate that after leaving Sebaste, Meletius lived elsewhere without occupation.[14] Socrates, on the other hand, speaks of an episcopal translation from Sebaste to Syrian Beroea.[15] But Rufinus speaks only of Meletius' transfer from Sebaste to Antioch[16] and negatively at that, because canon 15 of Nicaea had forbidden the translation of bishops. In the face of these uncertainties, most scholars accept Cavallera's opinion that Meletius was never officially transferred as bishop from Sebaste to Beroea.[17]

Nevertheless, even if scholars rule out a transfer from Sebaste to Beroea circa 358/359, Meletius' equivocal position as bishop of Sebaste (a position he seems to have abandoned without being deposed or formally resigning) creates difficulties for the assessment of Meletius' next reported activity, namely his participation at the council of Seleucia in the fall of 359. The evidence for Meletius' presence at this council is ambiguous. Socrates and Philostorgius explicitly claim that Meletius signed the creed of Seleucia,[18] which is generally described as Homoian because it outlawed the use of *ousia* language and declared the Son *homoios* to the Father.[19] Although Epiphanius insinuates that Meletius signed the creed as a member of Acacius' entourage,[20] he does not number Meletius among the bishops listed as signatories at the council.[21] Given that it is uncertain whether Meletius was recognised or functioning as bishop of either Sebaste or Beroea in 359, it is

[13] See Cavallera, 94–5.
[14] Theodoret, *HE* 2.31.2.
[15] Socrates *HE* 2.44.
[16] Rufinus, *HE* 1.24.
[17] Cavallera, 94–5.
[18] Socrates *HE* 2.44 and Philostorgius *HE* 5.1.
[19] See A. Hahn, ed., *Bibliothek der Symbole und Glaubensregeln der alten Kirche* (Hildesheim: Georg Olms, 1962), #165, 206–8.
[20] Epiphanius, *Panarion haer.* 73.23.4.
[21] ibid., 73.26.

questionable whether he could have participated at Seleucia as an episcopal colleague, and in this respect Cavallera's reservation with regard to this claim is justified.[22]

Nevertheless, Meletius' alleged links with Acacius at Seleucia may receive some confirmation through evidence that Meletius was elected to the see of Antioch under Acacius' influence. If it is true that Meletius came to Antioch under Acacius' patronage, then we may suppose that their relationship had some kind of prehistory. It is this earlier relationship that may be alluded to in the remark about Meletius' presence at Seleucia with Acacius.

Several sources report that Acacius engineered Meletius' appointment to the see of Antioch sometime after the council of Constantinople in early 360 in order to replace Eudoxius, who had been transferred to the latter city.[23] Why Acacius decided to appoint Meletius to the see is a mystery, given a curious remark in Philostorgius. One result of the council of Constantinople was a purge of Homoiousian bishops and the Heterousian Aetius.[24] But Philostorgius says that, having effected these measures, Acacius then set out to fill those sees vacated by the deposition of those who professed the *homoousion*. Meletius was appointed to Antioch, Onesimus to Nicomedia, Athanasius to Ancyra, Acacius to Tarsus, and Pelagius to Laodicea.[25] No such doctrinal stance could have motivated Acacius on this occasion, since Acacius played a major role at Constantinople in producing an anti-*homoousion* creed that explicitly prohibited any use of *ousia* or *hupostasis* language in

---

[22] Cavallera, 96.

[23] Epiphanius, *Panarion haer.* 73.28.1, Jerome, *Chron.* in PL 27: 503–504 and Philostorgius *HE* 5.1 specifically mention Acacius. *The Historia Acephala* (2.7), Theodoret *HE* 2.31.3 and Rufinus *HE* 1.25 speak of 'Arians'. Sozomen (*HE* 4.28) speaks of the partisans of Eudoxius, Meletius' predecessor, who had been sympathetic prior to 360 to the theology of Aetius and Eunomius and who had been allied with Acacius. On this alliance, see Sozomen HE 4.12.5 and Philostorgius *HE* 4.4. on a council held by Eudoxius in conjunction with Acacius of Caesarea and Uranius of Tyre confirming the decisions of the Sirmium meeting of 357. See also Sozomen *HE* 4.16.17 for the activities of Acacius and Eudoxius at court recommending the holding of the double council of Rimini and Seleucia in 359.

[24] On the exile of Aetius, see Socrates *HE* 2.35 and Sozomen *HE* 4.12, among others. On the deposition of Homoiousian bishops including Basil of Ancyra and Eustathius of Sebaste, see Socrates *HE* 2.42–43, Sozomen *HE* 4.24, Theodoret *HE* 2.27, and Philostorgius *HE* 5.1.

[25] Philostorgius *HE* 5.1.

theological discourse.[26] Philostorgius may be reporting as a motivating factor in 360 what became evident only afterward, that Meletius and several of his colleagues appointed by Acacius later explicitly endorsed the Nicene *homoousion* in a synodal letter to Jovian written in the fall of 363.[27]

In fact, the exact tenor of Meletius' theological views in 360 seems to have been indeterminate, and this indeterminacy generated conflicting perceptions of him that the sources report. Sozomen, Theodoret and Epiphanius all report that Meletius' patrons believed that at the time of his election Meletius held their Homoian views.[28] On the other hand, Theodoret and Sozomen relate that at the same time rumours were circulating that Meletius' doctrines were 'healthy',[29] and even that he held the *homoousion* position of the Nicene creed.[30] Philostorgius' report is the most damaging; he says that Meletius first espoused the *heterousion* associated with the doctrines of Aetius and Eunomius, but then ceded to the wishes of the emperor and subscribed to the tome of the Westerners (i.e., the Homoian creed of Seleucia), and finally became an enthusiastic exponent of the *homoousion*, but only after he became bishop of Antioch.[31] Cavallera, of course, dismisses Philostorgius' report immediately, but we should nonetheless consider the following. Cavallera argues that Philostorgius' reliability is vitiated by the fact that at the same time Meletius was allegedly espousing Heterousion

---

[26] Hahn, #167, 209.

[27] Socrates *HE* 3.25 and Sozomen *HE* 6.4. Manlio Simonetti, *La crisi ariana nel IV secolo*, Studia Ephemeridis 'Augustinianum' 11 (Roma: Institutum Patristicum 'Augustinianum', 1975), 375, notes that in addition to Pelagius, Athanasius and Eusebius of Samosata (who was involved in Meletius' election according to Theodoret, *HE* 2.29.5), several bishops signed this letter who had earlier signed the Seleucian formula, including Acacius of Caesarea himself.

[28] Sozomen *HE* 4.28.4–5, Epiphanius, *Panarion haer.* 73.28.1 and Theodoret *HE* 2.31.3.

[29] Theodoret *HE* 2.31.4.

[30] Sozomen *HE* 4.28.5.

[31] Philostorgius *HE* 5.1. At 5.5, Philostorgius goes on to say that Meletius was exiled as if he were convicted of perjury, since he preached *homoousios* at the same time as he pretended to embrace *heterousios*. The 'tome of the Westerners' seems a peculiar title for the Acacian creed of Seleucia. Philostorgius' usage may be traced to the kinship between the Seleucian formula and that of the western council of Rimini, ratified at Niké in Thrace. Both creeds take their point of departure from the Dated creed, produced at Sirmium in May 359. For more on the relation between these creeds, see J. N. D. Kelly, *Early Christian Creeds*, 3rd. ed. (Essex: Longman, 1972), 283–95.

theology, its chief exponent, Aetius, was expelled from the Antiochene diaconate and exiled.[32] We should recall, however, that in the aftermath of Constantinople, as Aetius was being punished with exile, his colleague, Eunomius, was elected bishop of Cyzicus.[33] Secondly, Cavallera's evaluation does not take into account the sequential nature of Philostorgius' report, that Meletius is said to have embraced Heterousion theology, and then Homoian, before his election to Antioch in 360. The evolution of ideas that Philostorgius outlines is entirely possible if Meletius was a protégé of Acacius, since Acacius is known to have colluded with the Neo-Arians in the late 350s, and then disassociated himself from them when it became clear that the emperor Constantius would not tolerate their radical views.[34] Granted, this interpretation of Philostorgius may be compromised by the lack of clear-cut data on Meletius' episcopal status and his relations with Acacius in the late 350s. Even so, it enables us to see that Cavallera's own biases may have blinded him to some of the doctrinal developments that are consonant with Philostorgius' report about Meletius' theological evolution.

There are further witnesses to Philostorgius' claim that Meletius did not openly profess the Nicene position on the Trinity until some time after he became bishop of Antioch. Socrates and Sozomen both contend that when he first ascended the *cathedra,* Meletius avoided all doctrinal questions and confined himself to ethical exhortation in his preaching.[35] This can only have increased the sense of anticipation among Meletius' parishioners and colleagues that he would eventually declare himself more precisely in the theological controversies that had preceded the Homoian victory at Constantinople and that only the continued rule of Constantius managed to suppress.

This brings us to the sermon on Prov. 8:22. The occasion on which

---

[32] Cavallera, 95–6.

[33] Philostorgius *HE* 5.3, Theodoret *HE* 2.29, Socrates *HE* 4.7 and Sozomen *HE* 6.8.

[34] For the history of this period and a more detailed treatment of Acacius' manoeuvres, see Kopecek, *Neo-Arianism,* 133–361; Simonetti, 313–14 and 326–35, where he discusses how Acacius formed a block with the Heterousians at Seleucia, while the Homoiousians made common cause with the supporters of *homoousios;* and Joseph T. Lienhard, 'Acacius of Caesarea: *Contra Marcellum', Christianesimo nella storia* 10 (1989), 1–21, especially 3–4. Lienhard also notes on p. 7 of his article that in 364 under Valens, Acacius moved back toward those sympathetic to Heterousian-type theology, including Eudoxius of Antioch, then bishop of Constantinople, and even taught the *anomoion.*

[35] Socrates *HE* 2.44 and Sozomen *HE* 4.28.6.

Meletius delivered this sermon is important because it may have a significant bearing on how we interpret the text of the sermon itself. Hence we must note the varying reports of the ancient historians on this occasion. The classic account is Theodoret's, who claims that either at his installation or shortly thereafter (it is unclear), Meletius participated in a preaching contest with George of Alexandria and Acacius of Caesarea at the emperor's request.[36] The set text was the controversial one favored by anti-Nicenes, Prov. 8:22.[37] Theodoret claims that on this occasion, Meletius, the last 'contestant', displayed the rectitude of the canonical doctrine and capped his discourse with a bit of show-and-tell. After holding up his hand and showing three fingers, he withdrew one, then another, and stated: 'In thought they are three, but we speak as one.' No other historian reports this contest, although Sozomen declares in an account apparently related to Theodoret's, that when Meletius finally pronounced in favor of the *homoousion,* a nearby deacon clapped his hand over Meletius' mouth, whereupon Meletius used the hand gestures (reported by Theodoret) to relate his meaning. When the deacon tried to restrain Meletius' hand, Meletius shouted his allegiance to Nicaea and a general free-for-all ensued, after which Eudoxius and his fellows decided to move for Meletius' depostion and exile.[38] Socrates does not mention the sermon on Prov. 8:22 as the pretext for Meletius' dismissal, only that when the emperor learned that Meletius asserted the *homoousion,* he sent him into exile.[39] Most significantly, Epiphanius, who provides us with the text of a sermon by Meletius in which he discusses Prov. 8:22, does not describe the preaching contest that Theodoret relates, nor any of the sensational aspects of Theodoret's and Sozomen's accounts. Epiphanius does say that the sermon was the first one Meletius gave in Antioch (and thus perhaps as part of his

[36] Theodoret *HE* 2.31.6–8. See Simonetti, 343, n. 78, for an explanation of Theodoret's error in naming the first contestant George of Laodicea instead of George of Alexandria.

[37] There are references to Prov. 8:22 in Arius' letter to Eusebius of Nicomedia 4–5 in Opitz 3, Urkunde 1, 3; in Eusebius of Nicomedia's letter to Paulinus of Tyre 4–5 in ibid., Urk. 8, 16; and Eunomius' *Apology* 12.2–3, 17.13–14, 26.15–16 and 28.23–24.

[38] Sozomen *HE* 4.28.6–10. Sozomen also reports that shortly afterward Eudoxius and his partisans recalled Meletius because they thought he had recanted and only definitively deposed and replaced him with Euzoius when it became clear that his devotion to the Nicene formula was unlikely to change.

[39] Socrates *HE* 2.44.

consecration ceremony) and that many say the sermon was orthodox (*orthodoxos*).[40]

Discerning the kernel of historical truth within these widely varying accounts is a difficult task. It would seem that if Theodoret's report about the preaching contest were true, Epiphanius would have reported something about it. That he does not may speak against the reliability of Theodoret. On the other hand, there is a reference within the sermon itself to 'those who have spoken before',[41] which might support the historicity of Theodoret's preaching contest. We should note that Theodoret and Epiphanius agree over against Socrates and Sozomen that the sermon Meletius delivered did not explicitly contain an endorsement of the Nicene *homoousios,* only a declaration of faith that was 'canonical' and 'orthodox'. If Meletius was deposed and exiled in response to some statement he made in support of the *homoousion,* as Socrates and Sozomen say he was, this statement was not the sermon extant in Epiphanius, which contains no mention of the Nicene watchword. One way of reconciling these conflicting reports would be to hypothesise that Sozomen's account conflates two separate occasions: one, perhaps Meletius' consecration ceremony, when he preached on Prov. 8:22 with other bishops gathered at Antioch for his installation, and another, at which Meletius preached in favor of *homoousios,* and which caused an outcry that precipitated his deposition. In any case, the comparison of sources frees us from the necessity of seeing in the preserved sermon a defense, however veiled, of *homoousios.*

2. Meletius' Sermon on Prov. 8:22: Epiphanius, *Panarion haer. 73.29–32*

Meletius begins his sermon (29.1) with the observation that it is better to finish a speech than begin it, a sentiment I take to reflect upon the considerable pressure Meletius must have been under to declare his theological allegiance at what may have been his first official appearance as bishop of the divided Antiochene church. With contradictory rumours regarding his views surrounding him and all eyes on him, one can well imagine his desire to have '*he peri to legein agonia*' behind him! Perhaps in acknowledgement of the tension

---

[40] Epiphanius, *Panarion haer.* 73.28.4.
[41] ibid., 73.31.2.

present in the community and in an effort to assuage it, Meletius launches into an extended moral exhortation on peace, which explores the themes of divine charity, mercy and truth (29.2–7). Returning to the theme of truth at the beginning of ch.30, Meletius goes on to describe the Antichrist as one who denies that Jesus is the Christ (30.1–3). Accordingly, Meletius concludes that it is necessary that true Christians confess Christ, a conclusion that leads to the first major theological statement of the sermon (30.4–7). This statement takes a confessional form, and although it focuses exclusively on the first part of the creed's second article (on the second person's pre-existence), it contains many elements that find parallels in creeds previous to or contemporary with it.

Meletius begins his confession (30.4) with a series of clauses that describe the Son at the same time as they intimate the nature of His relationship with the Father. The Son is 'God from God', a statement of the second person's divine status that is found in the Nicene creed, but also in virtually every eastern creed published from the time of the Antiochene Dedication council in 341 to the council of Constantinople in 360.[42] The description of the Son as *heis ex henos* appears to convey the distinctiveness of the two divine persons, a pre-occupation of fourth-century polemic against the apparent Neo-Sabellianism of Marcellus of Ancyra. Clear traces of this pre-occupation are evident elsewhere in the sermon. The phrase may be a variation of the *monon ek monou* formula that appears in the second Antiochene creed of 341, the Homoian creeds of Sirmium 359, Niké 359, Rimini 359 and Constantinople 360, as well as in Basil of Ancyra's Homoiousian synodal statement of 358.[43] Meletius' ascription of the title *monogenes* to the Son is entirely traditional, appearing in the Nicene creed and numerous subsequent eastern

[42] Hahn, #142, 161. See also the second, third and fourth creeds of the Antiochene Dedication council (341): #154–#156, 184, 186–7; the creed of Philippopolis (343), #158, 190; the *Ekthesis Makrostikos* (345), #159, 192; the creed of Sirmium (351), #160, 196; the creed of Sirmium (357), #161, 201; the Dated creed of Sirmium (359), #163, 204; the creed of Niké (359), #164, 206; the creeds of Seleucia, Rimini (both 359) and Constantinople (360), #165–7, 207–8. The phrase also appears in Acacius of Caesarea's *Contra Marcellum* in Epiphanius, *Panarion haer.* 72.7.1, and the Homoiousian document of 359 given by Epiphanius at 73.18.6 and 22.7.
[43] In Hahn, #154, 185, #163, 204, #164, 206, #166, 208 and #167, 208, and Epiphanius, *Panarion haer.* 73.5.7. See also the extract from Acacius in *Panarion haer.* 72.7.1.

creeds;[44] that the Only-begotten derives from the Father who is *agennetos* may have been more controversial in light of the use Aetius and Eunomius made of the term, seeing in the Father's unbegotten status the key to His *ousia* and superiority vis à vis the Son.[45] Basil of Ancyra and George of Laodicea criticise the Anomian (i.e., Heterousian) use of the term in their 359 statement.[46] Yet the term has an important pre-history of use even prior to the emergence of Anomian theology, for it figures significantly in Eusebius of Caesarea's anti-Marcellan polemic. Here Eusebius counters Marcellus' claim that preaching multiple *hupostaseis* entails polytheism by arguing that the two *hupostaseis* of Father and Son are not both *agennetoi* and so do not constitute two first principles.[47] As Ignace Bertin has demonstrated,[48] much of this polemic was incorporated into Greek creeds of the 340s and 350s, and so proscriptions against labelling the Son *agennetos* appear in the creed of Philippopolis (343), the *Ekthesis Makrostikos* (345), and anathema 26 of the creed of Sirmium (351).[49] Acacius of Caesarea also emphasises that the Son is not *agennetos* in the fragments that survive of his treatise *Contra Marcellum*.[50] In light of this background, it is not necessary to conclude that Meletius uses the term *agennetos* with its Neo-Arian connotations in mind.

In the next phrase, Meletius describes the Son as the 'most excellent offspring of the One who begot Him'. This is the first of the four times the term *gennema* appears in ch. 30. It is possible that Meletius uses the term with such frequency here (in conjunction with the complimentary adjective *exhaireton*) to counter the Arian notion of the second person's status as a contingent *ktisma* with a notion of the Son's genetic continuity with the Father ('genetic' in this instance

[44] In Nicaea, all four creeds of Antioch 341, Philippopolis, Sirmium 351, and 359, Niké, Seleucia, Rimini and Constantinople.

[45] On this, see Kopecek, *Neo-Arianism,* 83–93, 120–32, 229–97, 311–12, 343–6, 372–92. See also G. L. Prestige, *God in Patristic Thought* (London: SPCK, 1956), 25–54, 129–56, especially 37–54 and 135–56.

[46] Epiphanius, *Panarion haer.* 73.14, 19–20.

[47] Eusebius of Caesarea, *De ecclesiastica theologia* (= ET) 2.6–7 and 2.11–12. Eusebius' other anti-Marcellan work is the *Contra Marcellum* (= CM).

[48] Ignace Bertin, 'Cyrille de Jérusalem, Eusèbe d'Emèse et la théologie semi-arienne', *Revue des sciences philosophiques et théologiques* 52 (1968), 38–75.

[49] Hahn, #158, 191, #159, anathemas 2–3, 192–193, #160, 199.

[50] Epiphanius, *Panarion haer.* 72.7.4.

denoting some kind of transmission of the Father's divine nature and substance). The complimentary terms continue when Meletius characterises the second person as *axios huios tou anarchou*. *Anarchos*, however, is another term akin to *agennetos*, used even by Arius to stress the Father's transcendent, non-contingent nature in contrast to the Son's contingent nature.[51] The term re-appears in this sense in Eusebius of Caesarea,[52] and statements that there is only one divine person who is *anarchos* appear in anathema 3 of the *Ekthesis* and in the creed of Sirmium (357).[53] Later theologians sympathetic to Nicaea will re-interpret the term in a chronological, rather than ontological, sense (since the term can mean 'without beginning' as well as 'without source') and apply it to the Son in view of His eternal generation.[54]

Likewise, Meletius' description of the Son as 'ineffable *interpreter hermneus* of the ineffable' finds a parallel in the Homoiousian synodal statement of 359.[55] The source of this title lies in the dyohypostatic tradition's understanding of Christ's saving mission as one of revelation and education.[56] The chain of titles *logos, sophia,* and *dunamis* all derive from biblical titles for Christ and appear in various permutations in several Greek creeds from the 340s and 350s. The exact sequence in which Meletius presents them here appears in the fourth creed of Antioch (341), the creed of Philippopolis (343), the *Ekthesis* (345) and the creed of Seleucia (359).[57] That the Father of the Son who is Logos, etc., is Himself beyond (*huper*) *logos, dunamis,* etc., introduces a note of subordination into the sermon. Nevertheless the complimentary adjectives continue: the Son is a perfect and abiding *gennema* from the One who is perfect and abiding in identity *tautotes* (30.5.). The description of the Son as *teleion ek teleiou* finds parallels in the second and third creeds of Antioch 341, the two

---

[51] In Opitz, vol. 3, Urk.1.5.

[52] CM 1.1.17 and ET 1.2, 1.11.1, 1.20.12 and 1.20.33–4.

[53] Hahn, #159, 193, #161, 201.

[54] For example, see Apollinarius of Laodicea, *Kata Meros Pistis* (= KMP) 1. I owe the distinction between 'chronological' and 'ontological' interpretations of *arche* to Simonetti, 272. He makes this distinction in connection with Athanasius' defense of the Son's eternal generation in *Contra Arianos* 1.14, 2.34 and *De Decretis* 12.

[55] Epiphanius, *Panarion haer.* 73.12.6.

[56] See Lienhard, 'The "Arian" Controversy', 423–4.

[57] Hahn, #156, 187, #158, 190, #159, 192, #165, 207.

Homoiousian statements of 358 and 359, as well as Acacius' *Contra Marcellum*.[58] The phrase does not appear in any of the Homoian creeds from the years 357–360. In Meletius' sermon the phrase expresses his understanding that the Son is neither an incomplete part cut off from the Father nor an insubstantial word or energy of the Father, but a complete substantial entity existing in Himself, and as such is linked with the anti-Marcellan polemic that will later come to the fore in the sermon. Simonetti errs when he interprets Meletius as suggesting that the *tautotes* applies to the relationship of the Father and Son and so approximates the Nicene *homoousion*.[59] The phrase applies grammatically to the Father and specifies that He remains in His divine identity despite begetting the Son, suffering no change or division in the process, just as the Son remains and is not dissipated as soon as He is begotten (unlike the case of an ephemeral human word to which Marcellus wrongly compares Him). A variety of anti-Nicene critics found in the doctrine of the Son's being *begotten* from the Father the attribution of physical and animal notions to the transcendent immaterial godhead.[60] Meletius address this objection by insisting that as *gennema* of the Father, the Son neither emanated *aporreusan* from the Father, nor was cut off, nor divided from Him as if by a kind of cell-like fission (30.5). Interestingly, the denial that the Son emanated from the Father appears at least three times in Homoiousian statements of 358 and 359.[61] This concern to emphasise the non-physical nature of the Son's generation also conditions Meletius' next statement, according to which the Son comes forth *apathos* and *holokleros*. The dispassionate, non-corporeal nature of the Son's generation is another frequent theme in the Homoiousian documents,[62] and also appears in the creed of Sirmium (351; anathema 25), in the Dated creed of Sirmium (359) and the creed of Seleucia 359.[63]

---

[58] ibid., #154, 185, #155, 186 and Epiphanius, *Panarion haer.* 73.6.6, 15.7, and 16.4 and Acacius, CM in Epiphanius, *Panarion haer.* 72.6.1. and 7.1.

[59] Simonetti, 344.

[60] For example, Simonetti, 256–257, discusses this in relation to Eunomius' objections to the idea of the Son's eternal generation. Simonetti also (272) discusses it in relation to statements in Athanasius (*Contra Arianos* 1.15, 1.28; *De Decretis* 11, *De Synodis* 51).

[61] Epiphanius, *Panarion haer.* 73.6.1 and 73.17.5 and 18.5.

[62] ibid., 73.15.7, 17.5, 18.5.

[63] Hahn, #160, 199, #163, 204, #165, 207.

Chapter 30.6 initiates a line of argument whose roots in previous anti-Marcellan polemic is patent. This polemic continues with one break until the close of the chapter. The general thrust of the section is to counter the view (popularly thought to originate with Marcellus) that the second person of the Trinity was a 'mere word' uttered by the Father, which lacks substantial existence and its own activity. Marcellus did deny that the Word constituted another *ousia*, *hupostasis* or *prosopon* alongside that of the Father. He saw instead the differentiation of the Father and Word emerging only when the Word goes forth (*proserchomai* instead of *gennan*) *en drastike energeia* in creation and redemption.[64] As a result of these views, many thought that Marcellus taught that the Word is an incomplete part of or energy exerted by the Father. Meletius has already begun to counter these 'Marcellan' ideas in 30.5, when he insists that the Word is not an emanation or section of the Father, but an entity that emerges complete in all its parts from Him. Meletius rejects the view that the Word is merely a word, a *rema*, or a sound from the Father (*phone tou patros*). (The word *rema* appears in a similar statement in the Homoiousian statement of 359.)[65] Rather, he insists on the Word's own distinct personal existence as a Son, who subsists and acts in and of Himself (*huphestike gar katheauton kai energeia*) to create and preserve the universe. The particular idea that the Word does not exist 'in another' but 'in himself' appears in Eusebius of Caesarea[66] and the *Ekthesis* anathemas 5 and 6.[67] The ascription of the title 'Son' is deliberate; Marcellus preferred to apply this title to the second person after His incarnate birth from the Virgin, since only then can the Word be said to be truly born or begotten.[68] Likewise, the verb form *huphestike* is meant to convey the Word's substantial and enduring existence. The term is related in anti-Marcellan literature

[64] Marcellus asserts the existence of one *prosopon* in fr.76, and rejects Asterius' positing of two *hupostaseis* in fr.63. Marcellus only uses the word *ousia* in quotations from or references to his sources (frs.81–83, 96–7). Marcellus speaks of the Word going forth *en energeia* in frs. 52, 60–1 and 71. For the most recent treatment of Marcellus' theology, see Joseph T. Lienhard, '*Contra Marcellum:* The Influence of Marcellus of Ancyra on Fourth-Century Greek Theology' (Habilitationsschrift, Albert Ludwigs Universität zu Freiburg im Breisgau, 1986), 77–107.

[65] Epiphanius, *Panarion haer.* 73.12.3 (twice).

[66] ET 1.8.2 and 2.14.2.

[67] Hahn, #159, 193–4.

[68] Marcellus, frs. 31, 109. See Lienhard 'Contra Marcellum', 85.

stemming from Eusebius of Caesarea to the ascription of a second *hupostasis* to the Son. Given that the council of Constantinople had forbidden the use of *hupostasis* as well as of *ousia*,[69] Meletius may well be attempting to keep within the letter of the law by using the verb rather than the noun form here to express his thought.

The combination of references to the Son's subsistence and activity in 30.6 is paralleled elsewhere in anti-Marcellan literature, sometimes in combination with the description of the Son as 'living'.[70] In Eusebius, this reference to the living nature of the Son is ultimately linked with His status as image of God.[71] Meletius will first introduce this same theme at the end of ch. 30 and pursue it in more depth in ch. 31. The theme emerges in passing as Meletius reiterates his anti-Marcellan polemic. Just as the Word/Son is not simply a word or utterance from the Father, so He is not a resolution (*enthumema*) of the will or a movement of the mind (*kinesis tou hegemonikou*), or an activity (*energeia*). (Prohibitions against thinking of the Son as an *energeia* also appear in Homoiousian documents from 358–359.)[72] As Son, He exists as a *gennema* who acts to create and preserve all things. By way of glossing these observations, at the end of 30.6, Meletius describes the Son as a *'gennema homoion te tou patros kai ton charaktera tou patros akriboun'*. The phrase *gennema homoion* is of course a controversial one; some scholars (notably Schwartz)[73] have seen in Meletius' use of it here proof of his allegiance to the Homoian party. Although in using it Meletius obviously discards the outlawed alternatives *homoiousion* or *homoousion,* we should also observe that in coupling the term with *gennema* (which does not appear in comparable fashion in Homoian creeds), Meletius may again be seeking to emphasise the genetic continuity between Father and Son as the basis for their likeness. In this way he would counter the view that Father and Son are alike solely on the basis of

[69] Hahn, #167, 209.

[70] Eusebius of Caesarea, CM 1.1.14, ET 1.7.3,1.16.1, 1.20.25; Ps-Athanasius, *Contra Sabellianos* (= CS) 2, Basil of Caesarea, *Contra Sabellianos et Arium et Anomoeos* (= CSAA) 1, Apollinarius of Laodicea, KMP 32.

[71] ET 2.16.3 and 2.17.3.

[72] Epiphanius, *Panarion haer.* 73.4.4 and 12.6.

[73] Eduard Schwartz, 'Zur Kirchengeschichte des vierten Jahrhunderts' ZNW 34 (1935), 162.

their common will, a view compatible with that of the Son's creaturely status.[74]

Even more intriguing, however, is Meletius' description of the Son as *'ton charaktera tou patros akriboun'*. The reference derives originally from Heb. 1:3 (*hos on apaugasma tes doxes kai charakter tes hupostaseos autou*), which the RSV translates as 'He reflects the glory of God and bears the very stamp of His nature.' The term reappears in some important sections of Acacius' *Contra Marcellum*, which in turn seem to be the source for similar discussions in two other anti-Marcellan works, the Pseudo-Athanasian *Contra Sabellianos* and Basil's homily *Contra Sabellianos et Arium et Anomoeos*.[75]

Acacius wrote his treatise to defend Asterius the Sophist against the criticism brought against him in Marcellus of Ancyra's *Contra Asterium*, written shortly after 327.[76] The fragments of Acacius' work that are preserved in Epiphanius defend in particular Asterius' description of the pre-incarnate Word as 'unchanging image' of the Father's substance, power, will, and so forth. Marcellus had rejected the use of 'image' in this instance because he believed that an image is 1) always visible and 2) always other than that of which it is the image.[77] The term 'image' should only be applied to the body of the incarnate Word. In chapter 9 of the fragments, Acacius says that when Asterius describes the Son as the *unchanging image,* it is as if he were saying that the Father's *charakteres* inhere in the Son, and as if the things conceived in the mind about the Father, which are not different from Him, are imprinted or bestowed on the Son.[78] Acacius returns to this theme later, reiterating that the Son is formed by the paternal *charakteres,* and that the being (*to einai*) of the Son lies in

---

[74] Socrates (*EH* 2.40) and Sozomen (*EH* 4.22) report that Acacius advocated this view at Seleucia, where he was in league with Neo-Arian sympathisers such as Eudoxius. On this, see Simonetti, 332, and Lienhard, 'Acacius of Caesarea', 4. According to the ancient historians, Acacius' opponents at the council chided him for inconsistency, since he had himself earlier said that the Son was like the Father in all things, including (presumably) *ousia.*

[75] Lienhard has recently studied the surviving fragments of Acacius' *Contra Marcellum* in some depth and this brief discussion draws on his more detailed observations; see, in particular, 'Contra Marcellum', 241–55. In 'Acacius of Caesarea', 8, Lienhard dates the Acacian CM circa 340–1, and in 'Contra Marcellum', 243 and 252, dates the CS circa 360 and the CSAA circa 374–9.

[76] Lienhard, 'Acacius of Caesarea', 8–9.

[77] Marcellus, frs. 90–7.

[78] Epiphanius, *Panarion haer.* 72.9.6.

these *charakteres*.[79] Acacius and Marcellus agree that the Son's status as the image of God the Father shows that He is distinct from the latter, though Acacius understands this distinction in a trinitarian sense, Marcellus in a Christological one. At the same time, however, for Acacius the Son's status as image ensures the close similarity between His pre-existent nature and the Father's. In fact, Lienhard concludes that Acacius' position in the *Contra Marcellum* approximates the Homoiousian one, including the frequent use of the *ousia* language that Acacius later advocated prohibiting.[80]

Although Meletius uses the term *charakter* in the singular instead of the plural as Acacius does, his thought in the sermon appears to echo the latter's. For Meletius to say that the Son is the *charakter* of the Father is a more concise way of saying the Father's *charakteres* constitute the being of the Son, and perhaps has the advantage of being more scriptural. Likewise, Meletius says that God the Father 'sealed' (30.7) the Son with this *charakter,* just as Acacius says that the Father 'impressed' his *charakteres* on the Son. Moreover, Meletius' addition of the adjective *akriboun* to the term *charakter* further emphasises the Son's likeness to the Father, and thus may act as an intensifier to the intentionally vague description of the Son as *homoios,* a term even Acacius was willing to use in the superlative in the *Contra Marcellum*.[81]

More evidence of the anti-Marcellan polemic shared by Eusebius and Acacius of Caesarea appears in the part of Meletius' sermon that begins at chapter 31. Here Meletius addresses the text that had become such a bone of contention in the doctrinal controversies of the fourth century: Prov. 8:22. He begins by speaking of those who distort the sense of Scripture and who disregard the divinity of the Son because they err in their understanding of the creation to which the Proverbs passage refers (31.1). Rather than deny outright that the Son can be called a creature, however, Meletius offers three hermeneutical principles that must inform the Christian exegesis of

[79] ibid., 72.10.1.

[80] Lienhard, 'Acacius of Caesarea', 17.

[81] Epiphanius, *Panarion haer.* 72.9.8, where Acacius speaks of the Son's *homoiotate mimesis* of the Father's life and activity. See also 72.7.4, where Acacius speak of the Son as *ektupos kai akribos homoiomenen pros patriken . . . theoteta kai pasan energeian.* Eusebius also speaks of the Son's *homoiotes* to the Father at ET 1.10.1, 2.14.7, 2.17.3 (the latter with the term *akribestata*).

the troublesome passage. First, one must interpret the term *he ktisis* according to the life-giving Spirit rather than the letter which kills (cf. 2 Cor. 3:6; 31.1). Secondly, one must remember that Scripture never contradicts itself (31.3). Thirdly, one must accept that no one metaphor or analogy is sufficient to represent the generation of the only-begotten Son; it is by the gradual accumulation of such images common to our everyday experience that we begin to acquire some comprehension of an event that is necessarily incorporeal and mysterious (31.3–4). With these principles in mind, Meletius settles down to his task, not in the belief that 'that matter has not been completely dealt with by those who have spoken before us' (31.2, perhaps a deferential nod to George of Alexandria and Acacius of Caesarea?), but out of a desire to share the gifts of the Holy Spirit with his listeners.

A restatement of the Homoian formula precedes Meletius' exegesis of Prov. 8:22, this time without the addition of the noun 'offspring' (*gennema*). Christians must believe that the Son is 'like (*homoios*) the Father', since He is the image of the One who is over all, the image which is through all and through whom all things on heaven and earth have been made (31.5). The reference to the Son's role in creation is typical and appears in all synodal creeds from the Greek East from Nicaea to Constantinople 360. The references to the Father as the 'One over all' occurs frequently in Eusebius of Caesarea's anti-Marcellan works with subordinationist connotations, which Meletius' use of the phrase here may also suggest.[82] The description of the Son as 'image' appears in the second creed of Antioch 341, the *Ekthesis,* the creed of Seleucia (359) and in the Homoiousian document of 358.[83] Yet the particular qualification here of the Son's status as image (but) *not as the lifeless image of that which is living* may draw on a criticism that Acacius, with Eusebius, makes in the *Contra Marcellum* of Marcellus' conception of the image. Marcellus' critics reasoned as follows: given that Marcellus believed the image to be other than its prototype, if the Son is the *image* of life, power, glory, and so forth, then He cannot *be* or *have* life, power, glory and so on

---

[82] CM 1.1.33, ET 1.7.2, 1.14.2, 2.1.1, 2.14.11, 2.17.2, 2.20.15, 3.5.19, 3.6.2. One can find overtly subordinationist statements in Eusebius at ET 1.11.2, 2.7.3, 2.14.3, 3.5.17.

[83] Hahn, #154, 185 (in fact, the phrase *aparallakton eikon* appears here), #159, anathema 5, 194, #165, 207 and Epiphanius, *Panarion haer.* 73.7.7.

in Himself. Marcellus thus renders the image 'inanimate' and 'lifeless' (*apsuchon* and *adzoon*), as though it was constituted only by human art or craft (*techne*).[84] Meletius appears to refer to this discussion, as well as to the doctrine popularly attributed to Marcellus that the Son is an impersonal activity (*energeia*) of the Father, when he further rejects the understanding of the Son's status as the image produced by *energeia technes* or *apotelesma energeias*.

Meletius' own argument against the 'Marcellan' doctrine of image returns to what I have called the 'genetic' understanding of the Son: the Son is the Image because He is the offspring of the 'begetting Father' (31.6), although Meletius continues to insist that Christians must not apply notions of human bodily generation to divine generation. Meletius' statement that the Son's generation takes place 'before the ages' once again echoes the non-Nicene theology of the era, since similar language appears (usually with the addition of 'all') in virtually all Greek synodal creeds between 341 and 360.[85] In Eusebius' anti-Marcellan texts,[86] this kind of statement marks an intermediate position between, on the one hand, the claim made by Alexander and Athanasius that the Son is eternally begotten and, on the other, the early Arian view that the Son did not exist prior to His creation.[87] Simonetti suggests that although Basil of Ancyra and his Homoiousian colleagues also use this expression,[88] they elsewhere articulate an understanding of the Son's pre-existence that moves them significantly closer to an open declaration of the Son's eternity.[89] Insofar as Meletius chooses not to gloss the phrase, we may conclude that he preferred the older and more conservative interpretation.

The influence of anti-Marcellan polemic may be found yet again in Meletius' insistence that the scriptural description of the Son as Wisdom does not imply that He is, like human wisdom, without real and separate existence (*anhupostatos* and *anhuparktos*). The allegation

[84] Epiphanius' account of Acacius' CM in *Panarion haer.* 72.7.3 and Eusebius of Caesarea, ET 2.17.3 and 2.23.2.

[85] In Hahn, all four creeds from Antioch 341, #153–6, 183–7, Philippopolis #158, 190, *Ekthesis*, #159, 192, Sirmium (351), #160, 196, Sirmium (357), #161, 200, Sirmium (359), #163, 204, Niké, #164, 205–6, Seleucia, #165, 207, Rimini, #166, 208, and Constantinople, #167, 208.

[86] ET 1.2, 1.8.2.

[87] On this, see Lienhard, 'Contra Marcellum', 231–2.

[88] Epiphanius, *Panarion haer.* 73.15.7, 18.6.

[89] ibid., 73.14.3 and 73.10.6–7. See Simonetti, 262.

that Marcellus teaches an *anhupostatos logos* appears in both of Eusebius of Caesarea's anti-Marcellan treatises, and in three other anti-Marcellan tracts.[90] The affiliated term *anhuparktos* appears in the writings of Eusebius of Caesarea,[91] in anathema 5 of the *Ekthesis*[92] and, perhaps most significantly, in the Homoiousian statement of 359.[93] *Anhupostatos* is another term that bears an obvious kinship with the term *hupostasis,* and at least two of the anti-Marcellan authors who use the term (Eusebius and Apollinarius) recognise more than one *hupostasis* in the godhead. Once again, Meletius does not use the word *hupostasis* in the sermon, but his use of its cognates in a clearly anti-Marcellan context strongly suggests that he would have accepted a plurality of *hupostaseis* in the Trinity, as the discussion in the *Tomus ad Antiochenos* will later indicate.[94]

This conclusion may find further support in the exegesis of Prov. 8:22 that Meletius now offers, which may in turn be related to the exegesis of the passage appearing in Homoiousian documents from 358 and 359. Implicitly appealing to the previously-stated principle that the words of Scripture cannot contradict themselves, Meletius states that the expression *ektise* (Prov. 8:22) and *egennese* (Prov. 8:25) can both be used to express different aspects of the one Son (31.6). *Ektise* expresses His subsistent nature, the fact that He is *enhupostaton* is rather than *anhupostaton,* as well as expressing the enduring, non-ephemeral character of His nature (this interpretation may itself be partially dependent upon Eusebius' exegesis of *ektise* in ET 3.2.8. There he argues that this expression does not (*contra Arius*) indicate that the Son/Word subsists (*uphestos*) and lives, and pre-exists and pre-subsists (*prohuparkton*) the foundation of the universe). *Egennese,* on the other hand, expresses the excellence and uniqueness of the Only-Begotten. In claiming that scriptural texts do not contradict

[90] Eusebius of Caesarea, CM 1.1.32, 2.2.32, 2.4.21, ET 1.20.15, 1.20.30; Ps-Athanasius, CS 5 and *Contra Arianos* 4.8, Apollinarius of Laodicea, KMP 13.

[91] ET 1.20.62.

[92] Hahn, #159, 193.

[93] Epiphanius, *Panarion haer.* 73.12.3–4 (twice).

[94] Recent scholarship on chapters 5 and 6 of the *Tomus* agrees that the trinitarian discussions at the council of Alexandria took place between representatives of the Meletian community, who supported the three *hupostaseis* formula, and those of the Eustathian community, who preferred the one *hupostasis* formula. See Martin Tetz, 'Über nikäische Orthodoxie: Der sog. *Tomus ad Antiochenos* des Athanasius von Alexandrien', ZNW 66 (1975), 205–8 and Luise Abramowski, 'Trinitarische und christologische Hypostasenformeln', *Theologie und Philosophie* 545 (1979), 41–7.

but mutually illuminate one another, Meletius approximates an idea expressed in the 358 statement from the synod of Ancyra. In the text preserved in *Panarion haer.* 73.8.1–3 the authors juxtapose the Proverbs text with the prologue of John's gospel, suggesting that the former text must be read in light of the latter in order to understand that the pre-existent Word is not merely an *uttered one* (another typical anti-Marcellan term),[95] but one which exists. Similarly, later on in the same document the authors say that both the expressions *ektise* and *egennese* can refer to the Son, but they contend that the force of the former expression should never outweigh that of the second. Therefore, one cannot point to Prov. 8:22 as justification for saying that the Word is only a creature and no longer a Son. Both expressions have as their subject *ton huion ton apathos teleion*.[96] Again, in the 359 Homoiousion document, the authors insist that Prov. 8:22 must be interpreted in light of 8:25. Interestingly, this chapter includes the same reference to Jn. 8:24 that Meletius includes in his sermon at this point.[97] While Meletius seems to evaluate the two expressions from Prov. 8:22 and 25 somewhat more even-handedly than the Homoiousians do (who vehemently assert the priority of *egennese* over *ektise*), he admits with them the value of both expressions, and suggests (as Basil of Ancyra does) that in combination they can serve to express the distinct and unique subsistence of the Son. While this interpretation of Prov. 8:22 ff. does not challenge the Arian position on the Son's created status head-on (Arius, for example, recognised the Son as a second, though created, *hupostasis* alongside the Father)[98] it nevertheless offers an interpretation of scriptural language that was fruitful in the long run for trinitarian theology. This interpretation also contrasts with exegesis of Prov. 8:22 by Athanasius, who sees in the verse a prophecy of the incarnation.[99]

[95] The contrast is between the *logos kata dianoian,* the word in mental conception, and the *logos prophorikos,* the word in speech. The contrast is a variation on the Stoic concept of *logos endiathetos* and *logos prophorikos* that his critics thought Marcellus' Logos doctrine reproduced. The reference to *logos kata prophoran* appears in Eusebius' ET 2.15.1 and Apollinarius, KMP l.

[96] Epiphanius, *Panarion haer.* 73.11.1.

[97] ibid., 73.20.5–7.

[98] See the quote in Athanasius, *De Synodis* 15.3 in Opitz, vol.2, 242, lines 24–25.

[99] See the *Contra Arianos* 2.16–22. Athanasius was influenced in this regard by Marcellus. See Simonetti, 278.

At the conclusion of chapter 31 of his sermon Meletius returns to the theme of the passionless nature of the Son's generation in a remark that recalls a discussion in the 358 Homoiousian letter.[100] He says that the name of Wisdom applied to the Son banishes any thought of passion from the godhead. With this remark, the doctrinal part of the sermon concludes and Meletius resumes the exhortatory tone of chapter 29. He begins by chiding himself for getting carried away in his trinitarian speculations and checks himself by quoting Paul: 'O the depth of the riches and wisdom and knowledge of God! How unsearchable are His judgments and how inscrutable His ways!' (Rom. 11:33; 32.1–2). A lengthy meditation on the need for humility before divine mystery follows (32.3–33.4), in which Meletius asserts that Christians can neither know or explain anything with certainty regarding the Son's genesis (32.5 and 33.3). Similar agnostic declarations appear in all Homoian creeds between 357 and 360.[101] It is sufficient, Meletius says, for Christians to profess belief in the Son's role as creator. The sermon closes with a prayer and a traditional doxology (33.5).

Conclusion

My own analysis has largely confirmed Schwartz' opinion that Meletius is one of the least clear of fourth-century ecclesiastical figures.[102] As the variety of sources and parallels cited in this study suggests, Meletius' theological position in this sermon eludes strict classification. Nevertheless, we can make the following observations:

1) Many elements in the sermon bear a marked kinship with those appearing in numerous credal statements from the 340s and early 350s, several of which stem from the critical second and fourth creeds of the Antiochene Dedication council of 341. The theology of this council, as well as that of many subsequent councils, as Bertin has shown, is strongly marked by the anti-Marcellan polemic and vocabulary devised by Eusebius of Caesarea. This theology was intended to articulate a clear distinction between the Father who is *agennetos* and *anarchos,* and a Son who is *gennetos.* The complete subsistence of each of these

---

[100] Epiphanius, *Panarion haer.* 73.6.

[101] In Hahn, Sirmium (357), #161, 200, Sirmium (359), #163, 204, Niké, #164, 206, Rimini #166, 208, and Constantinople, #167, 208.

[102] Schwartz, 162.

persons is usually expressed by the term *hupostasis*.[103] While Meletius will use much of the typical vocabulary of this theology (e.g., *teleion ek teleiou, anhupostaton*), he will stop short of speaking of the Father and Son as distinct *hupostaseis*. Like many of these conciliar decrees and anti-Marcellan tracts, Meletius' sermon teaches the subordination of the Son to the Father, albeit in an attenuated form.

2) Not surprisingly, this theology appears in the early anti-Marcellan tract of Meletius' alleged patron and Eusebius' successor, Acacius of Caesarea,[104] although with some elaborations that appear unique to Acacius (e.g., the Son as the *charakter* of the Father, not an *apsuchon eikon* produced by human *techne*). The appearance of these elaborations in Meletius' sermon suggest the direct influence of Acacius' *Contra Marcellum* on Meletius. The resemblances between the theologies of Acacius and Meletius that I have outlined strengthens rather than weakens the impression of a close relationship between these two that emerges from the ancient historians, despite Cavallera's attempt to minimize this relationship.

3) The theology of Meletius' sermon shares with the Homoiousian texts of 358/359 a number of significant points, such as Meletius' characterization of the Son as *hermneus* ('interpreter'), his denial that the Son emanated from the Father or that He is an *anhuparktos rema* or *energeia* of the Father, and the exegetical link drawn between Prov. 8:22 and 25. These common points suggest the influence of Homoiousian theology on Meletius, and highlight the common ground shared by both Meletius and the Homoiousians with the synodal documents of the 340s and the 350s.

4) On the other hand, Meletius consistently avoids explicitly endorsing the watchword of the theology represented by Basil of Ancyra, namely *homoiousios,* as well as any of the other compounds of *ousia* then available. For the most part, he remains faithful to the letter of the Homoian formula that the Son is 'like the Father', and he justifies this doctrinal modesty by an appeal to the agnosticism typical of the Homoian formulas of 357 to 360.

---

[103] See, for example, the statement from the second creed of the Dedication council (Antioch, 341) that the Father, Son and Holy Spirit are *te men hupostasei tria,* in Hahn, #154, 186.

[104] Lienhard, 'Acacius of Caesarea', 8, thinks Acacius may have read from the treatise at the Dedication council; similarly, I noted earlier that Lienhard thinks that early Acacian texts exhibit a proto-Homoiousian theology.

5) In large part I agree with Simonetti that Meletius' theology is a Homoiousian one couched in cautious Homoian terms. The theology of Meletius' sermon is largely continuous with that of Eusebius of Caesarea, the creeds of the Dedication council, the early Acacius of Caesarea and the Homoiousian writers of the late 350s. These documents all represent the attempt to steer a middle path between the errors of Neo-Sabellianism, which levelled the real distinctions between the persons of the Trinity, and 'Arianism', which emphasised these distinctions to the point of undermining any meaningful divine status for the Son and Holy Spirit. Given Meletius' emphasis on the distinctions between the divine persons, offered in ways characteristic of the Eusebian-inspired anti-Marcellan tradition, and the lack of endorsement for a doctrine of the eternal generation of the Son, as well as (*contra* Simonetti) his failure to speak of *tautotes* or *homoousios,* his theology is not truly 'Nicene', at least in the Athanasian (or Paulinian) sense of that title. On the other hand, Meletius' understanding of the Son's derivation from and close similarity to the Father, expressed in his description of the Son as the *eikon, akriboun charakter* and *homoios gennema* of the Father, distances him considerably from the theologies of Arius or Eunomius and Aetius, who share the wish to preserve the Father's transcendence although at the cost of levelling the Son's differentiation from creatures.

It was Meletius' basically Homoiousian, not Homoousion, theology that prompted his exile shortly after he delivered this sermon.[105] This conclusion fits better with the evidence of the sermon and the political circumstances at the time of its delivery. While the chief exponent of 'Nicene' theology, Athanasius, was marginalised in the late 350s, hiding out in the Egyptian desert,[106] the political scene in the East witnessed a ferocious battle between Homoians and Homoiousians that concluded in 360 with the rout of the latter and the triumph of the former. It is reasonable to assume that, under these circumstances, when Meletius ascended the see and started to preach a theology very close to that of the deposed enemies, this action would provoke an immediate negative reaction. If, sometime after the delivery of this sermon, Meletius went so far as to proclaim openly

[105] As Simonetti thinks, 375, n. 64.
[106] ibid., 345–7.

the *homoousion*, his action could only have solidified the hostility the sermon had aroused, and thus ensured his downfall.[107]

[107] This scenario may be supported by Sozomen's account (*HE* 4.28.9), according to which it was Eudoxius, one of the chiefs of the Homoian movement, and his partisans who agitated for Meletius' removal. Interestingly, Acacius is not mentioned in any of the accounts of Meletius' deposition. Simonetti, 345, no. 82, places Meletius' election in late 360 and his deposition in early 361.

Chapter 7

AMBROSE, EMPERORS AND HOMOIANS IN MILAN: THE FIRST CONFLICT OVER A BASILICA

Daniel H. Williams

The dramatic clash between Ambrose and the pro-Homoian court of Valentinian II during 385–6 is surely one of the most celebrated episodes of the bishop's career in the ancient sources.[1] Details about the actual chain of events are provided by the bishop of Milan through three letters: an epistle to Valentinian II, two epistles to his sister Marcellina; and a sermon, which he preached against the resident 'Arian' bishop, Auxentius (formerly of Durostorum).[2]

The fracas began with the court's insistence that Homoians in Milan should have a basilica in which to worship and baptise new converts. It was also argued that the emperor ought to have one basilica to which he could go,[3] inasmuch as all property under his jurisdiction, civic and ecclesiastical, was subject to his authority.[4] Ambrose flatly refused. He claimed that the churches under his care belonged to God, not the emperor, and as such he could not surrender the contested basilica. Under pressure from Justina, who was the young regent's mother and an ardent anti-Nicene, the court

[1] These notices, however, provide very inexact references to the complicated unfolding of events during this period. Rufinus, HE II. 15–16; Augustine, *Confessions* IX. 7.15; *Praefatio Gaudentii Episcopi ad Benivolum* 5; Paulinus, *Vita Ambrosii* 13; Socrates, *HE* V. 11; Sozomen, *HE* VII. 13; Theodoret, *HE* V. 13. Only the strange election of Ambrose to the episcopacy (in 374) received more attention.

[2] Using the enumeration from CSEL 82.3, these are epistles 75–7, and 75a (the sermon, *Contra Auxentium*, is preserved as a letter). O. Seeck has shown that all four were written in 386. *Geschichte des Untergangs der Antiken Welt*, Vol. V (Stuttgart: J. B. Metzlersche, 1937), 204ff.

[3] *Contra Aux.* 30 (CSEL 82.3 102).

[4] *Ep.* 76. 8 (CSEL 82.3 112).

127

took various forms of legal and military action against Ambrose and the Nicene supporters. During Holy Week of 385,[5] imperial banners (*vela*) were hung in the basilica, probably the Portian,[6] to indicate its sequestration as government property, after which soldiers were sent to occupy it. But the fear of starting a major riot in the city forced the court to abandon the basilica, especially when Ambrose declined to check the momentum of agitation which had whipped up the crowds.[7] Soon after Easter, the court made another desperate attempt to cower the Nicenes by ordering soldiers to surround the Portian basilica while Ambrose was presiding over its services. This is the particular incidence which Augustine, an eyewitness, recalls in the *Confessions:*

> The devout people kept watch in the church, ready to die with their bishop, Thy servant. There my mother, Thy handmaid, enduring a chief part of those anxieties, lived for prayer. Even we, yet unwarmed by the heat of Thy Spirit, were stirred by the sight of the amazed and disquieted city. Then it was first instituted that hymns and Psalms should be sung lest the people become faint through the tediousness of sorrow.[8]

The siege, which seems to have lasted for several days,[9] was lifted for reasons that are not stated but probably for similar reasons as the first attempt to seize the basilica. Fear of an invasion by Maximus,

[5] The best reconstruction of events can be found in a triad of articles by J. H. van Haeringen, 'De Valentiniano II et Ambrosio. Illustrantur et digerunter res anno 386 gestae: Valentinianus II Basilicam Adornitur (De Ambrosii Epistula XX)', *Mnemosyne* tertia series 5 (1937), 152–8; 'De Ambrosii Epistula XXI,' *idem.* 28–33; 'De Ambrosii Epistulis XX et XXI. Temporum Descriptio,' *idem,* pp. 229–40. Van Haeringen's views have been recently reaffirmed by A. Lenox-Conyngham in 'A Topography of the Basilica Conflict of A.D. 385/6 in Milan,' *Historia* 31 (1982), 353–63; and 'Juristic and Religious Aspects of the Basilica Conflict of A.D. 386,' in *Studia Patristica XVIII: Papers of the 1983 Oxford Patristics Conference,* ed. E. A. Livingstone (Kalamazoo: Cistercian Publications, 1985), 55–8.

[6] Lenox-Conyngham argues that the court first sought the Portian basilica in 385 since it was 'extramurana' and the law forbidding Arian assemblies within a city (*CTh* XVI. 5,6) had not yet been abrogated by the Valentinian administration. But in 386, after Valentinian had issued a new edict (*CTh* XVI. 1,4) proclaiming freedom of worship for all adherents of the Ariminium creed, Ambrose is ordered to hand over the New Basilica. Lenox-Conyngham suggests this was 'a psychological manoeuvre on the part of the court to obtain the Portian, since yet another request was made for it' (p. 357).

[7] *Ep.* 76. 10 (CSEL 82.3 113). Another factor was that those catholic soldiers guarding the basilica had been threatened with excommunication (76. 13 [114. 87–92]).

[8] *Conf.* IX. 7.15 (trans. from *The Confessions of St. Augustine* [New York: Book League of America, 1936], 189). Cf. *Contra Aux.* 4 (CSEL 82.3 84).

[9] *Contra Aux.* 10 (CSEL 82.3 88.109–15).

emperor of Britain and the Gauls and an outspoken proponent of the Nicene faith, must have also contributed to the court's sudden loss of nerve.[10]

It is not surprising that the above episode(s) should figure so widely and prominently in the memory of the early church since it served as a striking example of, as Paulinus put it, how the Lord 'deigned to grant triumphs to His Church over its adversaries'.[11] But this was not the only conflict over a basilica between Ambrose and the Homoians in Milan. Several years earlier, anti-Nicene elements, at the prompting of Justina, sought a basilica for their worship and were granted one by the emperor Gratian, despite Ambrose's pleas to the contrary. Ambrose eventually received control of the basilica only once Gratian decided to return it to him. The entire affair suggests the impotency of the bishop of Milan during the first few years of his episcopacy – a portrait hardly recognizable when compared to Ambrose's later political achievements, such as his successful campaign against the *praefectus urbis,* Symmachus, who sought the restoration of the Altar of Victory to the Roman Senate,[12] or when Ambrose demanded public penance from the emperor Theodosius for his massacre of citizens in Thessalonica.[13] Whatever lack of control or hesitancies Ambrose may have experienced in the early part of his episcopacy were eventually eclipsed by his subsequent 'triumphs'. So effective was this blackout of historical memory that if some recollection of the first conflict over a basilica had not been preserved by Ambrose (*infra*), we would know nothing at all about it from ancient writers.

Some 19th and 20th century treatments share this tendency to ignore the incident as insignificant or as incongruent with the great

---

[10] This is the occasion of Maximus' threatening letter which he sent to Valentinian, *Ep.* 39 (CSEL 35 88–90), on account of the latter's persecution of the catholics.

[11] *Vita Ambrosii* 13. 4–6 (text in *Vita di S. Ambrogio,* ed. M. Pellegrino [Rome: Editrice Studium, 1961], 68).

[12] See Ambrose's letters to Valentinian II, *Ep.* 72 and 73 (= Migne, 17 and 18).

[13] The details are related in Ambrose's letter to Theodosius (*Ep.* 11 ['Epistulae extra collectionem'; CSEL 82.3 212–18]) and to Marcellina (*Ep.* 1 [*idem;* 145–61]). Both confrontations with Symmachus and Theodosius are selected by Paulinus as typical of Ambrose's career. Given Paulinus' obvious hagiographic agendum, one must be suspicious about the weight which has been traditionally placed on Paulinus' *Vita* as a document valuable for Ambrosian reconstruction.

bishop's career.[14] The majority of historians acknowledge the occurrence, but present a scenario which has remained quite uniform since Tillemont's *Memoires pour servir à l'histoire Ecclésiastique des six premiers siècles* (1704). This scenario has essentially two parts. The first part begins in the autumn or winter of 378, when the court of the boy emperor Valentinian II and his mother Justina arrived in Milan, along with many others who were fleeing from the Gothic invasion of Pannonia. According to A. Paredi,[15] a basilica was 'seized,' certainly at the prompting of the empress, in order to accommodate the increasing number of 'Arians' in the city. 'Ambrose appealed to Gratian, but the latter was too concerned with preserving the peace to intervene . . . He ordered the vicar of Italy to close the basilica at Milan now occupied by the Arians but claimed by the Catholics.'[16] Older scholarship has stressed that the sequestration of the basilica came immediately after a direct request for it was made by the court of Valentinian.[17]

The second part of the scenario is the most problematic. It is claimed that when Gratian visited Milan in the summer of 379, he spontaneously returned the basilica to Ambrose and the Nicenes – only several months after he had sequestered it. This *volte-face* is attributed to the strong influence which Ambrose had gained over the young emperor, who is described at this time by Palanque as 'a faithful disciple' of the bishop of Milan.[18]

Three pieces of evidence are generally adduced to establish the reconstruction of this first basilica controversy. First, is the passage from Ambrose's *De spiritu sancto*, dated with some certainty to the

---

[14] E.g., P. De Labriolle, *Saint Ambroise* (Paris: Bloud, 1908) and R. Thorton, *St. Ambrose: His Life, Times and Teaching*, 2 Vols (London: SPCK, 1879).

[15] *Saint Ambrose: His Life and Time*, trans. M. Costelloe (Notre Dame: Notre Dame Press, 1964), 183–5.

[16] Virtually the same description can be found in Homes Dudden, *The Life and Times of Saint Ambrose*, Vol. I (Oxford: Clarendon Press, 1935), 190.

[17] Tillemont, *Memoires*, 124; G. Hermant, *Vita di S. Ambrosio*, Italian trans. G. F. Fontana, vol. I (Milano, 1750), 167: 'she [Justina] induced Gratian to sequester this church'; M. Baunard, *Histoire de Saint Ambroise* (Paris: Librarie Poussielque Frère, 1872), 97.

[18] In *The Church in the Christian Roman Empire*, trans. E. C. Messenger, vol. I (London: Burns, Oates and Washbourne, 1949), 360, and *Saint Ambroise et L'Empire Romain: contribution à l'histoire des rapports de l'église et l'état à la fine du quatrième siècle* (Paris: E. De Boccard, 1933), 64; 501.

early months of 381,[19] and which offers the only concrete evidence that Gratian removed and returned a basilica under Ambrose's episcopal jurisdiction.

> Since you, most merciful emperor, are so fully instructed concerning the Son of God ... especially when you recently showed yourself to be delighted by an argument (*adsertione*) of this nature, that you commanded the basilica of the church to be restored without any urging. So then we have received the grace of your faith and the reward of our own; for we cannot say otherwise than that it was of the grace of the Holy Spirit that, when all were unconscious of it, you suddenly restored the basilica. And I do not regret the losses of the previous time, since the sequestration of that basilica resulted in a sort of gain of usury. For you sequestered the basilica that you might give proof of your faith. And so your piety fulfilled its intention, having sequestered that it might give proof, and so gave proof in restoring. I did not lose the fruit, and I have your judgement, having been made clear to all that, with a certain diversity of action, there was in you no diversity of opinion. It was made clear to all, I say, that it was not of yourself that you sequestered, but it was of yourself when you restored it.[20]

These lines (and the surrounding context) give no precise indication when Gratian is alleged to have first sequestered the basilica, and then returned it. But Ambrosian historians are almost universally agreed that the basilica was restored during Gratian's brief stay in Milan at the end of July 379,[21] and that the above passage is a reflection of that event. Their view is based on the assumption that Gratian had moved his loyalties firmly to Nicene theology after reading Ambrose's treatise, *De fide* (Books I–II), written at the end of 378 or early 379.[22] The removal of the sequestration was a symbolic gesture on Gratian's part as an act of personal devotion to Ambrose and his faith.

The only surviving letter of Gratian addressed to Ambrose seems to confirm a warming of Gratian's pieties toward the Nicene confession

[19] See O. Faller, CSEL 79 15*–16*.

[20] *De spir. sanc.* I. 1.19–21. Trans. (altered) in NPNF X: 96 (Latin text in CSEL 79 24–5).

[21] On his way from Sirmium to Treves, Gratian is known to have gone through North Italy and stayed at the palace in Milan from the end of July to 3 August. O. Seeck, *Regesten der Kaiser und Päpste für die Jahre 311 bis 476 n. Chr.* (Stuttgart: J. B. Metzlersche, 1919), 252.

[22] This has been the traditional dating of the treatise, and has been reaffirmed by P. Nautin, 'Les premiers relations d'Ambroise avec l'empereur Gratien. Le *De fide* (livres I et II)', in *Ambroise de Milan: XVIe Centenaire de son election episcopale*, ed. Y. M. Duval (Paris: Études Augustiniennes, 1974), 229–44.

and was certainly written after the publication of *De fide* I–II.[23] But the proof usually cited as a corollary to the restoration of the basilica (the second piece of evidence) is Gratian's edict of 3 August 379 (*Codex Theodosianus* [= *CTh*] XVI. 5,5), which has been interpreted as anti-Arian in purpose. No group is identified by name, although the first line of the edict gives the appearance of being a general anti-heretical ban: 'Omnes vetitae legibus et divinis et imperialibus haereses perpetuo conquiescant'. If this served as an anti-Arian edict, it would provide a legal rationale for Gratian returning the basilica to Ambrose in 379.[24]

A third argument for the above interpretation is based upon Ambrose's response to Gratian's letter, probably written in 379 but certainly before Gratian arrived in Milan.

> You have returned to me the tranquillity of the church, for you have shut the mouths of the heretics; how I wish that you would have shut their hearts also. You did this no less as an act of faith as by the authority of your power.[25]

It is widely agreed that this passage is a reference to the returning of the basilica; a view accepted even by those scholars who are somewhat sceptical that Gratian fell under Ambrose's influence as early as 379.[26]

It must be admitted that the overall evidence for the first conflict over a basilica is meagre. We have already discussed why this might be so. There are, however, significant problems with the traditional reconstruction of the available data. Exactly when Gratian began to let his religious affinities inform his political policies is far from clear. One cannot ignore the political ideology which Gratian inherited from his father, Valentinian I, who strictly maintained a neutral position concerning the internal matters of ecclesiastical affairs.[27]

---

[23] *PL* XVI 913B: 'Docebit enim me ille, quem non nego, quem fateor Deum ac Dominum esse meum, non ei objiciens quam in me video, creaturam, qui Christo nihil me addere posse confiteor'. Tillemont argued that Gratian was so impressed with *De fide* that he lifted the sequestration of the basilica (124).

[24] So Palanque, *Saint Ambroise,* 501; Homes Dudden, 191–2; Paredi, 185; M. G. Mara, 'Ambrose of Milan', in *Patrology* IV. 146–7.

[25] *Ep.* (extra collectionem) 12. 2 (CSEL 82.3 219.22–5): 'Reddidisti enim mihi quietem ecclesiae, perfidiorum ora atque utinam et corda clausisti; et hoc non minore fidei quam potestatis auctoritate fecisti.'

[26] Faller, CSEL 79 13*; Hanson, *The Search,* 795.

[27] Gratian's application of this principle was, as Valentinian's, selective and subject according to the larger consideration of the well-being of the *res publica*. For example, the

Such a position must have some bearing on our treatment of *CTh* XVI. 5,5. Furthermore, the accepted interpretation of Ambrose's statement to Gratian about having returned to him the 'quies ecclesiae' need not have any relation to the basilica issue, especially when one considers the attacks Ambrose sustained in 379 from the Homoian community in Milan. Only after a examination of these points can we attempt to place the basilica conflict discussed in *De spiritu sancto* in its rightful context.

Gratian's Religious Politics

Reliable information about Gratian's religious allegiances at the time of his father's death (375) is difficult to obtain. There seems to be no question that he was a Christian, as portrayed by his boyhood tutor and friend, Ausonius, though little else is revealed.[28] The fact that Gratian maintained the Altar of Victory, an overtly pagan symbol, on the senate steps in Rome, as well as retained the imperial title, 'Pontifex Maximus', until 383, may bespeak of Ausonius' religiously moderating influence on his pupil.[29] But if Ausonius' description is too subtle, Ambrose's remarks about the emperor carry no nuance at all. When Ambrose speaks of Gratian *postmortem* in the funeral sermon delivered at the graveside of Valentinian II, he is said to have been 'faithful in the Lord, pious and meek and pure of heart'.[30] Later

---

so-called 'edict of [religious] toleration', issued just after Valens' death in the battle of Hadrianople, proscribed Manichaeans, Photinians and Eunomians, who were deemed threats not only to the religious peace, but to the social order as well (Socrates, *HE* V. 2 [*PG* 67 568A-B]: Sozomen, *HE* VII. 1.3 [GCS 50. 302]).

[28] *Actio ad Gratianum Imperatorem pro Consulatu* XIV. 63–7.

[29] Cf. A. Piganiol, *L'Empire Chrétien (325–95),* 2nd ed. (Paris: Presses Universitaires de France, 1972), 277. There is little to show for Ausonius' own commitment to Christianity save his yearly observances of Easter at Bordeaux, and the fact that Valentinian I chose him to tutor his son Gratian. We may assume that, like most of those in the later fourth century who did not allow the issue of religion to obstruct their careers or social mobility, Ausonius submitted himself to the Christianity of the Valentinian dynasty. Ausonius' own family traditions, however, were patently Pagan. And it seems that he was at least sympathetic to the view that such traditions should continue to influence Roman culture and learning. W. H. C. Frend is probably correct in saying that Ausonius represented a conventional and non-assertive form of Christianity which eventually alienated him from the more strident and ascetic piety found within many families of the Christian nobility. 'The Two Worlds of Paulinus of Nola', in *Latin Literature of the Fourth Century,* ed. J. W. Binns (London: Routledge and Kegan Paul, 1974), 101; 108–10.

[30] *De consol. Valent.* 74: 'fuit enim ipse fidelis in domino, pius atque mansuetus, puro corde' (CSEL 73 364.10–11).

in the same sermon Ambrose expresses his personal grief over Gratian's decease (during the usurpation of Maximus in 383), telling his listeners of the 'many signs' of piety which Gratian gave to him.[31] In both cases, it is evident that the epithets 'faithful' or 'pious' are applied to Gratian because of his acceptance of the Nicene faith, and the 'plurima insignia' may represent those occasions where his personal religion benefited Ambrose's ecclesiastical control in Milan.

Ambrose's homilectical reflections were penned years after Gratian had committed himself publically to patronise the pro-Nicenes with imperial support, although we may well believe that Gratian shared his father's predilection for Nicene Christianity. The sermon, however, tells us nothing about the progression by which Gratian came to know of ecclesiastical politics in North Italy and eventually alter the legal conditions which had given toleration to Nicene and 'Arians' alike. The question is when exactly did Gratian abandon the Valentinian political policy toward religious plurality. An edict directed against the 'Arians' would supply proof of the Ambrosian-imperial relationship for which so many scholars have sought. Does *CTh* XVI. 5,5 provide the evidence for a dramatic departure from religious toleration as Gratian fell 'under the spell of Ambrose'?[32]

In a monograph, *Ambrosius von Mailand und Kaiser Gratian* (1973), G. Gottlieb has demonstrated that *CTh* XVI. 5,5 was not a general anti-heretical edict, and thus anti-Homoian in intent, but directed against the Donatists. The line, 'Quisquis redempta venerabili lavacro corpora reparata morte tabificat, id auferendo quod geminat . . .', according to Gottlieb, is an unmistakable reference to the practice of rebaptism and closely parallels terminology used in previous anti-Donatist legislation.[33] Gratian's rescript to the *vicarius* Aquilinus states, concerning the Donatist bishop Claudianus, 'cum religionis sanctissimae disciplinam non cumulet iteratio, sed evertat . . . perdit animos corporum redemptorum.'[34] That rescript was issued in response to the Roman synodical letter of 378 which sought

[31] ibid., 79b (366.18). Cf. *De obitu Theod.* 39.

[32] As stated by A. Ehrhardt, 'The First Two Years of the Emperor Theodosius', JEH 15 (1964), 4.

[33] *Ambrosius von Mailand und Kaiser Gratian* (Göttingen: Vandenhoeck & Ruprecht, 1973) (= *Hypomnemata* 40), 60 ff.

[34] *Coll. Avell.* 13. 8 (CSEL 35 56.17–23).

imperial action, *inter alia,* against Claudianus as one of the 'sacrilegious rebaptisers from Africa'.[35] Also in *CTh* XVI. 5,5, Gratian accuses the 'teachers and ministers of this perverse superstition' of having abused the priestly office by referring to themselves with the appellations of 'episcopus', 'presbyter' or 'diaconus'. A similar accusation against the Donatists was made in 373 by Valentinian in an edict to the proconsul of Africa.[36]

A major weakness in Gottlieb's argument is his insistence that only the Donatists practiced rebaptism at the end of the fourth century.[37] There exists clear testimony that the Eunomians and Homoians were practicing rebaptism on those who converted to their sects at least as early as the 380s. The Eunomians, according to Philostorgius and Sozomen,[38] in no way recognised the baptism of the homoousians (or their ordination) and so required initiates to be baptised in conformity with their rites. Ambrose explains how the Homoians in Milan, under the leadership of the rival bishop Auxentius, received ex-Nicenes into their communion by annulling their previous baptism: 'Why, then, does Auxentius claim that the faithful ought to be rebaptised since they have been baptised in the name of the Trinity. . . ?'[39]

One could reasonably object that *CTh* XVI. 5,5 refers to the rebaptism of 'Arians', not only the Donatists. There is, however, a statement from the edict which leaves no doubt that the Donatists

[35] PL 13. 580A.

[36] 'Antistitem, qui sanctitatem baptisti inlicta usurpatione geminaverit et contra instituta omnium eam gratiam iterando contaminaverit, sacerdotio indignum esse censemus.' ('We judge to be unworthy of the priesthood that bishop who repeats the sancity of baptism by unlawful unsurpation and, against the teachings of all, contaminates this act of grace by repetition.' [Pharr, *The Theodosian Code,* 463] *CTh* XVI. 6,1 (20 February 373). This edict probably provided the precedent by which Gratian publically condemned the Donatists three years later in *CTh* XVI. 5,4: Olim pro religione catholicae sanctitatis, ut coetus haeretici usurpatio conquiesceret, iussimus . . .' ('Previously, on behalf of the religion of catholic sanctity, in order that the illicit practice of heretical assembly should cease, we commanded . . .' [Pharr, 450]) That Gratian is referring to the Donatists here, see Piganiol, 227–8, n. 7; Gottlieb, 77.

[37] 'Die Donatisten waren damals die einzigen, welche die Taufe zu erneuern pflegten' (61). Only after A.D. 400, Gottlieb says, were there other groups, such as the Novatians and Eunomians, accused of renewing baptism.

[38] Philost. *HE* X. 4: Sozomen, *HE* VI. 26.7; 26.9.

[39] *Contra Aux.* 37 (CSEL 82.3 107.58–61). The *Contra Auxentium* is an expansion of the sermon delivered in 386. See also M. Meslin, *Les Ariens d'Occident 335–430* (Paris: Éditions du Seuil, 1967), 388, for other instances of Homoian rebaptism.

alone are the object of the condemnation: 'And all teachers or ministers of that perverse superstition . . . let these abstain from assemblies of an already condemned view'.[40] Only one sect fits the above descriptions of rebaptisers and who had an 'already condemned view' in the west. As was noted above, the Donatists had been proscribed by Valentinian in 373, and again in 376 by Gratian.[41] No such legislation would be aimed at the Homoians until Theodosius' religious uniformity edict on 27 February 380, and then in January 381, a specifically anti-Arian law was issued.[42] And even though the Eunomians had been outlawed earlier under Valens,[43] it appears that the Eunomians were not an issue in the west and are never a target of legislation passed in the west.[44] The fact that Gratian renews their condemnation in 378, along with the Manichees and Photinians, presents no exception in that the edict issued from Sirmium was meant to address eastern religious concerns now that Valens was dead.

From our brief examination of CTh XVI. 5,5, it can be concluded that Gratian was making no changes in the Valentinian political policy concerning religion. And if the edict had no relation to the struggle between Nicenes and Homoians in Milan, there is no reason to think that it had any connection to the first basilica controversy. Whatever growing influence Ambrose exercised over the emperor, it was not yet affecting Gratian's political decisions against the Homoians. In fact, Gratian was just as ready to placate anti-Nicenes in Milan in the interests of public tranquility.

[40] 'Omnesque perversae istius superstitionis magistri pariter ministri .. hi conciliabulis damnatae dudum opinionis abstineant.'

[41] CTh XVI. 5,4 (22 April 376).

[42] The first edict (CTh XVI. 1,1 'cunctos populos') spelled out that the standards of orthodox religion were henceforth to be measured by the faith of Damasus of Rome and Peter of Alexandria. The other edict, CTh XVI. 5, 6, mandated Nicene catholicism as the only acceptable religion of the Roman (eastern) empire and forbade Photinians, Arians and Eunomians to hold assembly. Gratian seems to have endorsed the same edict or passed a similar one in the west about this time.

[43] As implied in Gratian's edict in 378 granting religious toleration to all sects previously condemned (under Valens) except Eunomians, Manichees and Photinians. See note 27.

[44] All known imperial edicts passed against the Eunomians in the fourth and fifth centuries are directed to eastern officials. This includes CTh XVI. 5,17 (4/5 May 389), a condemnation of Eunomian eunuchs, issued to Tatianus while Theodosius is still in Milan. It is obvious that Theodosius was not addressing a problem in the west, since Tatianus was praetorio praefectus orientis (388–92).

In the perilous aftermath of the Roman defeat at Hadrianople (3 August 378), Gothic troops completely overran Thrace, spreading panic throughout the Illyrian provinces. Many fled west across the Alps. Among the refugees was the court of Valentinian II and his mother Justina, who left Sirmium and arrived in Milan probably during the autumn of 378.[45] Gratian was in Sirmium at the time and it is quite possible that he ordered their transfer to the imperial residence in Milan until order could be restored in Pannonia. Once in Milan, it seems that the court began to patronise the Homoian community. New needs for religious accommodation had to be secured which were soon expressed in the form of a request to Gratian for the use of a basilica in the city.

Unfortunately, Ambrose is our only source of information at this point, who tells us that Gratian responded by ordering a church to be sequestered;[46] an action which leaves some doubt as to Gratian's intent. The most common understanding of sequestration was the placing of the disputed property into neutral hands until the rightful ownership of that property could be determined.[47] The *sequestrum* was deposited with a third person, or some mutually recognised authority, who had no personal interest in the outcome and thus safely guarded the deposit. Until a decision was made the property in question was out-of-bounds to both sides involved in the dispute. It is almost certain that this is the kind of situation which Ambrose meant to conjure up by his description of Gratian's sequestration of the basilica. And virtually all modern scholars have accepted the language of Ambrose's description, especially since we have no other sources for comparison. A good illustration is Glaesner's explanation of the events, who recounts how Justina sought a basilica for the 'Arians', but when the Catholics also claimed the basilica, and the conflict became increasingly bitter, Gratian placed the church under sequestration.[48]

[45] M. Simonetti, *La crisi ariana nel IV secolo* (Roma: Institutum patristicum Augustinianum, 1975) (= Studia *Ephemeridis 'Augustinianum'* II), 438; Palanque, *Saint Ambroise,* 60.

[46] 'Etenim basilicam sequestrasti, ut fidem probares,' et passim (*De spir. sancto* I. 19–21). Full citation above.

[47] See *CTh* IV. 8.6 (7); XI. 36,25.

[48] 'L' empereur Gratien et Saint Ambroise', *Revue d'histoire et ecclésiastique* 52 (1957), 471. Baunard (*Histoire de Saint Ambroise,* 97) also observes the significance that Gratian's act of sequestering the basilica equally closed it off to both Arians and Nicenes. However, Baunard vitiates the point by stating, 'En attendant, Gratien se declara très energiquement pour Ambroise'.

Glaesner is quite correct in thinking that such an act of sequestration was consistent with the policy of religious tolerance which still characterised Gratian's reign. There is no need to imagine that the Homoians suddenly 'seized' a basilica under Justina's direction. But if Gratian actually sequestered a basilica, was not the intent to allow the Homoians to have unimpeded use of one basilica? Two arguments can be marshalled in favor of this interpretation.

First, it must be recognised that Gratian's actions are portrayed in the *De spiritu sancto* passage as euphemistically as possible. Ambrose blames the emperor's decision to impound the basilica on the influence of others, whereas Gratian's return of the basilica to the Nicenes is regarded as an act of his own will and proof of the Holy Spirit at work in the emperor's faithful heart. Indeed, Ambrose claims that the very loss of the basilica resulted in a kind of victory for his side, since its restoration presented Gratian with an opportunity to demonstrate later his commitment to orthodoxy. Ambrose never admits that the Homoians might have had use of the basilica after its sequestration. To claim two years later in 381 that Gratian simply sequestered the basilica leaves the question open – and retrospectively neutral in light of the emperor's restoration of the same.

Secondly, from our opening account of the controversy over a basilica in 385–6, it seems that a similar process of sequestration was attempted in order to appropriate a basilica for the Homoians. When the contested basilica was seized by military authorities, imperial banners were hung and soldiers were posted to mark the edifice as government property.[49] People were not allowed to enter, but that was probably a temporary measure until tensions settled. Once the basilica was under imperial jurisdiction, the court would have the right to dispose of it, or allow select groups to meet therein who were in accordance with the government's sympathies.

Gratian too enjoyed the imperial prerogatives which gave him ultimate authority over all public property such as church buildings.[50] It was wholly within the realm of possibility for him to have ordered the sequestration of a basilica in Milan with the purpose of permitting Homoian assembly. Such a move would not violate

---

[49] *Ep.* 76. 1–4 (CSEL 82.3 108–10).

[50] A right which Valentinian II was said to be exercising in his seizure of the contested basilica. *Ep.* 76. 8 (CSEL 82.3 112.46–7).

Gratian's public policy of religious toleration, since, as we have seen, a policy of tolerance is not the same as non-interference.

Ambrose's Letter to Gratian

Once we have established that Gratian was willing and able to meet the Homoian request for a place of worship, the questions which remain are when did Gratian return the basilica to Nicene hands and why. If Gratian made no changes in his political policies toward anti-Nicenes in 379 when he spent several weeks in Milan, what then did Ambrose mean in his letter to Gratian, 'You have restored to me the tranquility (*quies*) of the church'?[51] Clearly Ambrose cannot have been referring to an anti-Arian edict which would have effectively prevented Homoians from the right of maintaining ecclesiastical property.

The question can be best answered by proposing that Ambrose's statement is a direct allusion to a promise that Gratian's father, Valentinian I, is said to have made to Ambrose if he accepted his election for the episcopal office of Milan.

> quia pater pietatis tuae quietem futuram spopondit, si electus susciperet sacerdotium. hanc fidem secutus sum promissorum.[52]
> (the father of your Piety promised a peaceful future if the one chosen [namely Ambrose] would assume the bishopric. I have kept faith in these promises.)

At the time of Ambrose's sudden election to that see in 374, Homoian Arian and Nicene factions were vigorously contending for their own candidates, throwing the city into an uproar.[53] Ambrose was being urged to accept on the grounds that his ostensible neutrality as governor (*consularis*) of the region would bring a resolution to the deadlock over a successor. In exchange, it seems that Valentinian offered Ambrose a pledge of security or 'quies' against public disruption, preserving the bishop from unjust attack. Ambrose accepted.

But now, four years later, Valentinian was dead and Ambrose was under attack. P. Nautin has convincingly argued that Ambrose was

---

[51] Full citation in note 25.

[52] *Ep.* 75. 7 (CSEL 82.3 77).

[53] Rufinus records after Auxentius' death that a 'dissenio gravis et periculosa seditio' was racking the city over the choosing of a successor. *HE* II. 11 (PL 21 521B).

being accused of heresy by the Homoians, and that the purpose of publishing *De fide* (I–II), which was written in direct response to Gratian's request for information about Ambrose's theology,[54] was to exonerate himself of these charges.[55] Between the years of 376–8 there is ample evidence that Ambrose was being increasingly opposed by pro-Homoian elements in Milan.

The chronology of events is impossible to determine with any certainty, but we are told that a certain Julian Valens arrived in the city at this time, having come from the Illyrian city of Pettau (Poetovio), where he was rejected as bishop by the congregation on account of his heterodox views.[56] Since our only knowledge of Valens' activities before he came to Milan is derived from hostile sources, such an evaluation must be considered in light of the fact that the bishop's entry into North Italy was no more remarkable than any other refugee who fled to the west during the Gothic unrest in Pannonia. More certain however, is Valens' anti-Ambrosian campaign once he arrived in Milan, evidently establishing himself as bishop of the Homoian minority. By means of 'illicit ordinations' and preaching anti-Nicene doctrine,[57] Valens posed a threat sufficient enough that the Council of Aquileia in 381 sought his expulsion from the city.[58]

Nor was Julian Valens alone in his efforts to bolster the Homoian community. For reasons that are not understood fully, Ursinus, the arch-rival of Damasus for the Roman see, also appeared in Milan and joined Valens in the task of covertly nurturing anti-Ambrosian sentiments. Another synodical letter from the Council of Aquileia describes Ursinus' activities:

[54] 'Tu quoque, sancte imperator Gratiane . . . fidem meam audire voluisti'. *De fide* I. praef. 1 (CSEL 78 3–4).

[55] *Les premiers,* 240. Elsewhere I have shown the implausibilities with the standard arguments (as seen in Homes Dudden and Paredi) that Gratian's motive in wanting a doctrinal explanation from Ambrose was because of the bishop's wide reputation as a defender of the Nicene faith. See chapter four in *Ambrose of Milan and the End of the Nicene-Arian Conflicts* (Oxford University Press) (forthcoming).

[56] *Ep.* 2. 9–10 (CSEL 82.3 322–3).

[57] ibid., 10: 'qui nunc illicitis ordinationibus consimilis sui sociat sibi et seminarium quaerit suae impietatis atque perfidiae per quosque perditos derelinquere . . .' (CSEL 82.3 323.119–21).

[58] Ibid., 10 (CSEL 82.3 323.115–19).

He . . . had embraced and joined with the Arians at that time. In an alliance with Valens, he tried to undermine (*turbare*) the Milanese church, by means of detestable meeting(s), sometimes before the doors of the synagogues, sometimes in the homes of the Arians, sharing secret plans and bringing his supporters together.[59]

We know of no other details about Ursinus' participation in the anti-Nicene movement in Milan, but the degree of his success can be gauged by the pressure which the Aquileian council put on the emperor, as in the case of Valens, to officially ban him from the city.

The culmination in galvanizing the Milanese Homoians came when the court of Valentinian II arrived in the autumn of 378. Justina seems to have wasted no time in expressing her favoritism for the Homoians, who enthusiastically received her patronage and her manifest opposition to the bishop. There is no reason to doubt ancient historical accounts, even though they tend to conflate the events of 378–9 and 385–6, that Justina initiated a campaign of hostility towards Ambrose and his supporters.[60] Indeed, it may have been the result of Justina's prompting that Gratian removed a basilica from Ambrose's jurisdiction for Homoian worship.[61] It is equally plausible that her influence was behind the accusation of heresy; a charge which if sustained, would effectively undermine Ambrose's episcopacy and leave the door open for the court to select a successor sympathetic to Homoianism. Glaesner believes that Justina herself was responsible for flooding Gratian with a series of objections to the homoousion views of the bishop.[62] Whatever the source, a charge of heresy, such as tritheism,[63] would certainly draw the attention of the emperor, just as Hilary of Poitiers had done a decade earlier when he

---

[59] *Ep.* 5 (extra coll.). 3: 'qui . . . cum Arrianis copulatus atque coniunctus erat eo tempore, quo turbare Mediolanensem ecclesiam coetu detestabili moliebatur cum Valente, nunc ante synagogae fores, nunc in Arrianorum domibus miscens occulta consilia et suos iungens. . .' (CSEL 82.3 183–4).

[60] Rufinus, *HE* II. 15 (*PL* 21 523fi–C); Socrates, *HE* V. 11. See Meslin, 46, for other aspects of Justina's hostilities against the bishop.

[61] As implied in Ambrose's statement in *De spiritu sancto* I. 1.21: 'Patuit, inquam, omnibus et tuum non fuisse, cum sequestrares' (CSEL 79 25.25–6).

[62] 'L'empereur Gratien et Saint Ambroise,' 272. This is much more likely than Nautin's argument that Palladius of Ratiaria was the accuser.

[63] The most persistent of accusations made by Homoians against Homoousians was that of tritheism because the latter's insistence that God was three equal and eternal *ousiai*. See the 'Scholia ariana' 345v, 128–9; 303v, 36 (SC 267 310–12; 230–2); and Ambrose's defense against tritheism in *De fide* I. 1.10 (CSEL 78 8.25–29).

brought charges of heresy against Auxentius (then bishop of Milan) during the reign of Valentinian I. Even if Gratian was personally disposed to the Nicene form of the Christian faith, such accusations against the metropolitan of North Italy could not be ignored. Ambrose was therefore asked to present a clarification of his views with the result that he produced *De fide* (I–II) in his defense.

Gratian's favorable reception of Ambrose's treatise is made known in a brief letter[64] which the emperor reportedly wrote with his own hand. Unambiguous confirmation is bestowed upon Ambrose's episcopal authority, punctuated with epithets such as 'religiose dei sacerdos', and 'parens et cultor dei aeterni'. Not only is Ambrose reckoned as one who teaches 'true doctrine', but the emperor requested further elaboration on the Nicene doctrine of the Holy Spirit.

Such a commendation must have provided a welcome relief to Ambrose, and is the context in which we must understand Ambrose's letter to Gratian. Sometime before the emperor arrived in Milan in the summer of 379, Ambrose hastily penned a response to Gratian acknowledging the latter's approval of the two books which were sent and the glad tidings that there was now no danger to be feared.[65] To be sure, Ambrose writes how 'much grace' which was shown to him and how his strength was refreshed by the emperor's profession of faith. For now Gratian is said to 'have shut the mouths of the heretics' and returned to Ambrose the 'quies ecclesiae'. This is clearly not a reference to returning of the basilica, but the dropping of charges laid against the bishop. In effect, Ambrose's letter is an expression of gratefulness to Gratian for restoring to him a state of affairs which he once enjoyed under Valentinian I. There is, therefore, no connection between the first controversy over the basilica and Ambrose's letter to Gratian, except to say that the removed basilica is evidence of Ambrose's dire need to procure Gratian's goodwill towards his situation.

A criticism made against Ambrose in the 'scholia ariana' may offer further corroboration of the above interpretation. Gottlieb has suggested that one of Palladius' complaints in his 'Contra de fide' is

---

[64] 'Cupio valde' (PL 16 913–14; CSEL 79 3–4).

[65] 'Misi autem duos libellos, quorum iam quia tuae clementiae sunt probati periculum non verebor.' *Ep.* 12. (extra coll.) 7 (CSEL 82.3 221.61–2).

directly parallel to the comments in Ambrose's letter to Gratian.[66] Palladius blames Ambrose for having obtained immunity from charges of impiety through a *praeceptum* of the emperor so that 'no catholic or doctor of the truth is heard by anyone if they speak against you.'[67] Since Palladius is directing his criticisms toward the *De fide* I–II at this point, there is a strong possibility that Palladius is referring to Gratian's approval of Ambrose's treatise and how the emperor dropped the charges of impiety pending against him. Such events were taking an ominous direction from the Homoian perspective.

The Events of 381 and the De spiritu sancto

If there is no known anti-Homoian legislation before 381 that presupposes Gratian's hostilities toward the Homoians, and if the 'peace of the church' which Ambrose once again received pertains not to the basilica affair, when did Gratian return the contested edifice to the pro-Nicenes?

The answer, I suggest, will be found by returning to the *De spiritu sancto* and the events which led up to it. For the publication of this work in early 381 represents a major turning point in Ambrose's political aspirations to gain undisputed hegemony over his enemies in Milan. It is very different from *De fide* III–V, written between 379–380, which was little more than a sophisticated expansion of books I–II. As Ambrose points out in the preface, he was still in the position of defending himself against the assaults of (Homoian) critics.[68] Incidentally, there is no mention in *De fide* III–V about the restoration of the basilica which leaves an inexplicable silence if the basilica had been recently returned. Given the polemical nature of these books, it is hardly possible that Ambrose would have neglected to parade such an auspicious reversal – if it had happened yet.

By 381 the religious and political climate had changed for Ambrose, and the reader of *De spiritu sancto* cannot help but notice a tone of triumphalism in the treatise. The emperor Gratian had moved his imperial residence from Treves to North Italy[69] and, significantly, was present in Milan for the Easter season. It is at this time Ambrose

---

[66] *Ambrosius von Mailand*, 44ff.
[67] *Scholia* 336v, 44–8 (SC 267 270).
[68] *De fide* III. 1.2 (CSEL 78 108).
[69] Seeck, *Regesten*, 256. There is no record of Gratian returning to live in Treves again.

chose to publish *De spiritu sancto* in three books,[70] a work which was the acknowledged fulfilment of Gratian's initial request (in 'Cupio valde') that the bishop of Milan expand his discussion in *De fide* I–II to include arguments for the divinity of the Holy Spirit.[71] Noticeably absent is the terse apologetical style which characterised the books of *De fide*. Rather, it is explained in the preface how God through his loving-kindness has redeemed the whole world from heresy and cleansed each of its cities from the Arians' poison: 'Quantos in urbe Roma, quantos Alexandriae, quantos Antiochiae . . . [q]uantos ergo et Constantinopolim, quantos postremo toto hodie in orbe mundasti!'[72]

The radical change of fortune for the Nicene faith across the Roman empire was also felt in Milan. Among the many works of the Holy Spirit, Ambrose states, the emperor independently commanded the basilica to be restored to the church; an event which is said to have occurred 'recently' (*proxime*).[73] When exactly Gratian ordered the contested basilica to be returned to Ambrose's jurisdiction is difficult to say, but we can surmise that it occurred in the early months of 381 and certainly before Easter. As we discussed above, Gratian seems to have followed suit with Theodosius' anti-Arian legislation issued in

---

[70] Several allusions in the prologue show that it was delivered as a speech at Eastertide, e.g., 'ipso paschatis die' (see Faller, CSEL 79 l6*l7*), even though the body of the work had already been completed sometime after Athnaric's death and burial in Constantinople (*De spir. sancto* I. prol. 17 [CSEL 79 23.167–9]). The reference to 'the enemy himself' undoubtedly pertains to the feared Gothic king Athanaric, who, having made peace with the eastern emperor Theodosius, entered Constantinople on 11 January 381 and died exactly two weeks later (Zosimus, *Historia Nova* IV. 34.4 [F. Pashoud, *Zosime: Histoire Nouvelle*, Paris: Societé d'Edition 'Les Belles Lettres', 1979, 298]; Socrates, *HE* V. 10 [PG 67 584B, conflated]).

[71] 'Cupio valde', 3 (CSEL 79 4.15–18).

[72] ('How many in the city of Rome, how many in Alexandria, how many in Antioch. . . how many also in Constantinople, how many, finally, have You cleansed by this time in the entire world'.) *De spiritu sancto* I. prol. 17 (CSEL 79 23.161–2; 170–1).

[73] ibid., I. 1.19 (CSEL 79 24.11–12). Of course the 'proxime' is in reference to Gratian's agreement with the arguments which Ambrose had put forth for the pro-Nicene interpretation of the Trinity: 'praesertim cum ita te adsertione istiusmodi testificatus sis proxime delectatum'. This may be a reference to the *De fide*, which is why so many scholars have concluded that the restoration of the basilica occurred soon after the publication of that work. But this reference to *De fide* is not at all certain, nor is there a need to believe that Gratian took action immediately after the reading of *De fide*. Indeed, there is every indication that Gratian's political policies were affected not until later.

February 381.[74] Given the new legal situation in the western empire which now condemned Homoianism as heretical, Gratian was no longer in a position of needing to placate the religious sensitivities of the Milanese Homoians or their imperial patrons.[75] The returning of the basilica was symptomatic of the 'cleansing' which was now occurring in the west: a clear sign, in Ambrose's mind, of Gratian's pledge to orthodoxy and piety.

Once it is resolved that Gratian did not restore the basilica to Ambrose until much later than the usual scenario allows, our understanding about the relations between Ambrose and the Homoians in North Italy is open for reconsideration. We may agree with R. Lizzi's theory of an 'Ambrosian sphere of influence in North Italy,'[76] which enabled the bishop to secure some western sees with bishops who shared his theology and politics. But prior to 381 the bishop's influence had many limitations outside of his circle of ecclesiastical sympathisers. It should not be assumed that the power Ambrose wielded at the council of Aquileia was normative for the earlier part of his career. Furthermore, the fact that Gratian freely handed a basilica over to Homoian control and that this standoff was maintained for over two years challenges the long-standing assumption that Ambrose worked from an authoritative position informing western imperial opinion from 378 and onwards. On the contrary, it seems that Gratian was quite independent of the bishop even in religious affairs that concerned political policy, and there is no compelling reason why Gratian would have suddenly turned to the bishop of Milan for guidance much before 380.

It also has to be admitted that Ambrose's struggle with the Homoians in Milan was more complicated and hazardous than is depicted by most biographical treatments of the bishop. Even under Gratian's reign, Ambrose had to compete with the court of Valentinian II to maintain control of his see and was forced at one

---

[74] See note 42.

[75] Not until after the death of Gratian (383) is Valentinian II able to change this legal situation. On 23 January 386, Homoian assemblies are given the right to exist (*CTh* XVI. 1,4) which paved the way for the pro-Homoian court in Milan to once again contest Ambrose's jurisdiction over a basilica.

[76] 'Ambrose's Contemporaries and the Christianization of Northern Italy', JRS (1990), 156–73.

point to defend himself against charges of heresy. Clearly, the loss of the basilica in 378 was only one part of a campaign mounted against him. While we will probably never know all the details of the attacks launched against Ambrose during those difficult years preceeding the anti-Arian legislation,[77] we can say that they were sufficiently effective in promoting anti-Nicene interests in Milan. This is a far cry from Gwatkin's influential assessment that in the west 'Arianism scarcely had any legitimate footing at all.'[78] Milan itself was one of the remaining western strongholds for anti-Nicene sympathies, well before the arrival of imperial support in the person of Justina – a fact that has long been understated.[79] We are not surprised therefore at the enthusiasm with which Ambrose received Gratian's letter of commendation and approbation for his position in *De fide* (I–II).

Ambrose would not have his imperial ally for long, however. Just two years after Ambrose received back the basilica, Gratian was assassinated, leaving the government of Italy to Valentinian II, and thus setting the context for the day when Ambrose would have to defend his jurisdiction over a basilica in Milan for a second time.

---

[77] Despite the hagiographic embellishments that abound in Paulinus' *Vita Ambrosii*, one is still impressed with the sheer number and ferocity of attacks with which 'Arian' opponents attempted to unseat the bishop of Milan.

[78] H. M. Gwatkin, *Studies in Arianism* (Cambridge: Deighton, Bell and Co., 1882), 3. So convinced was Gwatkin of this assessment that he almost completely ignores ecclesiastical events in the west after the council of Ariminum (359).

[79] See Meslin, *Les Ariens,* 51–8; "Introduction" in Williams, *Ambrose of Milan.*

III
LITURGY AND ASCETICISM

Chapter 8

BAPTISM AND THE
ARIAN CONTROVERSY

Rowan Williams

A very frequent theme in fourth century polemic against those unwilling to accept the creed of Nicaea is the appeal to the Church's baptismal practice. In what is perhaps the best-known example of such an appeal,[1] Athanasius used the threefold baptismal formula to show that the 'Arian' doctrine of a single primordial divine person acting independently makes nonsense of what the Church actually does in its ritual practice; and the same sort of argument reappears elsewhere in Athanasius, in Basil and Gregory of Nyssa, and is presupposed by Hilary of Poitiers. Together with the appeal of these authors to the practice of addressing prayer and worship to the divine Son,[2] this suggests quite strongly that the enemies of Nicaea were conscious of resisting the weight of liturgical practice, that 'Arian' theologies were bound to be counter-intuitive to the Christian worshipper. However, if we stop to think about this for a moment, we should realise that it is an odd claim. With one exception – to be discussed later in this essay – we have no evidence that pro-Nicenes and anti-Nicenes habitually used radically different liturgies; did Nicaea's critics find it so easy to kick against the goads for decade after decade?

In fact, there is evidence that liturgical practice in general and baptism in particular was appealed to by both sides in the debate. Liturgy, like Scripture, was a common ground for disputation, and, just as biblical phrases in their pre-controversial innocence could be deployed by theologians of totally opposed commitments, so could the formulations of public worship. Unless we take this seriously, we

[1] *Or. con. Ar.* II. 41–3 (PG 26 253A–259C).
[2] E.g. *Or. con. Ar.* II. 23–4 (PG 26 193C–200A); Gregory of Nyssa, *Ref. conf. Eunomii* 30 (GNO II 323–4 = PG 45 480A) and 69–72 (ibid., 340–2 PG 45 497C–500A).

shall fail to understand how and why liturgical composition so flourished in the fourth and fifth centuries that the great liturgies of Eastern Christendom are almost inaccessible, as far as terminology and imagery goes, to someone with no knowledge of the doctrinal issues disputed in this period. We need to beware of a naive view of the relation between doctrine and worship, of giving to either a simple, undialectical priority. What I hope to do in this paper is, first, to examine the Nicene appeal to baptismal practice, second, to look at how Nicaea's opponents understood the baptismal formula, and third, to offer a few reflections on the difficult case of the alleged modifications of baptismal practice by Eunomius and his followers. This cannot pretend to be more than a preliminary survey of one area in a very rich and very little explored field: there is room for much fuller treatment of how not only the Nicene dispute in the strict sense, but also the controversies over the Spirit's status affected liturgical revision and creation. Baptism, however, has a particularly obvious centrality, and it is a point at which liturgical and exegetical concerns are closely interwoven; so it seems a reasonable place to start.

1. The Nicene Appeal to Baptismal Practice

1. Athanasius' encyclical letter of 339 significantly informs his readers that he is going to relate outrages unparalleled in the Church's history since the risen Christ commanded the apostles to baptise 'in the name of the Father and of the Son and of the Holy Spirit' (Matt. 28:19).[3] He does not develop the point; but the implication is clear. Not until the present troubles has the Lord's command been so manifestly disobeyed. But Athanasius' own distinctive theological glossing of the formula does not appear until the second book of the *Orationes contra Arianos,* where it forms part of the wider discussion of how the Father acts in or through the Logos. Athanasius (II.41) poses a dilemma for his opponents: if the Father can do what he wants to do without the Son, why bother to associate the Son with his actions? If the Father cannot do what he wants to do without the Son, this suggests (on the non-Nicene account) that the only and only true God is not 'all-sufficient' (*autarkēs*). Baptism focuses the question very neatly: if God can make the Logos a son directly by grace, why

[3] *Ep. encyclica.* (PG 25 225AB).

does he need this adopted son to make *us* adopted sons and daughters? Athanasius' (very Alexandrian)[4] response is to insist that, when the Father acts through the Son, he does not employ something other than his own resources to do his work; if you ask whether it is the sun or the sun's rays that shine, you should see at once that the question reveals a misunderstanding. For the sun to shine is for the sun to give off light; for the Father to bestow his loving grace is for the Father to act in the Son. It is not that the Father has to turn to 'someone else' for help. The Father is what he is in generating the Son, and giving away the divine life by that generating act. We cannot abstract from this to the Father 'alone'. Thus in baptism, the Father can only act to give us adoptive grace through the work of the Son (and the Spirit – though Athanasius is less clear about this: he seems to be saying that the Spirit is the concrete actualising of the Son's work as the Son is of the Father's[5]). There is one act of graceful giving (11.42), unintelligible except as the Father's act through the reality that eternally and by definition flows from him. To deny this eternal outpouring of divine life is to know neither the Father nor the Son. Thus, even if Athanasius' opponents use the right words, they cannot truly come into the baptismal relationship to God as Father: what could it mean to be baptised 'into' or 'in the name of' a created Logos who does not exist eternally and necessarily? What use is it to be united to a being who is not united to the Father (43)?

Athanasius allows that 'Arians' share the same baptismal formula as 'Catholics', but so do Manichaeans, Montanists and Paulinians (43). The Arian perversion of truth is, however, even worse than that of these other heretics, for here we have to do not simply with distorted views of the incarnate Son, but with offence against the Father. If 'Father' and 'Son' are replaceable terms, if they can be rendered as 'creator' and 'creature' (42), then the baptisand is deprived of a real contact with the Godhead: the threefold divine naming in baptism does not tell the truth about God, if the non-Nicenes are to be

[4] The image of the sun and its rays for the Father's relation to the Word is implicit in the long Alexandrian tradition of applying Wisd. 7:26 (and its echo in Heb. 1:3) in a trinitarian context; see Origen. *Peri Archon* I.2.9–11, passim; Dionysius, as cited in Athanasius' *De sententia Dionysii* 15 (Opitz, Athanasius Werke II.1.57.4–19), and Alexander of Alexandria's *hē philarchos* encyclical (Opitz, III. 1: *Urkunden zur Geschichte des Arianischen Streites*, no. 14.23.23–4, 24.4–6)

[5] Cf. *Or. con. Ar.* III.15 (PG 26 353B).

believed. It merely represents a loose analogy; the relation of the first and second hypostases could be more accurately expressed. Athanasius is thus doing something considerably more here than appealing to common practice alone to settle the argument. He is deploying at least two further presuppositions, both integrally connected with the whole of his theological polemic. The first is the conviction that *one* agency alone is involved in the work of salvation: there is only one eternal and all-sufficient agency, wholly dependable and irresistible, and only if it is this agency that acts for our redemption can we be confident that we are indeed saved.[6] To introduce an extraneous and contingent force, the independent will of the Logos, is at best confusing and at worst destructive of truthful belief about the nature of God. The second assumption is that salvation is union with the divine life, directly and without intermediary: failure to grasp the nature of that life (i.e. to understand that the Father is eternally and naturally generative)[7] means that I cannot learn to see myself as a child of the eternal Father, the object of that immutable love in which he beholds the eternal Word. The baptismal formula – like the words of Scripture[8] – must be interpreted in the light of a global construal of the logic of Salvation, which for Athanasius is above all bound up with the unity and direct accessibility of God's action. As I have already hinted, Athanasius stands very clearly in a particular kind of Alexandrian tradition, deeply preoccupied with the unity of God's work. It is perhaps in this respect that he stands closest to Origen.

If we turn to his correspondence with Serapion, a similar picture emerges. Through the Spirit given in baptism (1.4), Christ unites us 'with himself', and, through himself, to the Father (1.6) The Spirit cannot be an angel because Christ, in the Matthaean formula, sets the

---

[6] This motif in Athanasius' doctrine of salvation is lucidly set out in R. C. Gregg and D. E. Groh, *Early Arianism. A View of Salvation*, (Philadelphia and London: Fortress Press, 1981), 170–83. In a period when the memory of failure and betrayal in time of persecution was still vivid, the emphasis on immutable reliability has particular force. Even if there are questions to be asked about Gregg's and Groh's main thesis, this point certainly holds. The citation of *Or. con. Ar.* I.51 (PG 26 117C) on the need for an 'image' of changeless righteousness is apt.

[7] *Or. con. Ar.* II.2 (PG 26 149B–152B).

[8] Cf. the remarks on hermeneutical debate in the Arian controversy in Williams, *Arius*, 107–13.

Spirit alongside Father and Son; and we cannot be united to Father and Son by the mediation of a creature (I.11; cf., I.25). When we mention the Father, we necessarily mention the Son, and also mention the Spirit who is 'in' the Son (I.14, III.5): there is a single action of grace inseparably enacted by the three together, the Spirit realising in us what belongs by nature to the Son (1.19), marking us with his 'seal' (I.12, III.3). From the foundation of the Church, the baptismal formula has taught Christians to set the Spirit alongside the Father and the Son (I.28; cf. II.6, III.6). I.19 transfers the argument of *Contra Arianos* II. 43 to the Spirit: if we are baptised in the name of a created spirit, how can we be united to the creator? And if the Spirit as a creature can be named alongside the divine persons, who would not postulate an unlimited multitude of equal sharers in divinity? Once again, unclarity about the status of the divine hypostases reveals, to Athanasius, unclarity about the logic of salvation. Without a unified or coherent profession of faith in the unity of the Trinity, what becomes of baptism? do we have to suppose a 'divided' profession of faith, directed simultaneously to creator and creature, a dual baptism deriving at once from Father and Son and from an angelic creature (I.30, cf. III, 6, IV. 3,7)? Athanasius repeats several times the formula 'baptism is one as faith is one' (alluding to Eph. 4, 5) or some closely similar phrase. The argument turns once again on the unity of the divine action: if baptism does one thing for us and is associated with a once-for-all profession of faith, the persons named in baptism must perform one indivisible action. They are not an alliance of ontologically hybrid subjects.

All this leads Athanasius to a discussion in the fourth letter (8-end) of post-baptismal sin and blasphemy against the Holy Spirit, a discussion of some interest for the vexed history of the interpretation of Matt. 12:24–25. Sin against the Holy Spirit cannot be identical with post-baptismal sin, for two reasons: first, because baptism is performed in the name of all three persons, not of the Spirit alone, sin or blasphemy against the Spirit is indistinguishable from sin or blasphemy against the whole Trinity (12); second, closely related to this, Jesus is speaking to the unbaptised in the gospel who, by ascribing Jesus' works of power to Beelzebul, deny the presence in him of the Holy Spirit, and may thus be said to be guilty of an offence *specifically* against the Spirit (ibid. & 16). Athanasius is conscious of going aganst Alexandrian tradition (Origen[9] and Theognostus) in this matter: it is significant that both regard the essential feature of baptism as the gift of the Spirit (so that the unbaptised cannot sin against the Spirit, whom they have not yet encountered). Athanasius, in other words, recognises that his strongly 'unitary' account of baptism stands in some tension, if not with the practice of the Church as such, then at least with a well-supported glossing of that practice. That the issue had been raised by Serapion (IV.8) confirms the judgment that Athanasius' interpretation of the rite was not uncontroversial. As so often in his work, Athanasius triumphantly turns a problem into a polemical weapon: the Arians, in ascribing the works done by Christ to a created agency (the mutable and contingent logos) blaspheme against the Spirit no less than did the Pharisees (IV.22). And, once again, we are told that the failure to confess aright, the one divine action in the Spirit-filled life of Christ cuts the heretic off from true and eternal life.

It should be clear by now that Athanasius' deployment of the argument from baptismal usage in his polemic is not a wholly straightforward affair. He construes the meaning of the rite on the basis of his own very distinctive commitment to a theology of the three divine persons as the three ordered 'articulations' of one eternal act; and, while he certainly has Alexandrian precedent for such a theology, and might reasonably claim that a proper analysis of the baptismal event required such a theology, he is obviously making new connections and drawing new implications – sometimes also generating new problems, as in the discussion of Matt. 12. Liturgy does not simply determine the shape of doctrine: it is far more the contested material upon which doctrinal reflection must work, the subject of rival 'bids' for definition. Or, to put it rather more bluntly, liturgy does not settle arguments, whatever Athanasius (and his opponents) may have thought; but it does provide the *language* for argument. As I have indicated, this means that the use of liturgy clearly parallels the use of Scripture in the controversy of the period.

[9] At IV. 10, Athanasius claims to be quoting Origen; but the text is not verbatim from any work of Origen that we possess. It is possible that he is conflating *Peri Archon* I.3.2 (GCS 50.5–13) with I.3.7 of the same work (GCS 59.4.ff.). The conclusion Athanasius draws is that Origen held the baptised to be sinning against the Holy Spirit because the baptised person has come to be 'in the Spirit' (*en autó[i] genomenos*).

For obvious reasons, it is less prominent: there is no single, substantial widely-diffused corpus of accepted liturgical texts. However, in the absence of general credal formularies, the *pistis* confessed at baptism and the evidently unquestioned and scripturally-founded practice of invoking the threefold name[10] serve as a universally accessible point of reference. But before moving on to explore the ambiguities in this faith and practice which made it possible for both parties to claim the authority of the baptismal rite for their theologies, we shall look briefly at another Nicene apologist, to see how far Athanasius succeeded in establishing a clear convention of debate.

2. Basil of Caesarea's treatise *On the Holy Spirit* begins by mentioning a rather different kind of liturgical controversy, over the form of the doxology used in public prayer (possibly at the Eucharist).[11] Basil has apparently varied the traditional formula ('Glory be to the Father through the Son in the Holy Spirit') on occasions by the controversial alternative, 'Glory to the Father alongside (*meta*) the Son together with the (*sun*) the Holy Spirit'. That the former was traditional is clear from the fact that Basil is obliged to defend his usage as Scriptural and in some sense traditional,[12] and from the evident use of the more familiar formula to establish a kind of hierarchy between the divine persons: Basil, in III. 5 to V. 12 argues that the scriptural use of the prepositions 'through' (*dia*) and 'in' (*en*) is too loose to justify the drawing of exact theological conclusions unless one calls in the aid of something like an Aristotelian typology of causality, which is, of course (he says at III. 5), to import alien and heathen criteria into theology.

It is fairly plain from this that Basil's opponents (whether he has in mind non-Nicenes in general or 'Macedonians' in particular)[13] could

[10] On the history of the threefold invocation, see especially E. Riggenbach, *Der Trinitarische Taufbefehl* (Gütersloh: C. Bertelsmann, 1903), and various essays in ed., A. M. Triacca and A. Pistoia, *Trinité et Liturgie*, Eph. Lit. Subsidia 32, Rome 1984.

[11] *De spiritu sancto* I.3: *proseuchomenó[i] moi . . . meta tou laou* suggests a eucharistic context.

[12] See *De spiritu sancto* XXV. 58–60 (PG 32 173C–180B) on uses of *sun* in Scripture, suggesting that, as a simple conjunctive, it is no more offensive than 'and'; XXIX. 71–4 (PG 32 200B–208C) deals with traditional usages apparently supporting Basil's by speaking of Father, Son and Spirit in a co-ordinating fashion. Johnston's edition of the text (Oxford, 1892) has a useful note on interpretations of Basil's apparent concessions to other usages.

[13] On the unsatisfactory nature of this designation and the difficulty (so common in reading fourth century controversial texts) of identifying a single coherent school of

ARIANISM AFTER ARIUS

and did appeal to traditional liturgical practice and that pro-Nicenes were happy to improve on traditional usage by bringing into liturgical prominence what would have been at best a marginal usage.[14] When Basil turns to the discussion of baptism, he begins (X. 24) by emphasizing not so much the clarity of universal tradition as the demand for obedience to the plain words of Scripture. Jesus in Matt. 28:19 co-ordinates (*suntassein*) the divine hypostases, linking them by a simple conjunction; and 'We must obey God rather than men'. This is a skilful opening of the theme, which tacitly acknowledges that the appeal to practice alone is inadequate. If Basil's opponents are determined to argue about conjunctions and prepositions, the most unambiguous Scriptural statement of saving belief in the Trinity will support a co-ordinate and not a subordinate status for the Son and the Spirit. Only after this pre-emptive move do we turn to a more specific consideration of the rite itself (X. 26). Salvation is given to us exclusively through baptism, which involves the confession of the trinitarian faith, as well as being administered in the threefold name: to deny the plain implication of this confession is not only to disregard the Lord's words in Scripture, but 'to erase one's signature' (*tó[i] idió[i] cheirographó[i] machomenos*) to the contract of saving faith. Here Basil comes closer to Athanasius: XI. 27 picks up the point that there can be no salvation in the faith of someone who confesses the Father but denies the Godhead of the Son, and extends the same argument to the Spirit; and in XIII. 29, we find a strong statement, quite close to the thought of the letters to Serapion,[15] of the inability of created angelic powers to liberate us and give us familiarity and kinship (*oikeiotés*) with God as Father.

Basil's argument has moved generally into a more Athanasian key. Chapter XII. 28 has underlined the error in arguing from the fact that baptism in the New Testament is described regularly as being 'into

thought under this name, there is some helpful recent discussion in Hanson, *The Search*, 760–72, esp. 766–7.

[14] Theodore of Mopsuestia ascribes the introduction of 'Glory to the Father and to the Son and to the Holy Spirit' to Flavian of Antioch and Diodore of Tarsus, presumably in the 340s, when they were leading (lay) members of the dissident Eustathian party at Antioch during the episcopate of Leontius. (The fragment is preserved in Nicetas, *Thesaurus* V.30 [PG 139 1390C]). A Eustathian parentage for the 'co-ordinating' formula would have confirmed the worst suspicions of conservative pluralists.

[15] See above, p 153.

Christ' only, for 'mention of Christ is the confession of the whole [Godhead]'. In any case, various New Testament references to baptism 'in' or 'by' the Spirit do not lead us to doubt the equal significance of Father and Son. The essential underlying pattern in Scripture is clear: we receive the anointing Christ received from the Father. Salvation is being adopted by the Father, entering the divine life by assimilation to the life of the Son. For Basil, as for Athanasius, the argument turns finally on the character of salvation itself and on the inseparability of divine action. Basil has no difficulty (in XIV. 31 XV. 34) in refuting objections based on phrases about baptism 'into' Moses or even 'into' water. 'Baptism into Moses' is simply a rather artificial type of true baptism, which by definition involves dying and rising with Christ; the water (XV. 35) is the outward sign of the tomb from which the Spirit calls us back to life. Baptism (Basil adds) is performed once only because Christ died and rose once only – a point of some interest in the light of alleged Eunomian practice, as we shall see later. But it is perhaps in XVI. 38 that we find the clearest resonance with Athanasius: all that God does, he does in threefold unity, each act originating in the Father as *arché,* realised in the Son, completed by the Spirit. The Father has no 'need' of the Son as an extraneous reality to supplement his deficiencies: it is simply the case that what he does as Father he does through the Son. His will is made actual in the Son, as is the Son's in the Spirit. Whether Basil knew the *contra Arianos* is disputable;[16] but the closeness of this passage to *contra Arianos* II.41, where the same point about whether the Father needs the help of an independent agent if he works always through the Son is raised and answered, suggests a fairly direct connection.

Basil is no less aware than Athanasius that the baptismal argument is not completely clearcut. Faced with exegetical nitpicking about prepositions, he is able to adduce the dominical command to baptise as providing an apparently simple riposte; but when he wants to develop a serious case against the division of the trinitarian hypostases, he turns to very much the same points as Athanasius. His idiom in speaking of the Trinity is characteristically rather more pluralist than the Alexandrian bishop's, (*Or. con. Ar.* II. 41 lays far more emphasis than *de spir. sanct.* XVI. 38 upon the Son as the very

---

[16] Nothing in Basil's letters to Athanasius suggests extensive knowledge of the latter's written work overall. I know of no detailed modern treatment of the question.

form of the Father's action), yet the two main pillars of the Athanasian argument stand out the nature of salvation as incorporation into a single trinitarian complex of relations, and the cognate insistence on the unity of all divine action. To be saved is to be 'divinised' in the Son; no power less than God's can dispose of the divine life; salvation is thus the act of God and God only; therefore what realises in us the divine life must be always the single and indissoluble agency of God. Baptism is our entry into the status of Christ the Son, and so one action only is to be discerned in the grace there given. Two variations or amendments of the argument may be noted, one from the *De spiritu sanctu,* the other from a letter of Basil's. *De spir. sanct.* XVIII describes how the path by which we know God reflects (in reverse) the movement of the divine being: we are directed by the one Spirit to the one Son and thence to the one Father for the Son alone knows the Father, and the Spirit alone empowers us to confess the Son as Lord; and conversely, the divine goodness flows out from the Father to reach us through the Son and the Spirit. Basil's phraseology here suggests some consciousness of an anti-Nicene unease with what must have seemed like a potential telescoping of the divine hypostases into a single undifferentiated agent or subject (we shall see shortly how such an unease was indeed articulated by non-Nicenes): he is anxious that the differentiation in God's act, the order of revelation and the knowledge of God laid out in the New Testament, should not disappear, and in this respect he is more scrupulous than Athanasius in trying to do justice to the dynamic or narrative pattern of divine act and human response in Scripture which constituted so strong an element in non-Nicene apologetic.[17] The second, rather less significant, refinement is to be found in *ep.* CCX. 3–5,[18] where Basil has to cover his flank against Sabellianism. There are evidently some who use the formula of Matt. 28:19 in a far too enthusiastically unitive fashion, arguing that, since Christ enjoins baptism in the *name* – not the *names* – of Father, Son and Spirit, there is no

[17] Is he also influenced by the Plotinian account of the One's self-differentiation? On Basil and Plotinus, see J. M. Rist, 'Basil's "Neoplatonism": its Background and Nature', in *Basil of Caesarea: Christian, Humanist, Ascetic,* ed. P. J. Fedwick (Toronto: Pontifical Institute of Medieval Studies, 1981), 137–220, esp. 190–202. Rist's conclusion suggests caution in assuming direct and positive Plotinian influence.

[18] Cf. also *ep.* ccxxxvi. 4 for the same point more briefly put.

nameable hypostatic divine reality designated by 'Son' or 'Christ'; there is one divine subject only. Here Basil has to appeal in a rather different way to the force of the co-ordinating conjunction: they set the hypostases alongside each other, but posit them as distinct, each name corresponding to a reality. Otherwise, why offer glory in the doxology to a threefold name, if one would do? Basil is once again redressing what must have been quite widely perceived as the imbalance of the Nicene-Athanasian idiom.[19] His response is lame and inadequately thought through; but it does at least reinforce our awareness of how Athanasian enthusiasm for the singleness of divine agency needed nuancing in a region where the teaching of Marcellus was still perceived as a major threat. At least one of Basil's letters to Athanasius (*ep.* lxix) effectively begs the Patriarch to distance himself from Marcellus and to encourage Rome to do the same.

For Basil and Athanasius (as for other Nicene apologists) the baptismal invocation is a significant item in theological controversy; but its use requires the prior privileging of a quite close definition of the nature of salvation, whose roots are more diffuse than liturgical usage alone. The territory continues to be disputed in the fourth century not least because the view of divine action presupposed by Athanasius and (with qualifications) Basil seems to threaten some erosion of the differences between the divine hypostases, and thus a doctrine of God dangerously far removed from the revealed pattern of Scripture. We turn next to the examination of the ways in which baptismal practice and the formula of Matt. 28:19 figured in the non-Nicene polemics of the century.

2. The Baptismal Formulary in Non-Nicene Literature

Matt. 28:19 appears in several credal statements of the early fourth century – the creed of Eusebius of Caesarea as submitted to the Nicene fathers,[20] the statement of faith drawn up by Arius and Euzoius, probably in or around 327,[21] and the second creed of the Antiochene

---

[19] And Basil's own linking of Apollinarianism to Sabellianism (*epp.* cxxix.l and ccxxiv.2) indicates his clear sense of where the anxieties of the region lay.

[20] *De decretis* 33.4–6 (Opitz 29.11–28); also Socrates, *HE* I.8 and Theodoret *HE* I.12.

[21] Socrates, *HE* I.26.8, Sozomen *HE* II.27; for a later dating, dependent on the questionable conviction that Arius was not rehabilitated by any authority prior to 335, see Annik Martin's substantial and painstaking study, 'Le fil d'Arius: 325–35,' RHE LXXXIV (1989), 297–333, esp. 316–18.

synod of 341, often called the 'Creed of Lucian,'[22] and thus quite possibly the earliest in date of these three. What is immediately striking is the way in which all three explicitly associate the baptismal injunction with the belief that Father, Son and Spirit exist *alethós* – as actual individual subsistents, not as names for 'phases' of a single divine life. Each formula concludes its exposition of the faith by claiming to believe 'as the Lord Jesus Christ' taught when he delivered the commission of Matt. 28:19, and each glosses the text in this emphatically pluralist fashion. The Antiochene creed gives the fullest exposition, insisting that baptism is given in the name 'of a Father who is truly Father, a Son who truly is Son, a Holy Spirit who truly is Holy Spirit,' and that 'these names are not assigned casually or idly, but designate quite precisely the particular subsistence (*hypostasis*), the rank and the glory of each of those named'. The latter phrase reflects, almost certainly, the anxieties of the council fathers at Antioch in 341 rather than any earlier text directly related to Lucian and his circle: they have a specific concern to combat what they see as the neo-Sabellian teaching of Marcellus. However, the association of the word *alethós* with the gospel quotation in the two other formulae strongly suggests a convention pre-dating Nicaea. Although Eusebius uses Matt. 28:19 elsewhere,[23] in anti-Marcellan polemic, he does not use *alethós* in these contexts. It is a term which also appears in the surviving fragments of Asterius,[24] and was evidently significant before and after Nicaea as a test of pluralist trinitarian orthodoxy. It must be highly probable that its association with Matt. 28:19 originates in a confessional statement of the early fourth century (whether composed or merely subscribed by Lucian), perhaps drawn up in the aftermath of the Paul of Samosata controversy and diffused fairly widely in Syria (including Palestine) and Asia. Within a very short time after Nicaea, the problem of Marcellus gave a vigorous new lease of life to this exegetical trope.

[22] *De syn.* 23, Opitz. 249.11–250.4; see 723A for the repeated *alethós*.
[23] *Contra Marcellum* I.1.9 and 36 (GCS 3.7,8.21), *De eccl. theol.* 3.5 (GCS 163.22), *Theoph.* 4.8 (GCS 177.2). For an admirably full and authoritative discussion of Eusebius and the Matthaean text, see H. B. Green, 'Matthew 28:19, Eusebius, and the lex orandi,' in *The Making of Orthodoxy*, ed. R. Williams (Cambridge: Cambridge University Press, 1989), 124–41 – a study to which I am much indebted.
[24] Frag. XX.c of Asterius in G. Bardy, *Recherches sur s. Lucien d'Antioche et son école* (Paris: Beauchesne, 1936), 349.

Athanasius' use of Matt. 28:19 thus appears in a rather different perspective. He is neither drawing on an agreed exegetical convention nor simply initiating *ex nihilo* a novel theological theme. If the Matthaean text was as widely familiar before 330 as it seems to have been, in the context of defending a three-hypostasis theology of a sort inimical to Nicaea, his reference to the text in the 339 encyclical is likely to be deliberately provocative; and the argument of *Or. con. Ar.* II. 41 ff. is a conscious attempt to apply to this verse his consistent exegetical principle,[25] that scriptural texts must be interpreted in and only in the light of what the Church's language about salvation as a whole entails. But, in this as in other cases, such an exegetical recasting involves a major (if implicit) critique of a tradition whose polemical interests were specifically focused on the refutation of one or another kind of modalism. A glance at the history of the exegesis of texts like Ps 45:7–8,[26] Jn. 14:28[27] and even Prov. 8:22,[28] which were so problematic for post-Nicene interpreters, will show that they have a respectable record of use in establishing the real difference between Father and Son. If the evidence of the non-Nicene confessions we have been looking at is taken seriously, Matt. 28:19 had a similar history; and Athanasius' tactic here is not, as with other texts, simply to explain it away and to qualify misleading first impressions, but to turn its history upside down and make it a weapon in his theological offensive (as certainly seems to be happening in the 339 encyclical).

2. Further confirmation of the traditional and non-Nicene use of Matt. 28:19 may be had from the *Apostolic Constitutions*. Metzger's

[25] Williams, *Arius,* 109–10.

[26] Discussed at length in *Or. con. Ar.* 1.46–52. It was being used in the earliest days of the Arian controversy (see Alexander of Alexandria, *hé philarchos,* Opitz, *Urkunden* no. 14, 24.31); Origen examines it in *Com. Jn.* I. 28, *Peri Archon* II.6.4 and IV.4.4 and *Con. Cels.* VI.79, and it may lie behind fragments 6, 8 and 25–27 of Paul of Samosata as given in H. de Riedmatten, *Les actes du procès de Paul de Samosate* (Fribourg, 1952), 137, 138, 153. See also Irenaeus, *Adv. haer.* II.vi.1.

[27] See, e.g., M. Simonetti, *La crisi ariana nel IV secolo* (Rome: Institutum patristicum Augustinianum, 1975), 58–9, 185, n.58, for brief discussions. A longer treatment can be found in Simonetti's article, 'Giovanni 14.28 nella controversia Ariana,' *Kyriakon. Festschrift Johannes Quasten,* ed. P. Granfield and J. A. Jungmann (Münster, 1970), 151–61.

[28] Simonetti, *op. cit.* 66, n.73 and *Studi sull' arianesimo,* 9 ff. The text was apparently debated in the controversy between the two Dionysii as recorded in Athanasius, *De decr.* 26 (Opitz 23.1–4) and *De sent. Dion.* 10–11, 20 and 21 (Opitz 53–4, 61–2).

recent edition of the text[29] attempts to cut through the thickets of debate about whether and in what sense this compilation can be called 'Arian', underlining its archaizing features and noting[30] that most churches in the fourth century would be unlikely to mould their liturgies *in extenso* in response to the 'Arian crisis' as if it were a single and coherent programme or threat. Other and older problems (Judaism, Gnosticism, Sabellianism) dominated the horizon (and, we might add, the concrete catechesis of even the most dedicated Nicene apologists fully bears this out[31]). The problem is the same as with authors like Cyril of Jerusalem or Eusebius of Emesa[32]: they refuse to be located on an anachronistic map in which a clear frontier runs between Nicene Orthodoxy and everything else. It is in the next generation (broadly speaking, after 381) that liturgy becomes more sharply self-conscious in respect of the doctrinal crisis – and even then, extraordinary archaisms survive in unexpected places[33].

However, Metzger does a little less than justice to the strength of the case proposed by several scholars for a specifically Eunomian milieu for the *Constitutions*. This case has its best and most recent statement in the work of Dieter Hagedorn on the Job Commentary ascribed to a certain Julian, but some further considerations are explored in an article by T. A. Kopecek[34]. Hagedorn provides ample evidence of parallel phraseology in the Commentary and the *Constitutions* (and also in the Pseudo-Ignatian corpus), and concludes

[29] M. Metzger, *Les Constitutions Apostoliques* (SC 329), 3 vols. Paris 1985–7; vol. II, pp. 10–39, discusses the theology of the text.

[30] Ibid. II, pp. 16–18.

[31] See, e.g., the prologue to Gregory of Nyssa's *Great Catechism* (PG 45. 9A–11A), where the Anomoian threat takes its place among a host of others; in the text overall, the main polemical targets are Jews and pagan Hellenes.

[32] On the former, see R. C. Gregg, 'Cyril of Jerusalem and the Arians', in *Arianism, Historical and Theological Reassessments,* Philadelphia Patristic Foundation, 1985, pp. 85–109; on the latter, M. F. Wiles, 'The Theology of Eusebius of Emesa', *Studia Patristica XIX*, Leuven 1989, pp. 267–280.

[33] Very probably the *angelus* in the *Supplices te rogamus* of the Roman canon is a Christological title in origin; c.f. also the 'two most honourable living beings' in the pre-Sanctus of the Liturgy of St Mark, who almost certainly represent the primitive identification of the Son and the Spirit with the cheribum in the sanctuary, the seraphim of I.8 and the zóa of Hab. 3.2.

[34] Dieter Hagedorn, *Der Hiebkommentar des Arianers Julian*, Patristische Texte und Studien 14, Berlin/New York 1977, pp. XXXIV–LVII; and T. A. Kopecek, 'Neo–Arian Religion: The Evidence of the Apostolic Constitutions', Gregg, *Arianism*, 153–80.

that they have a single author; the Commentary exhibits hostility to both homoousians and homoiousians, and thus may well be a product of Eunomian circles; if so, the heterodox provenance of the *Constitutions* is clear. However, the case is not as clear-cut as at first appears. Hagedorn's impressive list of echoes and reminiscences falls some way short of establishing common authorship, which would require a far more detailed analysis of the texts on normal stylometric principles. Many of the parallels are in quintessentially formulaic patterns of words – doublets, liturgical redundancies – which constitute a very doubtful basis for conclusions about an individual style. Evidently the two texts have a common milieu, and Hagedorn is right to note that parallels to the *Constitutions* in the Commentary relate exclusively to those sections which do not simply incorporate *in toto* material from other texts (the *Didache* and *Didascalia*). In other words, Julian's phrases relate to what is distinctive in the sister text. But, as Metzger proposes in an all too sketchy discussion introducing his edition, this could indicate an *atelier* rather than a single author, a learned circle engaged in several more or less parallel enterprises not all dictated by an identical controversial animus. Textual material for the *Constitutions* might easily have circulated in such a group for a fairly long time, so that we do not even have to suppose a very close chronological proximity between the two works. And, although Julian's opposition to Nicenes and homoiousians is clear, this in itself does not tell us that he was a Eunomian, though he may have been the sort of person to whom Eunomius' teachings would have made some appeal. The very brief passages in which he touches upon controversial issues (245–6 and 270–1 in Hagedorn) provide little to go on, and certainly cannot be said to have much in common with the intensely dialectical polemic of Eunomius himself.

Kopecek stresses the fact that the liturgy of the *Constitutions* is much concerned with the importance of saving knowledge in a way that sounds reminiscent of Eunomius; but this is less telling in the light of the habitual idiom of the Jewish-Christian milieu, where the *Constitutions* often seem most at home (the *Didache* itself has the same emphasis upon knowledge and the revelation of the 'name' in Jesus).[35] The intriguing

---

[35] Ibid. pp. 172 ff.; on this question, see Metzger, op. cit. II, p. 22; and cf. Basil, de spiritu sancto XV. 35 (PG 32, 132A) for the language of divine knowledge and illumination in baptism. Examples from 'orthodox' sources could be multiplied.

verbal parallels between the *Constitutions* and the specific vocabulary of Arius and Aetius[36] must be balanced against a number of qualifications: Arius' confessional language is not that different from Alexander's,[37] which points to a common, probably liturgical, *Vorlage* to which all parties could appeal; Arius was not regarded by the Eunomians as an authority, and is unlikely to have been an obvious quarry for liturgical expressions; and the direct parallel between a phrase in *Constitutions* 39 VIII.5.1 and a syllogism in Aetius' *Syntagmation*,[38] a phrase once again found also in Julian, is still quite intelligible as a citation by Aetius from a liturgical text, rather than vice versa.[39]

But the piece of evidence most damaging to the Eunomian theory must be *Constitutions* VIII.47.50, from the 'apostolic canons': 'if a bishop or presbyter does not perform the single initiation by means of three immersions, but with one immersion only, a baptism "into the Lord's death", let him be deposed; for the Lord did not say, "Baptise into my death", but "Go therefore and make disciples of all nations, baptising them into the name of the Father and of the Son and of the Holy Spirit"'.[40] This canon is no Nicene interpolation: it is followed immediately by a gloss distinguishing the *agennétos Theos*, the Father, from the Son who is incarnate and who suffers in obedience to God's will, denying that the Spirit is *homotimon* with Father and Son, and repudiating any hint of two *anarchos* principles in a way that echoes some of the earliest polemic against what was to become Nicene theology. The canon cannot be directed against anything other than Eunomian baptismal practice (of which more will shortly be said); by

---

[36] Kopecek, art. cit., pp. 161–4.

[37] Compare the language about the transcendence of the Father (*monos agennétos*) in Arius' earliest Alexandrian confession (Opitz, *Urkunden* no. 6) and in Alexander *hé philarchos* (Opitz no. 14).

[38] Kopecek, art. cit., p. 163: *pasés aitias kai geneseós kreittón* is the phrase in the Constitutions; Aetius' syllogism argues that if God is above all causes, he must also transcend 'generation' – obviously understood here as a sub-class of casuality

[39] The exegesis of the period is characterised by what seems to us artificially close logical reading of casual phrases and idioms, not least parallelisms like the phrase from the Constitutions. I see no reason why Aetius should not hang a logical argument on a liturgical expression which allows him to represent *genesis* as a case of *aitia* (since no-one is likely to dispute God's transcendence of the latter).

[40] But note V.7.30, which splices Mt 28.19 with Rm 6.3 in a way which might seem to weaken the force of the canon. We must, however, remember the prevailing looseness of scriptural citation: V.7.30 does not, strictly, claim to be reporting the *ipsissima verba domini*.

the time there was a distinct Eunomian church and hierarchy, the church represented by the *Constitutions* had clearly rejected Eunomianism. This confirms the general impression that the *Constitutions* is shaped in significant ways by the old suspicion of Sabellianism – which is, in VIII.47.50, traced back to Simon Magus. The statement that Simon taught that 'God was one three-named being (*hena trionumon*)' seems to belong to the same world of disputation as that evoked in Basil's *ep.* CCX.

The *Apostolic Constitutions* thus show us further proof of the association of Matt. 28:19 with an hierarchical three hypostasis theology. Other citations of the 42 text in this work reflect the same general interest.[41] Thus, at V.7.30 (a curious blend of Matt. 28:19 with Rom. 6:3), Christ gives the command to baptise in obedience to 'the God of all things who is his Father, and by [or with] the witness of the Spirit' – a clear distinction between the roles of the three person. At VI.15.1–2, we have a text that at first sight might look Eunomian: there is 'one and only one baptism into the Lord's death'; and 'just as God is one and Christ is one and the Paraclete is one, and the Lord's death in the body is one, so let the baptism given into him [or it – i.e.the Lord's death] be one'. However, the context makes it clear that warning is being given against rebaptism, in very much the same terms as in Basil's *De spir. sanct.* XV.35, where Christ's death once for all is similarly invoked. And whatever the rhetoric of catechesis, fusing Matthew and Romans together, the canon already discussed rules out any suggestion that a single immersion could be in question here. Insofar as this passage bears on our main concerns here, it implies again a background assumption that Matt. 28:19 underlines the hypostatic distinctness of Father, Son and Spirit. VII. 40.3 is a bare quotation, with no polemical interest, and the one or two other allusions to baptism in the threefold name are not really exact enough to be considered citations. III. 17.4 does not quote the text, but sketches a theology of baptism fairly close to that of the gloss on the canon in VIII. 47–50; the Father is the cause (*aitios*) and sender (of the Son, presumably) and the Spirit is the witness; 'the

---

[41] Though at III.6.2 and III.9.4 a quite different point unexpectedly surfaces: the command to baptise is given only to the (male) apostles, so that no woman has the right to perform this or any other sacramental function. This is the earliest appearance of an argument rather dispiritingly familiar in more recent years.

Father is the God of all, Christ is the only-begotten God, the beloved Son, the Lord of glory, the Holy Spirit is the Paraclete sent by Christ, the Paraclete about whom he taught and who in turn proclaims him.'

What we have in the *Constitutions* is a consistent linking of the three persons to their roles in the economy of salvation, in a way designed to rule out any Sabellianizing suggestion that there is only one agent involved. VII. 39.2 rather awkwardly distinguishes between the three levels of knowledge of God through which the catechumen has to advance – the *gnósis* of the Father, the *epignósis* of the Son, and the *plérophoria* of the Spirit: this again appears to bind the trinitarian formula to the unfolding of revelation, and suggests that trinitarian catechesis was bound up with a schema not wholly unlike what Nazianzen sketches in a well-known passage.[42] The history of salvation or revelation is the progressive unfolding of the full knowledge of the divine world: through the two successive agencies of Son and Spirit. Kopecek[43] is correct to emphasise the strong focus in the *Constitutions'* baptismal liturgy on assimilation to Christ crucified and risen; but there is very little here indeed that would be alien to someone like Basil,[44] and the stress on conformation to Christ is set firmly within a trinitarian catechesis and ritual order. After the general remarks on instructing catechumens in VII. 39.23, which moves from the opening trinitarian formula to an account of creation, providence, rewards and punishments in the Bible, VII. 394 proceeds to the prebaptismal laying on of hands, which is accompanied by a prayer of thanksgiving to the one God for sending the only-begotten for our salvation, so that we may be adopted into his sonship *(eis huiothésian tén en Christó[i])* and into *koinónia* with his eternal life. The renunciation of Satan is followed by profession of allegiance to Christ which is at once elaborated in a trinitarian creed[45] of the conventional sort (it has verbal parallels with

[42] *Or.* XXXI.26–7 (PG 36 161–4).

[43] 'Neo-Arian Religion,' 166.

[44] See once again, *De spiritu sancto* xv.35.

[45] 41.3: 'I believe and am baptised in (*eis*) the one ingenerate (*agennéton*) only true God, the ruler of all, the Father of Christ, maker and shaper of all, from whom all things come; and in the Lord Jesus Christ, his only Son, firstborn of all creation, generated – not created – before the ages at the Father's good pleasure, through whom all things came to be . . . And I am baptised in the Holy Spirit, that is, the Paraclete, who has always been at work in holy people, and who was latterly also sent from the Father to the apostles, according to the promise of our Lord Jesus Christ, and, after the apostles, to all the believers within the holy

both the 'Creed of Lucian' and the confession of Arius and Euzoius).
The blessing of the baptismal water (43.1–4) follows a similar pattern
to 39.4: the one God of all is blessed, and then adoration is offered to
the only begotten *met'auton kai di' auton*. After baptism and (second)
anointing (45.1–3) the neophyte recites the Lord's Prayer, followed
by a simple invocation of the Father's grace and help, cast in a
trinitarian form and concluding with a doxology of the traditional
pattern – glory given to the Father through (*dia*) the Son and in (*en*)
the Spirit.

Certainly the emphasis of the *Constitutions* is Christocentric; but it is
a Christocentrism bound in with the confession of a trinitarian 'story' in
which the mediation of the Son is the hinge of everything. Through the
Son all things are made (note the repetition of *di autou* and *dia Christou*
in the eucharistic liturgy of VIII. 12). Through the Son, communion
with the Father is opened to us; through the Son, we are able to offer
praise to God. A good deal has rightly been made of the importance in
the *Constitutions* of the theology of Christ as High Priest and paradigm
worshipper of the Father (as in VII. 35.10, VII. 47.2, VIII. 12.17, VIII.
12 27–30) – a theme discernible in Arius' *Thalia*,[46] as well as in
Eunomius,[47] but anchored in a far older and more widespread Jewish-
Christian idiom. It is, in the *Constitutions*, part of a general picture in
which the natural ineffable transcendence of the *agennētos* God is
surpassed by this God's will to provide a means of access to the divine
nature by bringing into being an intermediary. To deny the hypostatic
independence of this intermediary is to jeopardise salvation: there would
be no prototype for us, no one to hold our place open before the glory
of the Father. If the Trinity is a manifestation only, collapsing back into
the unity of a single divine agent, the history of salvation is rendered
empty and there is no foreordained place for us in heaven, the place of
the glorious and faithful Son. If baptism were not an event setting us in
the 'space' defined by the heavenly High Priest, opened for us by his
earthly life, death and rising, it would be meaningless. No wonder, then,
that the Lord, instituting the sacrament, enjoined that it be bestowed in
the name of the three hypostases!

catholic and apostolic Church; in (*eis*) the resurrection of the flesh, the forgiveness of sins,
and in the kingdom of heaven and in the life of the age to come'.
   [46] *De syn.* 15 (Opitz, 243.13).
   [47] *Apologia* 20 (Vaggione, 61).

Such would appear to be the way in which the *Constitutions* understand the interweaving of trinitarian confession and 'Christomorphic' focus in baptism: just as much as for Athanasius, the exegesis of Matt. 28:19 is dictated by the priorities fixed in the way salvation is conceived, the new life of adoptive sonship begun at the font. And this requires some nuancing of the earlier conclusion that Athanasius is simply overturning an older convention in his use of Matt. 28:19. He is certainly doing at least this; but he is also taking for granted and appealing to the clear consensus that baptism is the beginning of adoptive sonship in Christ, access to the Son's place in heaven. To the non-Nicene contention that a 'natural' unity of the three hypostases dissolves such a schema, Athanasius in effect responds by insisting that union with Christ is union with Christ's relation to the Father, and by challenging any theology which assimilates the latter to the relation between maker and thing made. If our destiny is to be children, in Christ, of the Father, and if the Father is the unchangeable God, then fatherhood belongs naturally and timelessly to God (the argument of the beginning of *Or. con. Ar.* II).

The *Constitutions* represent a theology neither speculative nor polemical. What they do is to show us with some vividness why baptism and the understanding of the saved life required, in the eyes of many Eastern Churches, a firmly pluralist, 'serial' and, in a sense, hierarchical reading of the baptismal warrant of Matt. 28:19. The threefold formula is not a pointer to inseparable unity, but functions almost as a code for the stages of salvation history. That this could be turned to effective polemical use is apparent from some of the Latin Arian fragments published by Gryson. The theology of Christ as High Priest is found in several of these texts,[48] usually in a non-controversial context though cap. XIV of the *contra Judaeos* in the Collectio Veronensis may have an eye to Nicene as well as Jewish foes (*Et filius est patris et angelus eius dicitur, id est nuntius, et propheta et sacerdos et puer et aduocatus et uirtus et sapientia et cetera*).[49] Fragments 5 and 6 from the Bobbio Codex[50] set out with great clarity what is thought to be the scriptural pattern to which theology must conform: the Father commands, the Son obeys, and through the Son the work

[48] CCSL LXXXVII, 108, 116, 136, 241.
[49] ibid., 115.
[50] ibid., 236–8.

of creation and redemption is perfected. The Father's 'rule' over the Son is the model for the Son's rule over us (*Regimur a patre per filium, quia pater iussit filium et filius regit nos*).[51]

The Son's task is to pass on God's decisions, to bring them into effect without delay (*Dedit nobis pater sp<iritu>m sanctum per filium, quia pater iussit filio et statim filius dedit nobis sp<iritu>m sanctum*).[52] The claim that the Son is equal to the Father is the target of this writer's polemic, presumably because it would make nonsense of the strongly narrative focus of his understanding of Father and Son: there is a pattern of action and interaction clearly established in Scripture, which would be reduced to a matter of appearances only if the Son were not truly second in the order of things. Much use is made (frs 8, 9 and 17, for example) of texts from the fourth gospel about the Son's being 'sent' by the Father and as praying to the Father to ground a polemic against both Macedonians and *qui dicunt se esse orthodoxos*. Where the Holy Spirit is concerned, these fragments naturally concur with 'Macedonianism', however: in a way rather reminiscent of the 'creed of Lucian,'[53] the emphasis is consistently upon the Spirit's role as sanctifier and illuminator, the one who inspires the prayer of Christians and 'carries' that prayer to the Son. Just as the Son alone worships the Father without intermediary, so the Spirit alone directly adores the Son:[54] ... *adiuuante<m> orationem credentium et interpellantem pro hisdem gemitibus inenarrabilibus et adducentem sanctos ad filium, perducendos <per> filium ad patrem ... Necesse est ergo nos hanc trinitatem confiteri.*[55] The Spirit is thus the Son's minister as the Son is the Father's.[56] In all the Bobbio texts, it is taken for granted that a state of obedience to the will of another rules out the ascription of divinity in a strict sense: *regere, iubere, imperium* and *imperare* recur frequently in the discussion of trinitarian relations, and it is emphasised (in fr. 5 for example) that there can ultimately be only a single *imperium* or *potestas*.

[51] ibid., 237.
[52] ibid., 237–8.
[53] Where the Spirit is 'given to believers for *paraklesis* and sanctification and perfection'. [For more on the 'creed of Lucian', see W. Löhr's article, 'A Sense of Tradition: the Homoiousian Party' – eds.]
[54] Fr. 19 (Gryson, 259), 21 (ibid., 262).
[55] Fr. 23 (ibid., 264).
[56] Fr. 19 (ibid., 259).

Here, then, we have a clear statement of the 'serial' trinitarianism of the *Constitutions* and earlier texts given extra argumentative edge; and it is no surprise to find an appeal to the order in which the three persons are mentioned the formularies of the liturgy. Fr. 5 puts the point tersely: *Vnum autem d<eu>m et patrem omnium sic dicimus et credimus, ut istum sp<iritu>m sanctum, quem tertio loco a patre post filium in symbolo et in baptismo tradimus, non esse d<eu>m creatorem dicimus.*[57] But fr. 10 is perhaps the most interesting. This consists of a series of liturgical quotations from the baptismal and eucharistic orders, designed to show that the language of worship invariably accords the Father precedence over the Son. The Nicenes condemn all *qui praeponunt patrem filio,* yet they do this themselves in the pre-baptismal laying-on of hands, the baptismal interrogations, the solemn post-baptismal blessing (if that is what the text refers to, as seems highly probable; the Eastern baptismal texts, including the *Constitutions,* have no direct equivalent), and the preface of the eucharistic prayer (of which two versions are quoted).[58] The fragment evidently went on to adduce other cases, probably (following a fairly common order of proceeding) from the rites of ordination. This is one of the very earliest witnesses to the forms of Latin liturgy,[59] and has a particular fascination on that score alone. What it also offers is still further confirmation of how the order and implicit or explicit narrative structure of liturgical prayer formed a powerful element in the theological critique of Nicaea. If we assume, as we surely must, that fr. 10 represents a liturgy common to Nicenes and their opponents, the Bobbio texts are our most important witness to the fact that the common ground on which the two parties argued included, by the last quarter of the fourth century, not only Scripture, not only the baptismal commission of Matt. 28:19, not only the doxology, but a considerable range of traditionally accepted liturgical formulae.

---

[57] ibid., 237.

[58] ibid., 242–3.

[59] See K. Gamber, *Codices liturgici latini antiquiores* I (Fribourg: Schweitz, Universitatsverlag, 1968), for other early Latin material (these fragments are on 114–15).

3. Eunomian Baptism

We have numerous and fairly reliable sources for the statement that *hoi peri Eunomion* practised a distinctive baptismal rite, but little overall consistancy as to what exactly was involved. As we have already noted, the *Apostolic Constitutions* know and condemn the custom of baptising with a single immersion; and the seventh canon of the Council of Constantinople in 381 pronounces the same sentence,[60] identifying the culprits as Eunomians. Didymus the Blind knows of a Eunomian habit of baptising once 'into the Lord's death'. Epiphanius suggests that the Eunomians used an irregular and eccentric baptismal formula *(eis onoma Theou aktistou, kai eis onoma Huiou kektismenou, kai eis onoma Pneumatos hagiastikou, kai hupo tou kektismenou huiou ktisthentos)* and reports a story that the Eunomians baptise 'head first', immersing the candidate's head while lifting the feet.[61] They also rebaptise converts from catholic orthodoxy, other heresies and even other brands of 'Arianism'. Socrates reports briefly that the Eunomians, or some of them, particularly the followers of Theophronius, baptised not 'into' the Trinity but *eis ton tou Christou . . . thanaton*;[62] and Sozomen repeats this, confirming Epiphanius' mention of rebaptism.[63] He ascribes the particular innovation in the formula to Theophronius and Eutychius, though he knows that Eunomius was accused of changing 'customs'. Theodoret describes a single immersion *eis ton thanaton* and alleges that there is no *epiklēsis* of the Trinity; he also gives some odd details of the actual ritual which may support Epiphanius' bizarre story.[64] There is an account of the ritual also in the Syriac historian Barhadbešabba with close similarities to Theodoret.[65] R. P. Vaggione has argued with much plausibility that both depend upon the lost *Contra Eunomium* of

[60] The canon deals with the reconciliation of heretics with the Catholic Church, and distinguishes between Arians, Macedonians and others, who are to be received by chrismation, and Eunomians, Montanists and Sabellians, who must be rebaptised.
[61] *Panarion haer.* LXXVI.54 (GCS Epiphanius III 414, 3–11).
[62] *HE* V.24.
[63] *HE* VI.26.
[64] *Haer.* IV.3 (PG 83 42OB).
[65] *HE* XIV (PO 23, 281.8 f.; *E.T.* in Vaggione, 'Some Neglected Fragments of Theodore of Mopsuestia's *Contra Eunomium*', JTS n.s., XXXI.2 403–70, 428. [For further comments on the *Apostolic Constitutions*, see R. P. Vaggione's article, 'Of Monks and Lounge Lizards: "Arians", Polemics, and Asceticism in the Roman East' – eds.]

Theodore of Mopsuestia.[66] Philostorgius apparently mentioned the single immersion *eis ton thanaton* and the requirement of rebaptism.[67] Timothy of Constantinople refers to single immersion and the omission of a trinitarian invocation.[68]

What is to be made of this confusing bundle of material? We should note at once the extensive dependence on hearsay, admitted by Epiphanius and Sozomen in particular, where details are concerned; and we must allow for later developments in the many splinter groups stemming from the Eunomian party. What we can be sure of, as Vaggione concludes,[69] is that some groups associated with the name of Eunomius were baptising with a single immersion by the 370s. Were there earlier irregularities? Kopecek argues that there may have been, on the basis of the synodical letter of the council at Ancyra in 358 (preserved by Epiphanius)[70] but, as he allows, the terminology of the letter is indebted to Athanasius, and the thrust of the argument certainly does not require any actual liturgical usage to be in question.[71] The assembled bishops simply state that the biblical trinitarian formula as used in baptism names Father, Son and Spirit, not 'the fleshless' and 'the enfleshed' or 'the immortal' and 'the one who experienced death' or the *agennétos* and the *gennétos* or the creator and the creature'. The objection is evidently to the unscriptural use of dialectical oppositions in trinitarian terminology rather than to any actual baptismal practice. Something similar must underlie Epiphanius' version of a Eunomian baptismal formula. Quite apart from the unintelligible *hupo tou kektismenou huiou ktisthentos,* which can hardly correspond to any recognizable portion of a baptismal liturgy, the glossing of the trinitarian names sounds like the catechetical expansion of a formula rather than the formula itself. It is not out of the question that it was liturgically used, but it does seem unlikely (as for the detail of baptism being performed upside down – total inversion? – any lover of the pleasingly exotic in

[66] 'Some Neglected Fragments,' 426–49.

[67] *HE* X.4.

[68] *De recept. haer.* (PG 86 24BC).

[69] Vaggione, 'Aspects of Faith in the Eunomian Controversy' (Oxford, unpublished DPhil dissertation, 1976), 191–202, which contends that a change in liturgical *formula* is most unlikely.

[70] *Panarion haer.* LXXVI.54 (GCS Epiphanius III 414.3–11).

[71] Kopecek, *Neo-Arianism,* 160–1.

liturgical history must hope it is true). What this account does suggest, though, is that Epiphanius knows nothing of any omission of the threefold invocation. Likewise, since Philostorgius' hostile epitomiser does not mention such an omission, we cannot use Philostorgius as evidence for such a radical departure. The two canonical witnesses mention only the immersion question: whether the *eis ton thanaton* formula represents an actual utterance in the rite is not clear from the *Constitutions* and the Constantinopolitan canon does not mention it at all.

It seems, then, that (as Vaggione argues) only the single immersion is clearly identifiable as a 'Eunomian' innovation, at least in the early stages of debate. It is most likely to have been introduced at the point at which the followers of Aetius and Eunomius began to constitute an identifiably separate body i.e., after 361:[72] our reports are not sufficiently clear to justify the conclusion that Eunomius himself had already made such a major change in his early days as bishop of Cyzicus, prior to the Antiochene synod late in 361. This is by no means impossible; but since the practice of single immersion is regularly linked in a number of sources with the rebaptism of converts, it makes better sense to see it in relation to the organisation of a parallel jurisdiction. That no such issue ever arose between other non-Nicenes and their opponents (as Athanasius confirms, taking for granted a single general baptismal use and the absence of any convention of rebaptising[73]) should remind us yet again of of the anachronistic folly of treating the fourth century controversy as one between two clearly-demarcated 'churches' with firm and consistent ideologies. If Eunomianism stood alone, an enemy against which Nicenes and 'homoiousians' (and others) could increasingly unite, it is not simply because of doctrine, but because of that cardinal mark of schism, the refusal to accept the baptism of others.

If we ask what lay behind the Eunomian practice (whether instituted by Eunomius or by one of his disciples), the answer is not too difficult to trace. That baptism is 'into the Lord's death' is, as we

---

[72] When Julian the Apostate became sole emperor and all existing sentences of exile were lifted, Aetius was able to return from banishment and assist in the organising of a separate sect. See Philostorgius *HE* VII.5 ff., and Theodoret *HE* II.29.11; for discussion, Hanson, *The Search,* 603 and 615, Kopecek, *Neo-Arianism,* 416–25.

[73] *Or. con. Ar.* II.43 (PG 26 237BC).

have seen, something taken for granted throughout the theological milieu in which Eunomius moved, Asia Minor and the Mediterranean seaboard – broadly, the area of 'West Syrian' liturgical tradition. We have seen this theology in the *Constitutions* and in Basil, and it can be paralleled in Cyril of Jerusalem and Gregory of Nyssa, both of whom, ironically like the *Apostolic Constitutions,* use the threefold immersion precisely as a symbol of the 'three days' spent by Christ in the tomb.[74] Basil's *ep.* ccxxxvi clearly presupposes this typology as a catechetical commonplace.[75] We have seen already that Basil argues against rebaptism on the grounds that Christ died and was raised only once; and the same argument is found in the *Constitutions* (VI. 15. 1–2). That there is a certain tension between the single-event typology (Christ goes down into death and we are immersed; he rises and we emerge – as in *Constitutions* III. 17.3) and the threefold repetition may be what underlies the question from Amphilochius which Basil answers, or rather dismisses, in *ep.* ccxxxvi. But Eunomian practice had clearly made no difference at all to the importance of the paschal symbolism in catechesis.

The Eunomians can be seen as simply smoothing out a slightly unwieldy or overloaded symbolic structure in the ritual; but there must have been a more mediate political motive. Let us try to reconstruct the sort of argument that might have been developed by a logically astute critic of the traditional practice. 'Baptism is one', as Athanasius likes to say; everyone agrees that its primary point is to bring us once and for all into the life of God the Son through a participation in his death and resurrection.[76] Each of the three immersions represents the same thing, even if their totality represents the paschal event in another mode (the passage of time, the alternations of night and day between Calvary and Easter). But at yet another level, as, apparently, in *Constitutions* III. 17 and Basil's *De spir. sanct.* XV, the immersions are associated with the invocation or naming of each person of the Trinity in turn: we are baptised in or into the 'name' of each one, as Athanasius and Basil both insist – an

---

[74] See Gregory of Nyssa's *Great Catechism* 35 (PG 45 88CD), *Or. de bapt.* (PG 46, 585B), Cyril of Jerusalem, *Catechetical Lectures* XX.4 (PG 33 1080C).

[75] See above, p. 158

[76] I assume here the consensus in the Mediterranean world: on the rather different emphases of early Syriac Christianity, see my Excursus.

odd idea if immersion and invocation were not very specifically linked, presumably by the ritual form. The logical conclusion would be, putting these two symbolic levels together, that each person of the Trinity performed the same action – the precise antithesis of one of the most fundamental tenets of Eunomianism, that difference in name entailed difference in *ousia* and *energeia*.[77] It could also be argued that this interpretation undermined the conservative consensus about the threefold formula as enshrining the difference and the hierarchical order of the persons; if associated with immersion, it could not do this job.

So if we are right in thinking that the Eunomians initially at least continued to use the the threefold invocation but separated it from immersion so as to avoid the dangerous implication of equality and indistinguishability among the persons of the Trinity, they were not simply making a controversial innovation. They were disentangling two strands of tradition in the desire to be fully loyal to both the catechetical use of paschal typology,[78] and the conventional anti-monist exegesis of Matt. 28:19. They were in fact applying the same principles that motivated Basil, Flavian of Antioch and others to modify the doxology: controversy had so clouded the minds of Christians that traditions whose sense had once been quite clear within the wholelived balance of Catholic worship and practice had now become ambiguous. Long usage alone did not render a practice invulnerable. The Eunomian revision was a more drastic and disturbing one, claiming (as Basil is careful not to do) that alternatives were now illicit and invalid; but both kinds of change show us something of the character of fourth-century controversy, in which opposing extremists or militants so often had more in common methodologically than either group had with the conservative centre.

The appeal to the baptismal rite and its scriptural warrant bears out very fully what much of the rest of the fourth century doctrinal controversy suggests. In certain important respects, those who resisted Nicene theology, as represented above all by Athanasius, could quite plausibly claim both exegetical and liturgical tradition on their side.

---

[77] See, e.g., Eunomius' *Apologia* 9, 12, 14–16, 18, 21, etc. [For more on the role of these terms in Eunomius' theology, see the article by M. R. Barnes, 'The Background and Use of Eunomius' Causal Language' – eds.]

[78] As in Cyril and Gregory of Nyssa cited above, n. 74.

The catechesis of the Eastern Mediterranean churches before the outbreak of the Nicene controversies seems to have treated the text of Matt. 28:19, especially in conjunction with the threefold immersion (regarded as a kind of commemoration of the three persons – see *Constitutions* III.17), as a confirmation of the real hypostatic differences between Father, Son and Spirit; and it is radical Nicenes on the one hand and Eunomians on the other who recognise the strains in this convention once the question is pressed of the sense in which baptism is a single event, both from God's side and from ours. Athanasius' dialectic in effect dismisses the possibility that threefold baptism in the threefold name is a sort of cumulative co-operation between three agents: its unity is the unity of God's saving act to which the trinitarian name witnesses because its terms require and define each other. To mention one is, logically, to mention all, yet the oneness of the saving God can only be articulated by mentioning all. The Eunomian dialectic uncouples naming and immersion because of the risk of implying that the Trinity is one agent doing one thing under different names: the unity of baptism is the single event of transition to new life through participation in the Easter mystery. That this transition is effected by the hierarchically ordered work of the three persons is not in dispute, but the only way of strictly distinguishing them is by removing any hint that the work of one is indistinguishable from that of another. Whether or not this is Eunomius' own idea, it is his philosophy of substances, names and activities that underlies it.

I have tried to suggest elsewhere[79] that the entire complex of 'Arian' controversies (*not* a single phenomenon and *not* a debate about the teachings of Arius) can be better understood as a series of debates about how to be loyal to a tradition under strain. Both the accumulation of past debate (about Origen and about Paul of Samosata, for instance) and the new circumstances of the Constantinian empire reveal fault-lines in the deposit, points of unclarity about authority, unnoticed inconsistencies in exegesis or tensions between theology and liturgy, exacerbated as Christian teachers attempt to meet new questions. The majority would prefer to continue with a traditional practice, liturgical and exegetical, that may be riddled with tensions but is richly resourceful and hallowed

---

[79] Williams, *Arius,* 82–91, 233–41.

by usage (the most primitive usage of all, according to the myth of first century origins sustained by the *Apostolic Constitutions*); radical minorities press for clarification and resolution, even at the price of innovation in ways of praying and of reading the Bible. A *very* inchoate sense of the significance of history and its contingencies in the forming of doctrinal language is implicit.

What the use and counter-use of baptismal practice reminds us of is that a liturgical language concerned to do justice to the narrative and dramatic in Christian belief (the concern underlying the non-Nicene understanding of Matt. 28:19) is almost bound to fall foul of 'systematic' theology. To unscramble the levels of liturgical metaphor may be a necessary task of rational theology and apologetic, especially when the liturgical idiom is being used to sustain problematic or self-contradictory or intellecturally lazy theologies; but it is also, potentially, a diminution of imaginative and affective resource, and a step away from the dense and unavoidable plurality of perception generated by an authentically new moment of insight (or revelation?).[80] Tracing the disputes of the Nicene era, the drastically different clarificatory strategies of an Athanasius and an Eunomius, the intense ritual conservatism of the communities envisaged by the *Constitutions* or of the author of the Bobbio fragments, the cautious mediations of Basil, we may well recognise one of the most durable and obstinately difficult puzzles of theological methodology, business not only unfinished but (surely?) unfinishable.

Excursus

The fuller history of the association of Matt. 28:19 with the baptismal rite, and the issues relating to the significant of other texts such as Rom. 6:3–4 (baptism into the death of Christ) and Acts 2: 38 and its cognates such as 10:48 (baptism in the name of Jesus), constitute an enormous agenda for the liturgical historian.[81] I do not

[80] This is to echo the language of John Henry Newman in his *The Arians of the Fourth Century* (London: J. G. & F. Rivington, 1833); for a discussion of this ambiguity in the process of doctrinal definition as understood by Newman, see R. Williams, 'Newman's *Arians* and the Question of Method in Doctrinal History,' *Newman After a Hundred Years,* ed. Ian Ker and Alan G. Hill (Oxford: Clarendon Press, 1990), 263–85.

[81] Much helpful material in G. Bareille's article in DTC III on 'Baptême d'après les pères Grecs et Latins'; J. Crehan, *Early Christian Baptism and the Creed* (London 1950); H. M. Riley, *Christian Initiation* (Washington, 1974); and ch. 2 of A. Kavanagh, *The Shape of Baptism: The Rite of Christian Initiation* (New York, 1978).

intend to attempt even a summary here; but there are one or two aspects of the preceding essay which may bear upon discussion in this broader field. Gabriele Winkler, in a monograph deservedly regarded as something of a classic, stresses most emphatically the differences between primitive Syrian baptismal theologies and the way in which the rite was understood in the West, especially in Rome.[82] In Syria, where prebaptismal anointing and the association of threefold immersion with threefold invocation enjoy clear and early prominence, the heart of the ceremony seems to lie in the eschatological outpouring of the Spirit on the believer, paralleling what happens at Jesus' own baptism in the Jordan: in this context Matt. 3:17 ('This is my beloved Son') is of great significance for the rite.[83] The West in general shows more interest in the Pauline theology of sharing in Christ's death and resurrection, and, in Rome at least, language about being baptised 'in the name of the Lord', or 'in the name of Jesus' seems to have been common at an early date, and to have survived for a surprisingly long time.[84] As H. B. Green has recently argued, there is a very strong likelihood that the earliest texts of Matt. 28 (still known to Eusebius) did not in fact carry the injunction to baptise at all, and that therefore the Western practice could simply be read off from Acts 2:38 and other similar texts in the same book.[85] The longer text of Matt. 28:19 is an early but still secondary projection on the basis of an existing (Eastern) baptismal practice rooted in the threefold pattern of the narrative of Jesus' baptism (the descent of the Spirit as the Father's voice proclaims Jesus Son).

The broad outline of Winkler's thesis is indisputable; but the general comments on the sharp division between a Western *Todes-Mystik*, connected with 'cathartic' and 'apotropaic' elements, and a Syrian *Genesis-Mystik*, preoccupied with a new creation of the royal man (or woman) in the Spirit's power are,[86] I think, overdrawn. Winkler

---

[82] *Das Armenische Initiationsrituel* (Roma: Pont. Institutuum Studiorum Orientalium, 1984).

[83] ibid., 438.

[84] See, e.g., Cyprian, *ep.* lxxiii.14–18, CSEL III, 788–92, esp. 17, 790–1 for Cyprian's complaints about Roman tolerance on this issue.

[85] See n. 23.

[86] Winkler, 434–439, 444.

proposes that Western Syrian adoption of the paschal schema, of which Cyril of Jerusalem is the first witness, is a fairly late borrowing from the West, motivated by archaic themes in the region (the terror of the holy) disposing people towards a concern with apotropaic rites. However, this cannot be quite right. Obviously the process cannot have begun with Cyril (and Winkler makes no such claim).[87] Cyril can hardly be the source of an interpretation taken for granted in Cappadocia within two decades of the delivery of his catechetical lectures; and it would be surprising to find the *Apostolic Constitutions* adopting any very recent catechetical innovation. Again, despite Winkler's claim that Aphrahat shows no sign of a Pauline death-and-resurrection theology in his accounts of baptism, we do in fact find clear reference to just such an association: not only is baptism an integral part of the Christian passover celebration (which at least presupposes some connection), we also read of the sacrament as 'the mystery of our saviour's passion', and as a moment of rebirth from the dead, with ample quotation from Paul.[88] In other words, the paschal reading of baptism is widespread in the East before the middle of the fourth century: no one accuses Eunomius of innovation in respect of the *meaning* of the rite. We might also note that Origen's view of baptism is clearly aligned with Rom. 6:3–4[89] and that he also associates it with martyrdom,[90] just as Cyril later does.[91] Mark 10:39 and Luke 12:50 are texts that should not be overlooked here.

The *Todes-Mystik* understanding of baptism is difficult to fit neatly into a tightly-defined 'cathartic/apotropaic' mould: as we meet it in the texts examined in the present essay, it is allied very frequently to

[87] ibid., 435. Notice that Cyril of Jerusalem does not *replace* the idea of identification with Jesus in his baptism and the cognate imagery of anointing with the Spirit by his paschal typology: the two can be found side by side in his twenty-first lecture, 1–2 (PG 33 1088A–90A).

[88] Aphrahat, *Demonstrationes* XII. 13 (baptism and the Christian pascha), XII.10 (the sacrament of the passion), VI. 14 (new life from the dead).

[89] Rufinus' version of the Romans commentary has a full discussion of Rom. 6:3 (V.8, PG 14 1037C–43A); see also *Com. Jn.* VI.43 (GCS 152.11–153.2) on baptism into Christ's suffering, and compare the citation of Rom. 6:3 at I.27 (GCS 35.32–36.5); *Com. Mt.* XVI.6 (GCS 481.25–486.27), on sharing Christ's glory when we have shared his passion through baptism; also *Hom. Num.* 15.4 (CCS 136.16 ff.), *Hom Jos.* 4.2 (GCS 309.22–310.2), *Hom. Jud.* 7.2 (GCS 507.7–508.6), among many other examples.

[90] *Com. Mt.* XV.23 (GCS 413.6 ff.), *Exh. Mart.* 17, 30, 37 (GCS 15.28–16.23, 26.20–27.14, 34.9–35.25, esp. 35.6 ff.). Martyrdom is a form of baptism, and the baptismal promises commit the believer to the risk of martyrdom.

[91] *Lectures* III.10 (PG 33 440C) and XIII.21 (PG 33 797B–800A).

the theme of becoming a child of God, entitled to say the Lord's Prayer, as a result of putting to death the unredeemed, passion-ridden self. Baptism as remission of sin and purification, associated with Christ's death as a means to remission of sin, is certainly the focus of much (not all) Western discussion; but this is rather different from what we have been studying here.

The Eastern Mediterranean world sticks fairly close to the Pauline masterthemes – a paschal and adoptive *Mystik,* if we want a convenient slogan. Whatever its roots, it is not easily identified as simply a Western borrowing. Two points may illuminate the question of origins, though. First, in both Antioch and Asia Minor, we are dealing with an environment in which Pauline themes of various sorts have long been theologically prominent; and second, we are dealing with a region which, like Alexandria, where similar motifs are found, has a rich and persistent martyrological interest, from Ignatius and Polycarp and the Acts of Paul and Thekla to the heroes of the Great Persecution celebrated in Eusebius' work. It is hardly surprising that the Pauline theology of sharing in a redemptive or transformative death should colour thinking about baptism in this region. This is certainly not to say that Rome, Gaul or North Africa lack histories and theologies of martyrdom; but the indubitable connection of baptism with purification from sin in the practice and theology of the Western churches runs constantly alongside this theme, growing from a variety of factors in the self-understanding of these churches. This particular yoking of motifs (baptism and purification) is not at all prominent in the texts we have been looking at; and, although the whole subject is too prohibitively complex to permit of any very clear conclusions, there seems to be a fair case for regarding the fourth-century baptismal theology of Egypt, Palestine, West Syria and Asia Minor as fundamentally independent of Western influence, retaining something in common with East Syrian (especially Edessene) ideals of putting on the new identity of the Anointed Son, but having more interest in the narrative location (in the paschal events) of the transition to this new identity.

Chapter 9

OF MONKS AND LOUNGE LIZARDS: 'ARIANS', POLEMICS AND ASCETICISM IN THE ROMAN EAST[1]

Richard Paul Vaggione, O.H.C.

The historian Gibbon, in whose shade so many scholarly generations have laboured, could only respond to the monastic movement by expressing his horror at 'the swarms of monks, who arose from the Nile, <to> overspread and [darken] the face of the Christian world,'[2] and went on to describe in scornful tones the astonishing success of these wandering representatives of an ascetic revolution:

> The monastic saints, who excite only the contempt and pity of a philosopher were respected and almost adored by the prince and people. Every mode of religious worship which had been practised by the saints, every mysterious doctrine which they believed, was fortified by the sanction of divine revelation, and all the manly virtues were oppressed by the servile and pusillanimous reign of the monks. If it be possible to measure the interval between the philosophic writings of Cicero and the sacred legend of Theodoret, between the character of Cato and that of Simeon [Stylites], we may appreciate the memorable revolution which was accomplished in the Roman empire within a period of five hundred years.[3]

The extent of that revolution is more tangibly expressed, however, by the reflection that in some instances it was sufficient to change the landscape itself, for at Caesarea, the ancient metropolis of Cappadocia, the classical city lies abandoned, while some kilometres away the modern town occupies the site of a monastery once established on its outskirts by its formidable archbishop, St. Basil.[4]

---

[1] An earlier form of this paper was read to the history colloquium of the Department of History of the University of California, Berkeley in November, 1989.

[2] Edward Gibbon, *The Decline and Fall of the Roman Empire* (New York: Random House, n.d.), cap. xx, vol 1, p. 663.

[3] ibid., cap. xxxvii, vol. II, pp 363–364.

[4] Already in Basil's lifetime it was known as *tēn kainēn polin,* See Gregory of Nazianzus' *Orations* 43 63 (PG 36 577C). The *Orations* are hereafter cited as *Or.*

As with other revolutions, however, its very completeness has blinded us to the diversity of its origins, and in particular has eliminated from the historical record those other Christians who to one degree or another withstood the rising monastic tide. The exploits of so accomplished an ascetical showman as St. Simeon Stylites have tended to hide from the fascinated gaze of later generations the diversity of contemporary response, and to make it difficult to recognise that not all Christian asceticism was monastic. It is with one such ascetic alternative that the present paper deals.

If it is a childhood maxim that, having nothing good to say about someone, one should say nothing at all, it is also true that that 'nothing good' is extraordinarily revealing. The century which saw the rise of the monastic movement was the golden age, not only of ascetic and Trinitarian theology, but also of a vituperative Greek able to command the full resources of a rich classical heritage. Though it is easy to understand that a caricature which is unrecognizable serves no purpose, it is less readily acknowledged that the literary vituperation of one age can be as revealing as the political cartoons of another. Moreover, the so-called 'Arian controversy', the primary internal focus of the Christian community during the fourth century, generated an enormous quantity of such vituperation. Among the more prominent targets of such 'negative advertising' were two of the most controversial, Aetius and Eunomius, the one an Antiochene presbyter eventually ordained 'bishop-at-large', and the other a Cappadocian who had risen from a rural background to become briefly bishop of one of the major cities facing Constantinople across the Sea of Marmora. These uncompromising opponents of the doctrinal solution proposed by the Council of Nicaea were the targets of choice of some of the greatest figures of the age, among whom Basil the Great, Gregory of Nazianzus, Gregory of Nyssa, and the Antiochenes John Chrysostom and Theodore of Mopsuestia are the most prominent. A perusal of their works, however, reveals that several of these authors, in their apologetic zeal, chose vituperative themes which passed beyond the dogmatic to make Aetius and Eunomius as much the 'anti-monks' of the fourth century as Dostoevsky's Grand Inquisitor was the Antichrist of the nineteenth, and it is this feature of their works which is of interest to us.

Perhaps the most extravagant expression of this theme is to be found in the fragments of Theodore of Mopsuestia's great, lost *Contra Eunomium*. In the surviving fragments of this work Theodore's purpose was to undermine Eunomius' explanation of his behaviour at the Councils of Seleucia and Constantinople in 359 and 360. He was thus given an opportunity to discuss not only Eunomius' behaviour, but that of his teacher Aetius as well; and since not even his most ardent supporters could claim an upper class background for Aetius (very much a 'self-made man') Theodore focused most of his attention on him.

Passing over, therefore, the lively description of Aetius as an itinerant tinker's son picking up a few scraps of education so as to be able to write out his father's contracts,[5] we shall turn instead to Aetius as an adult. According to Theodore, this unfortunate cleric (who had in fact had some medical training) was a kind of rustic clown who spent his days hanging around the offices of physicians[6] and professional scribes, and wandering about the local squares and taverns in search of a free meals.[7] The description of his behaviour when successful in this quest is a classic of the genre and worth quoting in full:

> Aetius used to go to dinner parties not only when invited, but even crashed them by force and went in. He also increased his relations with those who lived disorderly lives. When he wanted to display the content of his faith, he used to pull up the skirt of his clothing right to the hips and slap his thighs. Indeed, he would lift up a foot and break wind to make the bystanders laugh. Whether by nature or because he used to work at it, he had a great facility for these things. He would say to those who were present in the dining-room, 'What faith do you want me to show you? Ours, or the heretics?' This is what he made of the rule of faith: he would lift up his foot and break wind while pressing his stomach. If they came out all alike, he would say, 'This is the faith of the Orthocycles!' (that is, of the heretics – that's what he called us). His own error was based on unequal things, so when he offered to demonstrate it, he did so with unequal sounds. That is, the first large, the second smaller than the large

---

[5] Theodore of Mopsuestia, *Contra Eunomium*, fr. i, gk. 1–17, syr. 1–5 (Vaggione 408).

[6] Interestingly, John Chrysostom too, *Adv. oppugnatores vitae monast.* I.2 (PG 47 322B), mentions the offices of physicians *(tois iatreiois)* as well as the agora as popular places of assembly. (Since Migne did not include column letters in his edition of Chrysostom, we have attempted to facilitate reference by supplying them at the points where they would normally occur [every 2.25 inches]).

[7] Theodore of Mopsuestia, *Contra Eunomium*, fr. iii, syr. 1–13 (Vaggione 413–4).

one, and the third less than both of them, in accordance with his opinion about the Trinity. This is why he was given the name Pileŝton, that is 'breaker of wind'. [8]

The passage ends with a mention of Aetius' snide reference to the fasts of the Nicenes as 'lentile-ness', 'bean-ness', 'chick pea(-ness)', and concludes with a description of his attachment to 'women who did not possess a name for virginity'.[9] Eunomius fares scarcely better. Incorrectly alleged to be of servile origin,[10] he is said to have acquired his education while serving as pedagogue to a wealthy Constantinopolitan household, and (in a story also told by Gregory of Nyssa)[11] is said to have been expelled after being caught in a compromising position with his charges.[12]

Other authors approach the matter differently. The Rabelesian gusto of Theodore, for instance, is in sharp contrast to the mordant wit of Gregory of Nyssa; but though Gregory later had the grace to feel ashamed of himself,[13] he not only enthusiastically rang the changes on the same themes, he borrowed still others from Athanasius in an attempt to turn Eunomius into an Arius *redivivus*.[14] In his view Eunomius was a mere clown[15] or drunkard,[16] with a theology better suited to a saloon or cocktail party circuit[17] than sober theological debate. His ornate literary style, moreover, could only be compared to the gyrations of an actor prancing onto stage and rattling his castanets,[18] while such ravings as could be understood were no more to be taken seriously than the belches of a glutton at

---

[8] ibid., fr. iii syr. 13–54, 62–4, cf. gk. 5–22 (Vaggione 414–16).

[9] ibid., fr. iii, syr. 65–77 (Vaggione 416–7).

[10] ibid., fr. iv, gk. 1–3, syr. 16–23 (Vaggione 420).

[11] Gregory of Nyssa, *Contra Eunomium* I (GNO I 39.21–3, cf. 56.20–24).

[12] Theodore of Mopsuestia, *Contra Eunomium*, fr. iv, gk. 8–28, syr. 37–63 (Vaggione 421–2).

[13] Gregory of Nyssa, *Ep.* 29.4 (GNO VIII.i. 88.3–8).

[14] Cf. Athanasius, *Or. con. Ar.* 1.3, 4, 5 (PG 26 16C–17C, 20A, 21A). The primary focus of these passages, of course, is the literary form of the *Thalia* and not (except by implication) Arius' behaviour; Athanasius' language, however, seems to have influenced Gregory significantly, e.g., *Contra Eunomium* I (GNO I 27.13, etc.).

[15] Gregory of Nyssa, *Contra Eunomium* I (GNO I 204.6–7).

[16] ibid. I (GNO I 144.26–7, 169.3–7); cf. III. viii (GNO II 260.4–6).

[17] ibid. I (GNO I 201.23–4, 202.16–19); cf. also Gregory of Nazianzus, *Or.* 27 3.15–19, 6.3–12 (SC 250.76, 84); cf. also *Or.* 21.5 (PG 35 1088A, 42.22, PG 36 484B).

[18] Gregory of Nyssa, *Contra Eunomium* I (GNO I 27.6–11).

dinner.[19] Similar portraits of other members of the school could be multiplied – George of Cappadocia, for instance, is consistently portrayed as a gluttonous and debauched embezzler.[20] But not to prolong matters unduly, we can perhaps summarise these classic portraits of Aetius and Eunomius, 'lounge lizards', by quoting Theodoret's graphic description of the arrival of Aetius at the court of Eudoxius of Antioch:

> ... and when Aetius discovered that Eudoxius was a co-religionist, and that in addition to his impiety he lived in Sybaritic luxury, he came to prefer the life at Antioch to any other, and together with Eunomius was practically nailed to the fellow's couches – for he affected the life of a professional hanger-on, and was constantly roaming about filling his belly, now to this, now to that person's house. [21]

For the Nicenes this behaviour was only a reflection of the theological orientation of these unhappy parasites; for – as they bitterly complained – in their well-known zeal for *akribeia* or doctrinal accuracy,[22] Aetius and Eunomius had reduced the faith to the dimensions of a single word:

> ... they don't care a fig for holiness of life, for fasting, the commandments of God, or anything else God commanded us for our salvation; the only thing important to them is to boil the whole thing down to a word ... [23]

That word, of course, was *agennētos* or 'unbegotten', the designation thought to describe God's essence most perfectly according to Aetius and Eunomius. Epiphanius' accusations were hardly new; Athanasius had long since complained that the only thing Constantius required of *his* bishops was a profession of

---

[19] ibid. III. viii (GNO II 261.19–21).

[20] Athanasius, *Apologia pro fuga sua* 26.4 (Opitz II. 86.6–8), *Historia Arianorum* 51.1, 75.1 (Opitz II 212.11, 224.9–225.3), *De synodis* 37.1 (Opitz II 263.30–264.5), cf. Gregory of Nazianzus, *Or.* 21.16 (PG 35 1097C–1100B), where George is said to have been dependent on the table of others, his price a barley-cake. A different, but equally unflattering account of him is given in Ammianus Marcellinus, *Res Gesta,* XX.11.4.

[21] Theodoret, *HE* II 27.9 (GCS 19 160.14–19).

[22] Cf., e.g., Eunomius, *Apologia* 8.2–3 (Vaggione 40–42), *Apologia apologiae* III (GNO II 284.20–25). Although Nicene assertions of the sole necessity of doctrinal accuracy for righteousness were certainly false, they were caricatures rather than inventions, for right-mindedness was certainly an important characteristic of the true servant of God; see pp. 193–4, 197–8 below and notes 70, 72, 109.

[23] Epiphanius, *Panarion haer.* 76.4.4 (GCS III 344.23–7).

impiety,[24] and accusations of monomania became a recurring theme of Nicene polemic. Later writers, indeed, went so far as to claim that Eunomians would condone anything, fornication included, if only their so-called 'faith' were kept entire.[25] Eventually this monomania was taken to be one of the distinguishing marks of the heresy, and later heresiologists claimed that according to their enemies no sin would be imputed to those holding the Eunomian faith.[26]

If to every antithesis there is a thesis, then to these somewhat disparate portraits of Aetius and Eunomius 'winebibbers and gluttons' we must oppose the answering picture of the Orthodox sage secure in his sobriety; for though in its positive expression this Nicene ideal was far from uniform, in the end it was one of the means by which Nicene Christians were able to accept and transform many of the popular ascetic movements then sweeping the Roman world. We can get a preliminary sense of the possibilities by looking at one such portrait, that of Basil the Great by Gregory Nazianzen:

> Such however, was the height of Basil's fame, that he became the pride of human kind. Let us consider the matter thus. Is any one devoted to poverty and a life devoid of property, and free from superfluity? What did he possess besides his body, and the necessary coverings of the flesh? His wealth was the having nothing, and he thought the cross, with which he lived more precious than great riches. For no one, however much he may wish, can obtain possession of all things, but any one can learn to despise and so prove himself superior to, all things. Such being his mind, and such his life, he had no need of an altar of vainglory nor of such public announcement as 'Crates sets Crates the Theban free.' For his aim was ever to be, not to seem, most excellent. Nor did he dwell in a tub, and in the midst of the market-place, and so by luxuriating in publicity turn his poverty into riches: but was poor and unkempt *(anerotos)* yet without ostentation: and taking cheerfully the casting overboard of all that he ever had, sailed lightly across the sea of life. [27]

---

[24] Athanasius, *Historia Arianorum* 75.1, cf. 51.1 (Opitz 11.224.9–225.3, cf. 212.11). Note also in *Apologia ad Constantium imperatorem* 20 (PG 25.632A–B) the sharp contrast between the bishops described as *monazontes kai askētai* who were evicted by Constantius and those installed by him.

[25] John of Damascus, *De haeresibus* 76 (PG 94 725B).

[26] Cf. the Auctor Praedestinati, *Praedestinatus sive Praedestinatorum Haeresis* I.54 (PL 53 606C), and Isidore of Seville, *Etymologiarum* VIII v.39 (PL 82 301C), followed by Honorius Augustodunensis, *De haeresibus* (PL 172 238A).

[27] Gregory of Nazianzus, *Or.* 43.60 (PG 36 573C–576A), translated in NPNF, Series II, VII:415.

Thus to the lounge lizards of contemporary urban society we are presented with the sage in his solitude, clinging resolutely to no possession save the cross, and offering the sharpest of contrasts to the theatrical denizens of the city squares and public banquets.

It takes no very extensive knowledge of the classics to recognise in the mention of Crates[28] an already venerable theme, that of the antithesis between philosophy and rhetoric. Already visible in the ancient rivalry between Plato and Isocrates, the baroque splendour of rhetoric's second century heyday rendered a traditional distinction far sharper and more urgent. The contrast between the contemplative and the active life, between scholarly retirement and civic duty, between the good of the intellect and that of the body, between, if you will, the underpaid professor of that age and the corporate lawyer, provided a fruitful source of invective. The rhythmic cadences of an orator's 'Asianic' style reminded Philostratus of an actor's castanets long before Gregory of Nyssa had read Eunomius,[29] and Marcus Aurelius, that most philosophic of Emperors, could only thank the gods that he had never fallen into the hands of a sophist.[30] Indeed, Dio Chrysostom (himself no mean orator) could publicly rebuke the Alexandrians for their attachment to rhythmic prose, and complain that, in their zeal for musical cadences, they had so confounded expectation that 'if you were to pass a courtroom, you would be hard put to decide whether a drinking party was in progress or a trial'.[31] Lucian's description of the ignorant rhetor possessed of a handful of Attic words who strides up and down intoning 'Gentlemen of the jury' in a sing-song while slapping his thighs and swaying his hips,[32] is no less effective than his portrayal of the itinerant philosopher in search of a meal:

'How do you suppose I feel,' says his Nigrinus, 'when I see one of [these selfstyled philosophers], especially one well on in years, among a crowd of

---

[28] The resemblance between monks and Cynic philosophers was early noted by both supporters (Gregory of Nazianzus, *Or.* 4.72 [PG 35 596Al]) and critics (Julian the Apostate, *Or.* vii, 224A–C). It may be that Eunomius' assertion that the philosophy of the Cynics is far removed from Christianity in *Apol.* 19.6 (Vaggione 56) is directed at his Christian rather than his pagan contemporaries.

[29] Philostratus, Vita Apollonii VIII.6.

[30] Marcus Aurelius I 17.8.

[31] Dio Chrysostom, *Or.* 32.68.

[32] Lucian, *Rhetorum praeceptor* 16–20.

toadies, at the heels of some Jack-in-office, in conference with the dispensers of his dinner invitations? His philosophic dress only makes him the more conspicuous' [33]

If Lucian was prepared on occasion to tar philosopher and rhetor with the same brush it was not because the distinction between them was unreal, but because in the nature of things it was not precise. This was a civil and not a foreign war. But though in every age there were attempts to combine the two (in Plutarch[34] no less than Libanius,[35] in Julian,[36] no less than Gregory Nazianzen),[37] the ideals themselves remained. We sometimes find 'rhetorical' philosophers and 'philosophical' rhetors (and others who are just unclassifiable) but they are characterised by the same polemical themes in each succeeding age. Perhaps we can summarise the distinction best by calling to mind the young man in Philostratus who, as long as he practiced philosophy, was abstemious in food and slovenly in dress, but upon his 'conversion' to rhetoric went out and bought himself a decent set of clothes and threw a party![38]

Such conventional literary brickbats would hardly seem the stuff of history at all but for two things: first, that all the participants in these controversies seem to have taken the distinction very seriously;[39] and secondly, that in this instance at least the literary *topoi* seem to have had a basis in fact – or at least there were persons who claimed to be 'Christian rhetors'.[40] If we ask what this might have meant, we can get some idea by looking at a nearly contemporary pagan 'philosophical rhetor', in this case Maximus, the friend of Julian the Apostate. As described by Eunapius, Maximus possessed not only the 'gravity of countenance' and 'expression of the brows' said by Philostratus to be the mark of a sophist,[41] but several of the features common to a similar description of Eunomius:

[33] Lucian, *Nigrinus* 24 (translation: LCL I 125).

[34] Plutarch, *De liberis educandis* 10 (7F–8A).

[35] Libanius, *Or.* 12.30 (Foerster II 19.3–10).

[36] ibid.; cf. also Julian, *Ep.* 53.

[37] Gregory of Nazianzus, *carm.* II i.xi.292–311 (PG 37 1049–1051).

[38] Philostratus, *Vita sophistarum* II 567.2.

[39] Gregory Nazianzen (!) for one was prepared to assert flatly, *Ep.* 11.6 (Gallay II 17), that rhetoric and Christianity were incompatible.

[40] Cf. Eusebius, *HE* VII xxix.2 (GGS II ii.704.10–18).

[41] Philostratus, *Vita Soph.* I 528; cf. also, more acidulously, Nazianzen's *Ep.* 233 1–2, 235.4 (Gallay II 124, 126).

[Maximus' voice, says Eunapius] was such as one might have heard from Homer's Athene or Apollo. The very pupils of his eyes, were, so to speak, winged; he had a long grey beard, and his glance revealed the agile impulses of his soul. There was a wonderful harmony in his person, both to the eye and ear, and all who conversed with him were amazed by both these faculties, since one could hardly endure the swift movements of his eyes or his rapid flow of words. In discussion with him no one ventured to contradict him, not even the most experienced and most eloquent, but they yielded to him in silence and acquiesced in what he said as though it came from the tripod of an oracle. [42]

Several of these same features are visible in Philostorgius' description of a meeting with his hero, Eunomius, for even through the hostile eyes of the ninth century Patriarch Photius we can still catch glimpses of the traditional description of an orator:

[Philostorgius] praises Eunomius extravagantly, and describes his understanding and character as 'incomparable'. He also speaks flatteringly of the great distinction of his facial appearance and of his limbs. He even likens the words of his mouth to pearls – though a little further on he admits (if unwillingly) that his voice had a lisp. Nor was he ashamed of the lisp; he extols it as extremely elegant [it may in fact have been a residual Cappadocian accent]. Likewise, the white blemishes which disfigured and spotted his face he strives to turn into a bodily ornament. He praises all his works extravagantly. [43]

Philostorgius' attempt to use the traditional figure of the rhetor in a Christian context was not unique. If we look at the closely related writings of Eunomius' western colleagues,[44] for instance, we find that St. Paul has become an 'orator Christi'[45] and Christ himself, the Word of the Father, 'mellifluous':

[Christ] indeed preached so beautifully, and spoke with such sweet and honied eloquence that the crowds not only approached him, they 'pressed upon him', for SO IT WAS THAT THE PEOPLE PRESSED UPON

---

[42] Eunapius, *Vita sophistarum* 473.

[43] Philostorgius, *HE* X 6 (GGS 21 128.10–20).

[44] Cf., ibid., II 5 (GGS 21 18.12–14).

[45] Arianus ignotus, *Expositio Evangelii secundum Lucam* 5:4. 138ᵛ 5–7 (CCSL 87.216): Praedica cum Paulo oratore Cristi, filosopho fidei et gratiae instructore . . .', etc. Nor were such descriptions exclusively found in the Latin West; the anomoean author of the two Easter homilies ascribed to John Chrysostom, for instance, describes Peter as entering the ranks of the rhetors to 'do battle' with the crowd and the apostle John as a *'theorhētōr'*, (Ps.–) Chrysostom, *hom. anom.* I 13.167–8, 21.301–2 (SC 146 72, 84). Peter, moreover, is portrayed as developing his discourse systematically, and his speech is later analyzed in rhetorical terms, ibid. I 18.264–5, II.24.311–27.364 (SC 146 80,122–6).

HIM. Like bees swarming onto thyme or other flowers so they 'pressed upon' the Virgin's saving Rose, the Father's sweetly smelling Lily – not just to see his graceful person, not just to admire the beauty of his countenance, but TO HEAR THE WORD OF GOD. . . [46]

If allusions to a divine Orator[47] and his earthly counterparts suggest that there was indeed a basis for Nicene descriptions of Eunomius as 'an accomplished and inventive rhetor',[48] we must still ask to what extent the more polemical features of their portraits were justified. The limited range and monochromatic character of Eunomius' own writing[49] make it difficult to seek an answer from that source, but in the closely related writings of his followers and imitators we may hope to transcend such limitations; for in those works, transmitted under names more orthodox and illustrious than those of their real authors, we are given a much greater insight into the mission and personal identities of those who wrote them. Two are well known; the third has only recently become available in its entirety. They are the so-called *Apostolic Constitutions,* the longer form of the Ignatian Epistles, and the *Commentary on Job* by Julian.[50]

---

[46] ibid., 5:1.155ʳ.22–155ᵛ.12 (CCSL 87 213). In other circumstances, however, these Western opponents of Nicaea were prepared to turn the tables and accuse Ambrose, for instance, of trusting in rhetorical skill, not apostolic faith, cf. Palladius, *Contra Ambrosium* apud Maximinus, *comment.* 86.337ʳ.29–87.337ᵛ.49 (SC 267 272–4): 'desine a similitudine monstruosa, qua in iactantiam litterariae scientiae garrulum exercuisti sermonem', etc.

[47] Cf. Arianus ignotus, *Expositio Evangelii secundum Lucam* 5:3.157ᵛ.20–158ʳ.9 (CCSL 87 215), where Christ is likened to a bishop preaching in his own basilica; cf. also ibid. 4:44.155m. 7–9, 18–22 (CCSL 87.212)

[48] (Ps.–) Chrysostom, *BMV* 2 (PG 59 712C).

[49] Cf. Vaggione, *Eunomius,* xv–xvii.

[50] That there was a connection between the final editor of the *Apostolic Constitutions* (hereafter, *Apost. Const.*) and the longer form of the Ignatian epistles has long been recognised. The recent publication of the *Commentary on Job* by Julian, however, has made it clear on literary grounds (cf., e.g., n. 106 below) that its author and the editor of these other documents must be identical; cf. Der Hiob-Kommentar des Arianers Julian, ed. Dieter Hagedorn, PTS 141 (Berlin: Walter de Gruyter, 1973), xxxiv–lii. Though earlier scholars had recognised that the editor of the *Apostolic Constitutions* might be an 'Arian' (cf., C. H. Turner, Notes on the *Apostolic Constitutions* (I & II)', JTS 16 [1914–15], 54–61, 523–38, 'Notes on the Apostolic Constitutions (III)', JTS 31 [1930], 128–41) or even specifically a Eunomian (cf. Georg Wagner, 'Zur Herkunft der apostolischen Konstitutionen', in *Mélanges liturgiques offerts au R. P. Dom Bernard Botte* [Louvain: Abbaye de Mont César, 1972], 525–37), the connection with Julian resolves the issue. The theological orientation of this author is not in question; not only was he clearly non-Nicene, he obviously had a close affinity to Eunomius and his school; cf. ibid., PTS 14 205.15–206.3, 245.10–246.7, 270.10–271.13, etc., and Hagedorn's comments, op. cit., lii–lvii. On a purely literary level we may also note the presence of two shared classical

If it comes as no surprise that we cannot find in any of them the libertine or bacchanalian creations of the Nicenes, what we do find is almost as interesting. The table-hopping social parasites of Nicene legend might indeed have been dismissed a *priori*, but a glance at Philostorgius is enough to suggest that Aetius and Eunomius' spiritual descendants regarded the traditional ascetical disciplines much as did their Nicene opponents.[51] The real question is one of context: in what context are we to understand a combination of *prima facie* ascetical normalcy and violent polemical attack? For a preliminary answer we shall turn to the book of Job, an 'image in writing' *(eikona anagegrammenen)*[52] of its eponymous hero.

It may not be accidental that of the four late fourth or early fifth century commentaries on Job two are non-Nicene.[53] Job was taken to

allusions: Plato, *Timaeus* 37C–39E (cf., Julian, Job [PTS xiv.254.4–61 with Eunomius, *Apol.* 10.6 [Vaggione 441] and Aeschylus, fr. 139 [Nauck 45] (Julian, *Job* (PTS xiv.255.16] with Eunomius' *Apol. apol.* III, [GNO II 205.17–20]). The most recent editor of the *Apost. Const.,* Marcel Metzquer (SC 320, 329, 336), has accepted the general interrelatedness of the three documents (SC 320.60–62) but then confusedly (and somewhat inconsistently, cf. SC 329.13 [204]) argued that the editor's orientation was practical and pastoral rather than heterodox (SC 329 10–39). We have no space to deal with this argument here (it is based largely on silence and a very simplistic view of 'Arianism'); instead we will refer the reader to a very thorough review by Thomas A. Kopecek in JTS 39 (1988), 611–18, which discusses the argument in detail. In what follows we will continue to refer to the edition of F. X. Funk because (in spite of its deficiencies) the presence of a parallel edition of the *Didascalia Apostolorum* makes it easier to identify the work of the fourth century editor. [For further comments on the *Apostolic Constitutions,* see the article by R. Williams, 'Baptism and the Arian Controversy' – eds.]

[51] Cf. Philostorgius, *HE* X 12 (GCS 21 131.1–8) where Philostorgius is not only an advocate of rigorous fasting, he holds up one Eudoxius (not the bishop) as an exemplar of the ascetic life. In *HE* X.1 (GCS 126.6–9), moreover, he portrays Eunomius as rejecting communion with Dorotheus and his followers on moral grounds (M. Simonetti, *La Crisi Ariana nel IV secolo* [Rome: Augustinianum, 1975], 454, n. 53, doubts the veracity of this, but for our purposes it makes no difference). Eunomius' rejection of the Ever-virginity of Mary, reported in Philostorgius *HE* VI 2 (GCS 21 71.3–9) and the *Opus Imperfectum in Matthaeum* i (PG 56 635C), seems to be based on Biblical literalism (cf. Eunomius, *Apol.* 17.12–14 [Vaggione 54]) rather than any hostility to virginity as such (cf. *Apol.* 27.7 [Vaggione 70], *Apol. apol.* III (GNO II 35.3).

[52] Julian, *Job* (PTS xiv 4.15–18), cf. Chrysostom, *Job* i.26.6–7 (SC 346, 148).

[53] The commentary by Julian cited in note 50 and the Latin commentary ascribed to Origen in PG 17 371–522; the remaining more or less complete Nicene commentaries are those of Didymus the Blind (*Kommentar zu Hiob,* edd. A. Henrichs, L. Koene, U. and D. Hagedorn [Papyrologische Texte und Abhandlungen 1–3, 33/1]; Bonn: R. Habelt, 1960ff) and John Chrysostom (*Commentaire sur Job,* SC 346, 348). There are also scattered fragments of others by Evagrius Ponticus (CPG 2458, 2), Theodore of Mopsuestia (CPG 3835), Polychronius of Apamea (CPG 3880), and Hesychius of Jerusalem (CPG 6551).

be, among other things,[54] the very model of an active lay spirituality:[55] an exemplary father and paterfamilias administering impartial justice to a household,[56] he was a true example of Christian leadership;[57] possessed of wealth, he was untouched by the money-madness of his fourth century analogues;[58] above all, in an unbelieving age[59] he was a true worshipper of his Creator.[60] That even Nicenes should think monasticism irrelevant in such a context is hardly surprising,[61] but it is in the non-Nicene portraits of Job's other admirers that we catch a first glimpse of the context of the Nicene polemic.

In the version of this portrait given by the Antiochene[62] 'Julian' we are presented with a Job who is something of a paradox: descended from a race with no inheritance in Jacob and unable to plead any nobility of descent,[63] he is nonetheless a *'theios* . . .

---

[54] He was also important as the human conqueror of an immortal bodiless being, the devil; see Arianus ignotus, *Job* I (PG 17 378B–379A, cf. 376D); cf. Didymus, *Job* 7.22–32 (Henrichs I 44).

[55] Cf. Didymus, *Job* 1.8–23 (Henrichs I 24).

[56] Arianus ignotus, *Job* I (PG 17 385B, 384C–387A, 396D–398A, cf. 388A, 393D); cf. Chrysostom, *Job* i.7.21–60 (SC 346 90–100).

[57] Arianus ignotus, *Job* I (PG 17 379B–C): a truly just 'dux ac princeps provinciae suae'. Cf. also Chrysostom's portrayal of Job as one who glories unsought in his function as judge and protector, in implied contrast to the decurions of contemporary Antioch: *Job* xxix.7.34–47 (SC 348.112).

[58] Arianus ignotus, *Job* I (PG 17 385D–386B, cf. 387D–388A); cf. Chrysostom, *Job* i.3.4–13 (SC 346 90). Note this interesting portrait of a bucolic Job dependent on landed wealth, spurning in his secure simplicity the money economy of later ages, and possessing a very 'paradisum divitiarum sicut et olim Adam' (PG 17 399A).

[59] Cf. Arianus ignotus, *Job* I (PG 17 378A): 'Cum esset inter infideles, non habuit infidelitatem.' Doubtless reflecting the situation of his audience, the author lays much emphasis on Job as a book intended to comfort a community under persecution (the Israelites in Egypt), ibid. I (PG 17 375A–C, cf. 382A–B); cf. also Chrysostom, *Job* prologue, 4.1–3 (SC 346 82).

[60] With regard to non-Nicene spirituality, note in Arianus ignotus, *Job* I (PG 17 394C, 397A, cf. 382C) the importance attached to prayer to the Creator.

[61] This is true even of so certainly pro-monastic an author as the Chalcedonian Olympiodorus, a sixth century presbyter of Alexandria, in whose extensive commentary the monks of the surrounding deserts appear but once (PTS xxiv 371.20–372.3) – not out of any hostility, but simply because in this context they were irrelevant.

[62] Or at any rate Syrian; cf. Hagedorn, PTS xiv, lvi–lvii, cf. xxxv.

[63] Cf. Julian, *Job* (PTS xiv 3.16–4.14). In the other non-Nicene commentary, obviously addressed to an aristocratic audience ('O viri periti' [PG 17 382A, 415D, cf. 384B–C]), the author lays much greater emphasis on Job's ignoble origins and the consequent unimportance of noble descent in seeking the favour of God: Arianus ignotus, *Job* I (PG 17 377B–378A, 389D–390A).

anēr'[64] an example *par excellence* of a truly fundamental virtue: *eunoia* or 'right-mindedness'.[65] As understood by Julian *eunoia* was more than general benevolence or earnest 'good will', it was an echo of the divine goodness.[66] It implied a mind as fully turned toward God[67] as the devil's was against – for the principle characteristic of that dark mind was its opposite: *kakonoia* or 'wrong-mindedness'.[68] A similar dichotomy is visible in the writings of Eunomius – there too God's enemies languish in *kakonoia*[69] while the right-minded are faithfully preserved in a 'partiality' for the truth'[70] by the Holy Spirit.[71] There is a closer affinity still, however. In portraying Job as truly 'veri Dei servus verax' (to quote another non-Nicene),[72] Julian identified Job's *eunoia* with the unswerving (aparatrepton) fidelity of the saints to God's will,[73] a will understood by both Eunomius[74] and Julian to be accessible only to the 'right-minded' – i.e., to persons who

[64] Julian, *Job* (PTS xiv 80.11, 96.10), cf. *ho hieros houtos anēr,* ibid. (PTS xiv 10.14). Cf. also *Apostolic Constitutions* v.7.21 (Funk I 259.21).

[65] Julian, *Job* (PTS xiv 3.4–4.14, 6.4–8, 14.19–20, cf. 21.15–16, 24.1–2, 20, 51.9–10).

[66] ibid. (PTS xiv 228.9–10).

[67] ibid. (PTS xiv.126.1–10).

[68] ibid. (PTS xiv 13.21–14.1, 20.15, 77.19–78.3, 161.15–16, 284.12–13, 298.15, cf. 224.10–12), cf. *Apostolic Constitutions* viii.7.5 (Funk I 482.13–17), (Ps.-) Ignatius, *Phil.* 11, 12 (in J. B. Lightfoot, ed., *The Apostolic Fathers* [Grand Rapids: Baker Books, 1981 rpt.], II iii.199.26–7, 200.13–14) (hereafter, Lightfoot).

[69] Eunomius, *Apol.* 6.10–13, 23.3–4, 27.40 (Vaggione 38, 62, 72), *Apol. apol.* III (GNO II 238.4–10); cf. Julian, *Job* (PTS xiv 229.1–6).

[70] Eunomius, *Apol.* 2.9–11, 20.12–14 (Vaggione 36, 58–60).

[71] Eunomius, *Expositio fidei* 4.22–4 (Vaggione 158).

[72] Arianus ignotus, *Job* I (PG 17 380B), citing John 17:3, a text much favoured by later non-Nicenes as emphasizing the necessity of worshipping, like Job, the one and only true God.

[73] Julian, *Job* (PTS xiv 24.20, 106.1–10, cf. 15.1–5, 248.18–20). Julian makes a distinction between those who are *atreptos* by nature and those who have become so *di' hekousion.* The latter are the saints, of whom Job is one.

[74] Eunomius shared with Julian and other writers of the period (e.g., Chrysostom, *Job,* prol. 4.8–14, cf. i.1.60–62, iii.5. 54–5 [SC 346 82, cf. 88, 212]) the conviction that some knowledge about God was inherent and represented by *koinōn logismōn* present in all human beings (cf. *Apol.* 10.8–10 [Vaggione 44] and the passages cited below in n. 77). Those who perverted such universal conceptions by wilfully misunderstanding them (e.g. *Apol. apol.* II [GNO I 316.8–11], III [GNO II 113.10, 115.12]) were guilty of *kakonoia* just as those who were faithful to them possessed *eunoia.* Thus, e.g., in *Apol.* 6.10–12 and its continuation 7.1–3 (Vaggione 38, 40) the enemies of the faith, blinded by *kakonoia,* are unable to see the truth innately accessible to them (a *physikēn ennoian*); cf. also *Apol. apol.* I (GNO I 201.3–5). This same truth was also confirmed by and accessible in Holy Scripture (see nn. 76–77 below).

understood aright the knowledge of God implanted in all human beings by the Creator.[75] Though this knowledge was later to be made explicit through the Scriptures, Job (who lived long before they were written)[76] naturally came to be seen as an example of those who were faithful to it from the beginning.[77]

Such fidelity was not without fruit, for in Job the result of *eunoia* was a moral wholeness which made him the very model of practical wisdom.[78] An *athlētēs* whose 'right-mindedness' could delight even God,[79] he did not flee possessions but used them rightly,[80] for right use increases the longing *(pothos)* for God.[81] Even the week-long feasts of his children were not occasions of sin but schools of sobriety – opportunities for instruction in the exacting disciplines of communal love.[82] Job's sacrifices were as much for thanksgiving as for penance.[83]

---

[75] Julian, *Job* (PTS xiv 220.8–9, 232.8–14, cf. 172.20–171.3, 310.17–19). The close connection of *eunoia* and knowledge is mirrored by the connection between *kakonoia* and ignorance *(agnoia)* in the *Apost. Const.;* cf. n. 112 below.

[76] It was commonly believed that Job had lived before Moses and that Moses had either written or translated the book, e.g., Julian, *Job* (PTS xiv 1.5–3.3); Arianus ignotus, *Job* I (PG 17 373B–374C); cf. Chrysostom, *Job,* prol. 1.1–2.12 (SC 346.70–80), xxx.8.16–17, xlii.9.2–8 (SC 348.126, 240).

[77] And not only for non-Nicenes; cf. Olympiodorus, *Job* i, fr. 3.3–5 (PTS xxiv.8), Chrysostom, *Job,* prol. 2.9–10, 4.6–7 (SC 346 80, 82), *hom. div.* 4.3 (PG 63 481C–D), where Job is portrayed as one who, in fidelity to the *physikēn kai ap' archēs ennoian* (Olympiodorus), keeps the Law before there is a Law to keep. Cf. also *Apost. Const.* vi.19.2 (Funk I 347.11–14), where the Law is a confirmation of *tou physikou;* cf. also ibid. vi.20.1, 4, 22.5, 34.2 (Funk I 349.14, 351.4, 357.26, 359.1), viii.8.8, 12.18, 25, 30 (Funk I 486.20–21, 500.33–502.2, 504.8–13, 506.15–16).

[78] Julian, *Job* (PTS xiv 172.17–171.3, 174.9–10).

[79] ibid. (PTS xiv 14.19–20).

[80] ibid. (PTS xiv 9.18–10.3).

[81] ibid. (PTS xiv 9.9–14, cf. 44.6–10).

[82] ibid. (PTS xiv 17.19–21, cf. 10.14–11.13). The idea that the banquets were expressions of *philadelphia* is fairly common (see Chrysostom, *Job* i.6.4–10 [SC 346 96]), but in the other non-Nicene commentary this idea evokes a parallel with the restrained communal banquets of the primitive Church. See Arianus ignotus, *Job* I (PG 17 393A, cf. 384D, 392A, D): 'omnes simul ecclesia sanctorum'. A similar theme is also found in the Alexandrian tradition; cf. Didymus, *Job* 10.25–33 (Henrichs I 52), Olympiodorus, *Job* (PTS xxiv 10, fr. 6.2–6) etc. Though Didymus certainly saw nothing wrong with the banquets (and indeed, regarded the presence of Job's daughters as a guarantee of their sobriety, *Job* 11.5–9 [Henrichs I 54], cf. Arianus ignotus, Job 1 [PG 17 392D]), the devil could think that their deaths in the midst of a feast would cause Job greater worry (Didymus, *Job* 31.12–17 [Henrichs I 106]). Didymus thus hedges his bets by describing the banquets as spiritual ones (ibid., 24.27–33 [Henrichs I 90]).

[83] Julian, *Job* (PTS xiv 11.11–12).

His goal was not to live without passions, but to use them in proper measure *(eulogōs)*.[84] Job was a living example of ordinate love.[85] Bound neither by wealth nor pleasure[86] he was unswervingly loyal to the soul's ruling part *(hēgemonikon)*,[87] but, while rejecting any inappropriate *(akairous)* sexual expression,[88] did not fail to join his wife in the licit delights (and burdens) of procreation.[89] If elsewhere in his non-Nicene guise Job is the perfect late Roman patrician,[90] in Julian he is something more: the truly 'right-minded' man – a sage with eyes as 'winged' as any philosophical rhetor,[91] yet one unfailingly just to the demands of everyday life.

The contrast of this figure with the nearly contemporary (and equally Antiochene) Nicene Job of Chrysostom[92] is startling: *this* Job is an ascetic philosopher,[93] his children as much disciples as progeny,[94]

[84] ibid. (PTS xiv 8.12–14).

[85] ibid. (PTS xiv 7.1–9).

[86] ibid. (PTS xiv 9.18–10.3, 57.13–58.1).

[87] ibid. (PTS xiv 190.2–4, cf. 6.14–17, 19.2–3).

[88] ibid. (PTS xiv 190.9–15).

[89] ibid. (PTS xiv 27.14–18); cf. Arianus ignotus, *Job* I (PG 17 382[B–]C): '. . . sancte et pudice secundum officium naturae, caste ac veraciter juxta Creatoris promissionem'.

[90] See nn. 56–60, 63 above. Whatever their other differences, however, both non-Nicene commentaries lay considerable emphasis on Job as an example of fidelity in right belief (cf., e.g., n. 72 above); though the Nicenes took Job's doctrinal orthodoxy for granted, for them his *theosebeia* was moral rather than doctrinal, cf., e.g., Didymus, *Job* 20.20–29 (Henrichs I.78–80).

[91] Job's status as a seer is established on the basis of the Theophany which concludes the book; Job (sharing a privilege accorded elsewhere only to Moses) sees the Only-begotten God face to face in the cloud, Julian, *Job* (PTS xiv 247.16–248.20, 301.12–15, cf. 280.11–281.8).

[92] These newly published homilies have long been known in manuscript and are almost certainly authentic (cf. PG 64 504–5). Any remaining doubts seem to be dispelled by the numerous parallels with the certainly authentic later homily *Adversus eos qui non adfuerunt*, etc. (*hom.* 4, PG 63 477–86; cf. SC 346, 70–71). This homily was preached in the Church of the Anastasis at Constantinople sometime after Chrysostom became archbishop in 398; there is every indication that the commentary was written much earlier at Antioch (cf. Quasten, *Patrology* III:433, and n. 101 below).

[93] Cf. Chrysostom, *Job* i.23.21, and i.21.21–4, i.23.22–4, iii. 5.20–22, etc. (SC 346 140, cf. 138, 140, 208–10, etc.), *hom.* 4.1, 3, 4, 5 (PG 63 477C, 481C, 482B, 483B, 484D). Abraham is treated similarly in *De virginate* lxxxii.3.46–9 (SC 125 384). Chrysostom's transformation of Job stands in marked contrast to that of the equally Nicene but Alexandrian Didymus; the Job of Didymus is certainly the servant of God in every sense (cf. Didymus, *Job* 18.1–14 [Henrichs I 72]), and a formidable opponent of the Devil (ibid. 7.22–32 [Henrichs I 44]), but he is not an ascetic in the sense that he rejects material things as such; in themselves they are mere *adiaphora*, ibid. 21.31–22.11, cf. 42.8–15, 49.19–21 (Henrichs I 82, cf. 134, 154). This is in general accord with the approach of a

his wife a temptress and instrument of Satan.[95] Where gluttonous Adam fell his abstemious descendant triumphs,[96] and, abhorring all intemperance,[97] regards no possession as his own,[98] viewing even the loss of children with detachment.[99] A true 'hero and athlete'[100] he displays a *dynamis* as potent as that of any Olympic victor,[101] and equally public;[102] for, deliberately seeking to excite the pity of the crowd, he sits continually exposed to its gaze and, with a determination worthy of a stylite saint, inhales a divine refreshment while enclosed in the decaying stench of a body.[103] Here is a Job

later representative of the same school, the sixth century Chalcedonian Olympiodorus, for whom Job is certainly an *athlētēs tou theou* (*Job* [PTS xxiv 14.22, 15.22, etc.]), but the focus of whose commentary is Job's *parrēsia* as a child relating to a parent (ibid., PTS xxiv 88.20–1, 103.4–6, etc.), not his ascetical rigour (cf. ibid., PTS xxiv 6.5–15). Job's family is assumed, not explained.

[94] Chrysostom, *Job* i.23.28–9 (SC 346 140).

[95] ibid., ii.9.1–66 (SC 346.174–8). Cf. *hom* 4.2, 3 (PG 63 480A, 481A); indeed, the attitude of Chrysostom toward all the women in Job's story is notably negative. In contrast to the prominent position accorded Job's daughters in other commentaries (see n. 82 above and Arianus ignotus, *Job* i [PG 17 382D–383B]), Chrysostom reduces them to servants at dinner, (ibid., i. 6.10–13 [SC 346 96]) and elsewhere regards wives in general as mere hindrances to their husbands' salvation (see *De virg.* xlv.2.33–xlvi.2.25 (SC 125 256–8). Perhaps after all the Empress Eudoxia had a case!

[96] Chrysostom, *Job* ii.9.24–9 (SC 346 176).

[97] ibid., xxxi.1.12–32 (SC 348.128–30).

[98] ibid., i.25.2–7 (SC 346 144).

[99] ibid., i .25.23–7, cf. i.26.54–60, ii.9.20–23 (SC 346.146, cf. 152, 174).

[100] ibid., ii.6.25–35 (SC 346 165).

[101] ibid., ii.3.21–2 (SC 346 160). The mention of the Olympic games is another indication of the Antiochene provenance of these homilies, for local Olympic games were celebrated there (with interruptions) from the time of Augustus until the beginning of the sixth century; during this period the games are known to have been celebrated in 380, 384, 388, and 404. See G. Downey, *A History of Antioch in Syria* (Princeton: The Princeton University Press, 1961), 168, 197, 440, etc., and J. H. W. G. Liebeschuetz, *Antioch, City and Imperial Administration in the Later Roman Empire* (Oxford: At the Clarendon Press, 1972), 136–140.

[102] Chrysostom, *Job* ii.7.19–27, cf. ii.8.19–28 (SC 346 170, cf. 172). Note that Chrysostom sees such public approbation as useful in the beginning for the encouragement of the weak, and later as of no danger because the ascetic no longer needs applause and may, by example, be of help to others; see *De virg.* xxii.2.22–3.30 (SC 125.166).

[103] Chrysostom, *Job* ii.8.9–16 (SC 346 172).

indeed who has left the walls of the city behind;[104] the losses of family, possessions, and friends are but stages in an emancipation. Chrysostom, by ruthlessly transforming a biblical hero, has captured him for a cause, and enlisted him in the army of a new, and equally transformed, 'philosophy'.

The drunken scoundrels of Nicene legend are thus indeed caricatures, but they are caricatures with a certain basis in fact. The radical gulf separating Julian's Job from Chrysostom's is an 'image in writing' of two strikingly different approaches to life in the late classical city:[105] Chrysostom's Job has left the city altogether; Julian's has learned to live in it wisely. On these two striking alternatives the traditional opposition of philosopher and rhetor was imposed (and modified) by Nicene and non-Nicene alike; but if the polemical details of these portraits cannot be accepted, the opposition underlying them remains only too real.

It is when we begin to look for the wider context of this opposition that our other documents become relevant. In the *Apostolic Constitutions*, for instance, we find that some of Julian's characteristic themes are prominent in just those portions of the work which must be ascribed to the non-Nicene editor:[106] God is accessible to those who approach him with *eunoia*;[107] only the 'right-minded' may

---

[104] ibid., ii.7.25–8.8 (SC 346 170–172), cf. *hom* 4.3 (PG 63 481A). In other commentators Job's departure from the city is neither particularly important nor voluntary: cf. Julian, *Job* (PTS xiv 25.16–19), Didymus, *Job* 45.7–12 (Henrichs I 142), Olympiodorus, *Job* (PTS xxiv 27.21–2). It is worth noting in this regard that not all ascetics were confined to the desert. There were others who, after achieving freedom from the passions, returned to the city, and, frequenting the public baths in an attempt to show their superiority to nature, tried to be men with men and women with women, and to share the nature of each sex; see Evagrius Scholasticus, *HE* 1.21 (PG 86 ii.2480B–2484A).

[105] For purposes of this article words such as 'city' or 'city dweller', 'urban', etc., refer not to the physical inhabitants of the cities, however numerous, but to those for whom the inherited social structures and culture of the city *(polis)* continued to be relevant in the changing context of early Byzantine society.

[106] Indeed, it may not be accidental that in *Apost. Const.* i.6.3, cf. vi.5.5 (Funk I 15.5–7, cf. 313.18) the editor has added Job and Proverbs to the list of Scriptural locations where *poiēseōs kai sophisteias pleiona anchinoian* may be found, for at v.7.21 (Funk I 259.21–8) he cites a saying of 'the most divine Job' (10:10–13), which is used in the same sense by Julian to prove that the soul is infused into the body by a divine act distinct from physical conception; see Julian, *Job* (PTS xiv 79.13–81.16).

[107] *Apost. Const.* viii.15.7 (Funk I 520.14–17); cf. viii.32. 16 (Funk I 536.18–19), where *eunoia* is a necessary part of study.

perform miracles;[108] true religion *(eusebeia)* is the fruit of right-mindedness *(eunoia)*;[109] those who, like Simon Magus, lack *eunoia* fall into 'simony,'[110] while those who possess it like Stephen attain martyrdom and the vision of God.[111] *Kakonoia* is the mark of the ignorant bishop[112] no less than of the Jew[113] or heretic,[114] and rejecting it is a necessary preliminary to entering the Christian Church,[115] and so on. All this goes a long way toward showing that the link between the two documents is a genuine one, but of more immediate interest is the fact that the *Apostolic Constitutions* is a Church Order, and as such represents what its non-Nicene editor believed the Christian Church in general (and that of Antioch in particular) ought to be. It is thus significant that at almost every point where the editor's hand can be detected the traditional ascetical disciplines have been retained and, if anything, strengthened.[116] This is consistent with what we know from non-Nicene sources elsewhere. Setting aside routine condemnations of fornication[117] and conventional allusions to the fasts of Daniel,[118] these sources generally represent an 'ascetical' view of Christian life: Peter and Paul are said to have rejected worldly delights and luxuries;[119] the other apostles never

[108] ibid., viii.1.3, cf. 26.2 (Funk I 462.4–8, cf. 528.16–18).

[109] ibid., viii.15.7 (Funk I 520.14–17).

[110] ibid., iv.7.2 (Funk I 229.2–4).

[111] ibid., viii.46.16 (Funk I 562.10–20).

[112] ibid., viii.2.4 (Funk I 468.11–12). It is worth noting that in the case of both the bishop and the heretic (see n. 114 below) the result of *kakonoia* is *agnoia*, a lack of positive knowledge, but in the case of the latter there are some who are merely irreligious *(asebeis)* and err through ignorance alone.

[113] ibid., v.16.18 (Funk I 283.18). There seems to be a heightened antipathy to Judaism throughout, e.g, ibid. ii.21.2 (Funk I 79.4).

[114] Ibid., vi.5.1 (Funk I 309.15–16).

[115] Ibid., vii.40.1 (Funk I 442.27–444.1).

[116] Cf., e.g., ibid., v.13.3, 14.20, 18.1–2 (Funk I 269.17–271.4, 279.1–281.4, 289.8–17), vii.23.1–4, (Funk I 408.1–13), viii.47.69 (Funk I 504.16–19), etc. Indeed, in keeping with the polemical themes discussed earlier, it may be no accident that the clergy are so strongly forbidden to set foot in a tavern (Ibid., viii.57.54 [Funk I 500.10–19])! Note, however, that fasting is strictly prohibited on the Sabbath in view of the characteristically Eunomian emphasis on the *katapausin tou dēmiourgou*, ibid. v.14.20 (Funk I 281.2–3), vii.23.4, 36.1, 4–5 (Funk I 408.8–14, 432.26–434.2, 14–27), viii. 47.64 (Funk I 582.27–584.2); cf. Eunomius, *Apol. apol.* III (GNO II 224.6–10, 227.22–228.4), *Apol.* 23.6–15, fr. i (Vaggione 62–4, 176).

[117] (Ps.–) Chrysostom, *hom. anon.* II 4.52, 6.67–7.84 (SC 146 98, 100–102).

[118] ibid., II 2.37–9 (SC 146 98).

[119] Arianus ignotus, *hom. sollemn.* XI.3.65.11–16 (CCSL 87 i.78).

ate to satiety;[120] Christ himself is a lover of chastity,[121] and Stephen as faithful in continence as in the more obvious charity.[122] That such descriptions are almost flat contradictions of Nicene polemic need no longer surprise us, but we must still try to understand what such contradictory pictures really mean.

If we turn to the *Apostolic Constitutions* and examine once again the whole range of persons and practices which might loosely be called 'ascetical', we find that almost all are in some way communal or 'domestic' – that is, they presuppose or are pursued within the context of a particular church or household.[123] To find a collectivist orientation in what is, after all, a Church Order is hardly unexpected, but a similar assertion could be made about Julian's portrayal of Job. For Julian Job's asceticism is the asceticism of one living in the midst of others;[124] of one who, like Zacharias and Elizabeth elsewhere,[125] is a paradigm of *married* chastity. If Job and his children are models of the right use rather than the abuse of this world's goods *(sōphrosunē)*[126] their asceticism is comprehensible only in the context of a community. True, within this community there are other persons whose leading role[127] is based less on formal status[128] than on

---

[120] Arianus ignotus, *Expositio evangelii secundum Lucam* 6:1.186ʳ.3–6 (CCSL 87 i.223).

[121] Arianus ignotus, *hom. sollemn.* XV.3.74ʳ.24–74ᵛ.6, cf. XV.3.75ʳ.10–13 (CCSL 87 i.88–9, cf. 89).

[122] Ibid., X.3.63ʳ .9–19 (CCSL 87 i.75).

[123] Cf. *Apost. Const.* ii.14.5–6 (Funk I 51.29–53.3), where strong emphasis is laid on not separating from the world; Christians are to be like their Father in heaven who causes his sun to shine on good and bad alike (Mt. 5:45).

[124] Cf. pp. 191–5 above.

[125] Arianus ignotus, *Expositio evangelii secundum Lucam* 1:6.9ʳ.19–20 (CCSL 87 i.201).

[126] Julian, *Job* (PTS xiv 10.14–15, 10.20–11.2, 17.19–21, 27.14–18, etc.).

[127] *Apost. Const.* iii.15.5 (Funk I 209.8–9); virgins and widows are listed as separate categories along with the clergy and laity (note that male ascetics are not so listed). Treatises dealing with virgins repeatedly emphasise that they ought to stay at home ([Ps.–] Basil, *De virg.* 27–34 [RB 63.41.9–43.1]), at least when young (Basil of Ancyra, *De virg.* 19 [PG 30 708D–709A]), but in fact we find them playing a significant role in contemporary controversies. They were prominent early supporters of Arius (Epiphanius, *Panarion haer.* 68.4.3, cf. 69.3.2, 7 [GCS III 144.13–16, cf. 154.17–21, 155.16–17]; cf. also Alexander of Alexandria, *ep. Alex.* 5, 58 [Urkunde 14, Opitz III 20.14–16, 29.5–8]), and we find them later (on both sides) conspicuously present in situations where violence was to be expected (Athanasius, *apol. sec.* 15.1–2 [Opitz II 98.29–99.8], *fug.* 6.3, 6–7; 7.2 [Opitz II 72.4–8, 15–18; 73.3–6]; cf., *Decretum sinodi orientalium* in C.A.P. A.I.iv.1.9.1 (CSEL 65. 55.12–19]).

[128] Or at any rate not on ordination; *Apost. Const.* viii. 24.1–2 (Funk I 528.5–7), Among those who were ordained note that female deacons represent the Holy Spirit just as male

thoroughgoing asceticism; but the asceticism of these persons is every bit as 'communal' as Job's.[129] Though some are male *(askētai)*,[130] the great majority (or at least the most frequently mentioned) are female: widows, who as recipients of the Church's alms could be reckoned altars of Christian sacrifice,[131] and virgins, who as instruments of prayer could be described as dwelling places of God[132] and altars of incense.[133] Though as a group the virgins were considered a *systēma* or 'company',[134] they continued in most instances to live at home with their families[135] and appear to have been as much a part of the non-Nicene as of the Nicene Churches.[136] In non-Nicene sources they are

deacons represent Christ, and that they are as subordinate to them as the Spirit is to Christ, ibid. ii.26.5–6 (Funk I 105.12–21). In (Ps.–) Basil, *De virg.* 41 (RB 65. 43.10–11, cf. note *ad loc.*), however, it is the consecrated virgin who is described as *pneuma hagion sesarkōmenon*(!). Does the feminine Holy Spirit of Syriac language and theology lie behind this imagery?

[129] Basil of Ancyra defines three categories of those who undertake ascetic disciplines in the Church: those who embrace virginity, those who afflict the body with fasts, and those who sell their goods for the sake of the Lord; see *De virg.* I (PG 30 669A, cf. 672A).

[130] *Apost. Const.* viii.12.44, 13.24, 15.5, cf. 10.11 (Funk I. 512.11–14, 516.12, 518.32–520.1, cf. 490.10–11); cf. also (Ps.–) Ignatius, *Polyc.* 5 (Lightfoot II iii.230.13–22) and the very interesting non-Nicene (Ps.–) Basil, *De virg.* 11 (RB 63.37.14–16), where both male and female ascetics seem to be intended; note also the male urban ascetics mentioned in n. 104 above.

[131] Along with the orphans, *Apost. Const.* ii.26.8 (Funk 1.105.26–8 [from the *Didascalia*]), cf. ibid. ii.57.12, iii.6.4, 7.7 (Funk I 165.7–8, 191.23, 198.5–8), (Ps.–) Ignatius, *Smyrn.* 13 (Lightfoot III.ii.227.40).

[132] *Apost. Const.* iv.14.2 (Funk I 235.8–10); cf. Basil of Ancyra, *De virg.* 41 (PG 30 749D).

[133] *Apost. Const.* ii.26.8 (Funk I 105.28–9); elsewhere they are *hōs hiereias Christou*, (Ps.–) Ignatius, *Tars.* 9, cf. *Ant.* 8 (Lightfoot II.iii.187.15–16, cf. 238.15–16) or like precious vessels; ibid., *Her.* 5 (Lightfoot II.iii.247.26); the Father who permits a daughter (or son) to embrace virginity thereby becomes a priest in the Temple of the Most High God, (Ps.–) Basil, *De virg.* 20, cf. 63 (RB 63.39.16–17, cf. 55.1). Such analogies, however, were not always so innocent: cf. (Ps.–) Basil, *De virg.* 34 (RB 63.43. 1) where the virgin, elsewhere called *parathēkēn* and *hagiastērion theōi naon Christou* (ibid. 28, 41 [RB 63.41.10, 43.9–10]), is also described as an *aichmalōton*, 'prisoner'.

[134] (Ps.) Ignatius, *Phil.* 15 (Lightfoot III.ii.202.16–203.1).

[135] Cf. the female ascetic Domnina who, though attending Church every morning and evening, continues to live in her mother's garden and is able to use her brothers' funds for charity, Theodoret (of Cyrus), *Historia religiosa* (hereafter *H. rel.*) XXX.1.1–13, 3.7–8 (SC 257 240, 244). It is worth noting in this regard that many treatises on virginity are addressed in whole or in part to men, in particular those who were in some way responsible for virgins within their households, e.g., (Ps.–) Basil, *De virg.* 11, 20 (RB 65.37.14–16, 39.16–17), etc.; cf. Basil of Ancyra, *De virg.* 65, cf. 39, 41 (PG 30.804A, cf. 748B–D, 749C–751A).

[136] Cf., e.g., for the West, Arianus ignotus, *hom. sollemn.* XV.7.77ʳ.19–20 (CCL 87 i.91), which clearly implies the existence of consecrated virgins: 'Quomodo illum uirgines

portrayed as moderately ascetic: the virgin, a living image of restraint (*sōphrosynēs eikōn*)[137] is warned that severe fasting will unfit her for the service of her neighbour[138] and that care of the body is a necessary part of 'philosophy';[139] fasting is nothing in itself,[140] and the virgin must be content with fulfilling the necessities of daily life.[141] Though it is fair to say that there was nothing very new in all this (the *Apostolic Constitutions,* after all, were as popular in Nicene as in non-Nicene Churches) what is conspicuously absent is any clear intent to alter traditional norms. More significant is the recurring presence in the midst of such normalcy of another and more sinister asceticism, this time one strongly condemned by our non-Nicene sources.

For instance, in the Pseudo-Ignatian Epistles, we find that while the targets of their fourth century editor are ostensibly the Docetists and Gnostics of the first century, his actual objects seem to have been contemporaries of his own in the fourth. These contemporaries are portrayed as practicing an asceticism which denied the goodness of marriage, procreation, and ordinary family life, for the editor is at pains to establish the goodness of sexual intercourse[142] and the positive value of married life,[143] even while honouring consecrated virginity and widowhood.[144] Moreover, he is careful to warn these more legitimate ascetics against regarding their consecrated state as a denigration of marriage.[145] Similar concerns are found in the *Apostolic Constitutions:* clergy who reject marriage, wine, or meat, as evil in themselves are to be excommunicated;[146] those who refuse to eat meat

amarent, quae in terra maritos non quaesierunt?' Elsewhere such prominent non-Nicenes as Acacius, Basil of Ancyra, Eudoxius, and Demophilus (among others) complained bitterly about the violence done by supporters of Marcellus to consecrated virgins, c. Sard., *ep. orientalium,* C.A.P. A. I.iv.1.9.1 (CSEL 65 55.12–19]).

[137] Basil of Ancyra, *De virg.* 22 (PG 30 716A).
[138] Ibid., 11 (PG 30 689B–692A).
[139] Ibid., 11 (PG 30 692B–C).
[140] Ibid., 12 (PG 30 693A–B).
[141] Ibid., 25 (PG 30 721A).
[142] (Ps.–) Ignatius, *Philad.* 6 (Lightfoot II iii.212.13–16).
[143] (Ps.–) Ignatius, *Tars.* 9 (Lightfoot II iii.186.12–187.21), *Phil.* 13 (Lightfoot II.iii.201.26–7), *Philad.* 4 (Lightfoot II iii.208.12–14), *Ant.* 9 (Lightfoot II iii.238.17–239.24).
[144] (Ps.–) Ignatius, *Tars.* 9 (Lightfoot II iii.187.1–2), *Phil.* 15 (Lightfoot II iii.202.16–203.1).
[145] (Ps.–) Ignatius, *Philad.* 4, 5 (Lightfoot II iii.208.6–8, 208.14–209.28), *Polyc.* 5 (Lightfoot II iii.230.17–22).
[146] *Apost. Const.,* viii.47.51 (Funk I 580.3–9).

on feast days are to be deposed,[147] and none is to fast on a Saturday or Sunday.[148] The sanctity of marriage is strongly affirmed,[149] as is intercourse within its bounds.[150] Widows and virgins are once again cautioned that their state implies no denigration of marriage,[151] and ascetics in general are warned that God has forbidden the misuse and not the use of the physical passions.[152] We have already seen a positive expression of these themes in Julian's portrait of Job, but we also find in the same work a strong condemnation of Manichees, false ascetics *(pseudenkratitai)*, and all who deny the goodness of the body or reject procreation as evil.[153]

The documents we have been examining are all Antiochene in origin, but if we look a little further afield we find that the situation they envisage is reflected in an influential if mysterious council in a neighbouring region, that of Gangra in Paphlagonia. The date of this council is difficult to determine. According to Socrates it took place after the Council of Constantinople in 360,[154] according to Sozomen before that of Antioch in 341.[155] Since its *acta* give the names but not the sees of the participants,[156] it is difficult to decide the issue on that basis.[157] Dates as late as 376 have been suggested, but if Sozomen is correct and the council took place before 341, then the 'Eusebius'

---

[147] ibid., viii.47.53 (Funk I 580.14–17).

[148] Ibid., viii.47.64 (Funk I 582.27–584.2), cf. C. Gangr., *ep. syn.* (Mansi II 1097–8b, ad pedem), Socrates, *HE* II 43 (PG 67 353A), Sozomen, *HE* III 14.33 (GCS 50 123.21–2).

[149] *Apost. Const.,* vi.14.3–4, 26.3 (Funk I 335.22–337.6, 369.4–6).

[150] ibid., vi.28.1–8 (Funk I 375.6–379.8).

[151] ibid., iv.14.1–3 (Funk I 235.4–15).

[152] ibid., vi.23.2 (Funk I 359.12–13).

[153] Julian, *Job* (PTS xiv 67.7–68.7). Compare the similar condemnation of Novatians and Manichaeans for denying the goodness of creation in (Ps.–) Chrystostom, *hom. anom.* II 11.129–137 (SC 146 106), and of stylites and other extreme ascetics in the *Opus Imperfectum in Matthaeum* 48 (PG 56 905C).

[154] Socrates, *HE* II 43 (PG 67 352B–C). Perhaps Socrates has confused this denunciation of the much-condemned Eustathius with that of a later Council.

[155] Sozomen, *HE,* IV 24.9 (CCS 180.10–12).

[156] C. Gangr., *ep. syn* (Mansi II.1095–6). Though Greek *acta* list 13 participants, the Latin versions give up to 16 in a different order. There is general agreement on the thirteen (assuming that 'Hilarius' in one manuscript is a corruption of Aelianus), but the Latin versions give up to another three, Heraclius or Heracles, found in all the manuscripts, Bassianus (a doublet of Bassus?), and, somewhat surprisingly, Osius Cordubensis (perhaps added because the council took place *'meta Tēn en Nikaiai synodon'*).

[157] For a brief discussion of some of the alternatives, see H. M. Gwatkin, *Studies of Arianism* (Cambridge: Deighton, Bell and Co., 1882), 185–188.

who presided was Eusebius of Nicomedia,[158] the disciple of Lucian, defender of Arius, and theological ancestor of Eunomius. The council's main target, indeed, was one of Eunomius' chief enemies, Eustathius of Sebaste,[159] once disciple of Arius[160] and mentor of Basil the Great.[161] Eunomius described him (in terms already venerable)[162] as a false ascetic, 'pale with fasting and murderous with rage', a figure 'cloaked in black, a saint accursed.'[163] The bishops at Gangra held him in no higher esteem, for they condemned him for doctrines not unlike those implied in the *Apostolic Constitutions* and Pseudo-Ignatian epistles: that no married person can be saved;[164] that meat is forbidden a Christian;[165] and that there is no salvation without renunciation of one's goods.[166] His followers' unconventional lifestyle, moreover (including cross dressing for the women[167] and separate assemblies for all)[168] gave additional cause for offense.

[158] Cf. Basil, *ep.* 263 3.9–14 (Courtonne III:123), Sozomen, *HE* IV 24.9 (GCS 50 180.7–10).

[159] C. Gangr., *ep. syn,* (Mansi II 1098, post initium).

[160] Basil, *ep.* 244 3.17–19, 263.3.3–6 (Courtonne III:77, 123). The statement in 244 3.19 that Aetius was Eustathius' own disciple seems to be an attempt by Basil to suggest where his (none too consistent) Trinitarian doctrine would sooner or later lead. Eustathius does seem to have had a remarkably diverse collection of disciples, and Sozomen ascribes the extravagances condemned at Gangra to these disciples rather than Eustathius personally at *HE* III 14.33 (GCS 50 123.18–26); Basil the Great, even as a youth, seems unlikely to have been attracted by the life-style condemned by the council (see following note).

[161] Cf. Basil, *ep.* 244 1.7–10 (Courtonne III:74), where Basil describes himself as a perfect slave to Eustathius in his youth. Sozomen asserts that some people even considered Eustathius to be the author of Basil's ascetical works, *HE* III 14.31 (GCS 50 123.15–16).

[162] Cf. Chrysostom, *De virg.* vi.1.16–17 (SC 125 110), Libanius, *or.* 30.8 (Foerster III 91.12), Eunapius, *Vita Soph.* 472, etc.

[163] Eunomius, *Apol. apol.* I (GNO I 32.18–33.1, cf. 32.6–8). Accusations of an unnatural pallor were standard features of this polemic; cf. the similar description of Basil the Great mentioned by Nazianzen, *Or.* 43 77 (PG 36 600A), and nn. 170 and 196 below. Note also that (in a story not without difficulties) Eustathius is said to have been deposed by his own father (a bishop) for dressing in a manner unbecoming a member of the clergy, Socrates, *HE* II 43 (PG 67 352B), Sozomen, *HE* IV 24.9 (CCS 50 180.5–7).

[164] C. Gangr, *can.* 1, cf. 4 (Mansi II 1102, cf. 1101b); cf. also Socrates, *HE* I 43 (PG 67 352C–353A), Sozomen, *HE* III 14.33 (GCS 50 123.19–21, 123.26–124.2).

[165] ibid., *can.* 2 (Mansi II 1102); cf. Socrates, *HE* II. 43 (PG 67 352D–353A), Sozomen, *HE* III 14.33 (GCS 50 123.23–24).

[166] C. Gangr., *ep. syn.* (Mansi II 1012b, ad initium); cf. Sozomen, *HE* III 14.33 (GCS 50 123.22–3).

[167] ibid. (Mansi II.1098 post medium); the men also wore unconventional clothing, Socrates, *HE* II 43 (PG 67 353A), Sozomen, *HE* III 14.33, cf. 36 (CCS 50 123.24–6, cf. 124.5–8), cf. Basil, *ep.* 223 3.4–8 (Courtonne III:11).

[168] ibid. (Mansi II 1098 ante medium); cf. Socrates, *HE* II 43 (PG 67 353A), Sozomen, *HE* III 14.33 (GCS 50 123.22).

To this almost complete transvaluation of all ancient society's
values the documents we have been studying opposed a communal
asceticism of studied moderation. The solutions proposed by others
were as different as their portraits of Job. The 'heretical virgins'
observed by Chrysostom at Antioch[169] in the 380s were as pale-faced
as Eustathius and no less somberly dressed; but if the great Doctor
was as ready as Pseudo-Ignatius to discern in them the marks of a
perverted Gnosis,[170] his proposed solution was strikingly different.[171]
The condemnation of marriage was indeed heretical,[172] but wedlock
itself could never be more than a tolerated alternative to
fornication.[173] For Chrysostom marriage had entered the world in the
funeral train of Adam and Eve leaving paradise,[174] and remained
within it only as a consolation prize for those unable to embrace the
full rigour and angelic joys of virginity.[175] Chrysostom's, then, is a
solitary and not a communal ideal, an attempt to return in actual fact
to the paradisal state of Adam and Eve in their seclusion and
innocence.[176] Like his Job, Chrysostom's virgin has left the secure
ramparts of the city to engage in single combat outside it; spectators
may watch from the walls but the virgin may never again be admitted
within[177] – she can no more abandon her post than an athlete leave
the stadium during a contest.[178] The communal delights of Job's
children at the supper table have been replaced by the abstemious
repasts of a philosopher and his disciples; what for Julian was a right,
in Chrysostom has become a concession. The virgin has been taken in
hand and transformed as radically as the patriarch, and having
embraced 'philosophy'[179] has left family and city behind; she is now
free, if only in spirit, to join the monk in the desert.[180]

[169] Chrysostom, *De virg.* i.1.6–7, 2.16–21 (SC 125.92, 94).

[170] ibid., vi.1.16–17, vii.1.11–12 (SC 125.110, 112).

[171] ibid., iii.1–9 (SC 125.100–102), cf. iv.2.22–3 (SC 125.104) where they are said to
be worse than pagans because they have rejected the real God and brought in many.

[172] ibid., viii.4.47–9 (SC 125.118), cf. viii.1.3– xi.2.26 (SC 125.114–28).

[173] ibid., xix.1.2–2.21, cf. ix.1.3–10 (SC 125.156–8, cf. 120).

[174] ibid., xiv.5.55–67 (SC 125.140–42) cf. xiv.5.55–67 (SC 125.140–42).

[175] ibid., x.3.22–xi.2.26, lxxix.1.3–2.37 (SC 125.124–8, 376–8).

[176] ibid., xiv.4.43–5.55 (SC 125.140).

[177] ibid., xxxiv.3.29–33 (SC 125.200).

[178] ibid., xxxviii.1.13–24 (SC 125.224–6).

[179] ibid., lxiii.2.22–6, cf. xlvii.1.17–21, 2.32–36 (SC 125.328, cf. 264–6).

[180] ibid., lxxix.1.11–14 (SC 125.376).

It is in this repeated contrast between patrician patriarch and 'athletic' philosopher, home-bound ascetic and 'warrior' virgin, that we begin to catch a glimpse of the reality behind the polemic. The temptation to apply the traditional contrast between philosopher and rhetor in such a context must have been well nigh irresistible. But if this does much to explain the form of the polemic, it does little to explain its vituperative depth or emotional intensity. There must have been more at stake. If considerations of space make it impossible to answer such a question in the course of a single article, we can at least outline some of the possibilities.

Almost all the documents we have been studying date from Antioch or its environs in the final decades of the fourth century. It would be easy to regard them, therefore, as exclusively concerned with the problems of eastern Asia Minor or Syria; but behind the ecclesiastical asceticism of the non-Nicenes and the 'athletic' individualism of Chrysostom another figure is visible, that of Gibbon's 'swarms of monks'; monasticism did indeed present the Roman world with an unparalleled crisis, if not quite that envisaged by Gibbon. Gibbon's philosopher might well look with pitying eye on the insect-like hoards of ascetics descending on the civilization of Cato and Cicero, but though condescending, his image serves to draw attention to the one indisputable fact about the movement, its immense popularity.[181] The philosophical and rhetorical elites of the Roman cities lived their lives in virtual ignorance of the vast, non-Hellenic populations which surrounded and supported them. Philostratus' description of Tyana as 'a Greek city in the midst of a population of Cappadocians'[182] could have applied as easily to any city in the Roman East. Even the great Athanasius, living in the capital of Egypt and bishop of a city with a significant Egyptian population, could describe the indigenous inhabitants of his native land with all the detachment of a foreigner.[183] The arrival of monasticism made such detachment impossible. The withdrawal of

[181] ibid., xxii.2.14–16 (SC 125 164).
[182] Philostratus, *Vita Apoll.* I. iv.
[183] Athanasius, *Oratio contra gentes* 23. 23–25 (Thomson 62–4).

thousands[184] of Christians, and smaller numbers of pagans (as
Cynics) from active participation in communal life threatened to
undermine the very fabric of the classical city. The urban loiterers
who attacked monks,[185] and who are said by Chrysostom to have
preferred a return to paganism to accepting them[186] feared that the
success of this movement would leave the cities abandoned.[187]
However unlikely as fact, this fear is a fitting symbol of the dilemma
faced by the urban elites of Roman society in the face of a largely rural
and non-Hellenic ascetic revolution.

It is said that history is written by the victors and this is as true of
monastic history as of any other. It is all too easy, therefore, to read
the early history of the monastic movement through the twin eyes of
Graeco-Roman culture and coenobitic monasticism. The same
process which produced the neat succession of *diadoxoi* in Diogenes
Laertius' history of the philosophic schools produced an equally
ordered series of monastic founders leading back to the 'first monk',
Antony of Egypt. Attempts by Jerome and others to assert the priority
of non-Egyptians were politely ignored, and Gibbon's monastic
swarms were free to rise from the Nile without opposition. The
increasing availability of Coptic and Syriac sources, however, has
shown that this pleasant uniformity is almost wholly incorrect and
that monasticism had a number of foci, the most important being the
enduring polarity between Egypt and Syria. The comparatively
moderate coenobitic monasticism of Egypt stood in marked contrast
to the theatrical and highly individual asceticism of Syria, where
communal living was a late development and the individual ascetic
always held pride of place.[188] The Antiochene provenance of many of
our sources is not accidental. The background of the polemic we have
been studying is not the moderate and ordered communal life of

---

[184] As usual most of the evidence comes from Egypt; though it is impossible to establish
detailed statistics, at a very early date many Egyptian and, later, some Syrian monastic
settlements numbered in the thousands. There is a convenient summary of the more
accessible evidence in A. H. M. Jones, *The Later Roman Empire* 284–602 (Baltimore: The
Johns Hopkins University Press, 1986), II:930–931.

[185] Chrysostom, *Adv. oppugn.* I.2 (PG 47 322B–C).

[186] ibid. (PG 47 321B).

[187] ibid. I.8 (PG 47 329C); cf. *De virg.* xiv.1.2–2.31 (SC 125 136–40).

[188] Cf. A. Vööbus, *History of Asceticism in the Syrian Orient*, in CSCO, subsidia 17, vol.
197 (1960), 146–58.

Egypt's Pachomius, but the public defecations of the Syrian ascetic James,[189] and the pillar of St. Simeon Stylites.[190]

Reactions to such ascetic *pièces de théâtre* varied considerably. The enthusiasm of the Syriac speaking countryside, where it was not unknown for one village to 'steal' the ascetic of another,[191] was not so visible in the Greek speaking towns. For every well-born lady who, like Theodoret's mother,[192] held the ascetics in awe, there were others who regarded them as a fit butt for jokes,[193] and though the Emperor might long to visit a Syriac-speaking ascetic[194] the Greek-speaking inhabitants of his largest cities were more ambivalent. Opposition was particularly strong among the wealthy and often still pagan members of the city councils – and not only because (in an age when it was possible to be *condemned* to a city council) some of their number had escaped by fleeing to the desert.[195] Libanius describes the monks of the Syrian hinterland in almost the same terms as Eunomius: they are violent black-robed gluttons hiding their excesses beneath an artificial pallor,[196] cave dwellers whose monotonous chanting[197] could disrupt even a court of law.[198] Indeed, according to Eunapius, anyone who was prepared to put on a black robe and make a public display could count on almost tyrannical power,[199] and Zosimus, echoing the complaints of some Christians,[200] thought the

[189] Theodoret, *H. rel.* XXI 5.1–10 (SC 257 76).

[190] It is interesting to note in this regard the evolution of Chrysostom's picture of Job once he left Antioch. When called upon to preach on Job as bishop of Constantinople his focus became Job the perfect patrician; for though still a philosopher (*hom.* 4.1, 3, 4, 5 [PG 63 477C, 481C–D, 482B, 483B, 484D]), in the Empire's capital this Job was an ideal example of the generosity needed to bridge the gulf between rich and poor, *hom.* 4.1, 4 (PG 67 478D, 482C–483D).

[191] Theodoret *H. rel.* XIX 3.1–10 (SC 257 60).

[192] ibid. VI 14.5–8 (SC 234 364).

[193] ibid. IX 9.13–16 (SC 234 424).

[194] ibid. XVII 9.1–7 (SC 257 46).

[195] Cf. *Codex Theodosianus* XII 1.63 (Mommsen 1.2.678), a law of 370 or 373 referring to certain 'ignaviae sectatores' in Egypt who, 'desertis civitatum muneribus captant solitudines ac secreta et specie religionis cum coetibus monazonton congregantur'; they are to be returned to their civic duties by force.

[196] Libanius, *or.* 30.8 (Foerster III 91.12–19); cf. Julian the Apostate, *ep. ad sac.* 288B (cf. also nn. 163, 170 above). Jerome, with his usual gusto, rang the changes on this theme in dealing with his own monastic enemies, Hieron., *ep.* 22.34 (CSEL 54 196.16–197.13).

[197] Cf. Chrysostom, *Adv. oppugn.* II 2 (PG 47 334A).

[198] Libanius, *or.* 45.26, cf. 2.32 (Foerster III 371.24–372.5, cf. I.249.5–8).

[199] Eunapius, *Vita Soph.* 472.

[200] Cf. nn. 185 and 186 above.

monks as useless for war as for any other public endeavour.[201] Though
it was some time before the authorities realised the fact, the black-
robed followers of Eustathius and the equally somberly clad virgins of
Chrysostom were outrunners of a popular ascetic revolution which
was indeed to challenge the civilization of Cato and Cicero.

If the traditional forms of Graeco-Roman society were to survive in
the face of this onslaught, the movement itself would have to be co-
opted, and both Church and State made strenuous efforts to do so.
Throughout the 370s the imperial government made a concerted
effort to recall its recalcitrant citizens to their duty. Decurions were to
be returned to the cities by force,[202] ordinary monks subjected to the
draft,[203] and all resistance to be greeted with severe penalties. Later
emperors tried (unsuccessfully) to forbid the monks even to enter a
city.[204] The bishops were no less zealous, though with a different end
in view: theirs was the difficult task of integrating a dangerously
disruptive movement into existing ecclesiastical structures. Control
by ordination became a favourite device,[205] and on a political level
almost all sides attempted to capture the monks for themselves. At the
Council of Alexandria in 362, for instance, we hear of 'Apollinarian
monks'[206] and at roughly the same period of 'Arian' efforts to
influence the monks of Egypt.[207] Later, and suspiciously similar

[201] Zosimus, *historia nova* V.23 (CSHB 47 278.23–279.6).

[202] See n. 195 above.

[203] Orosius, *Historiarum adversum paganos*, vii.33 (PL 31 1144C–1145A); Prosper of
Aquitaine, *chron.* i (PL 51 583A); Paul the Deacon, *Historia miscell.* xi (PL 95
931D–932A). The date, four years after the death of Valentinian I (A.D. 378 counting
inclusively, said to be A.U.C. 1128), is suspicious in that it seems to be designed to provide
a religious explanation for Valens' defeat and death at Adrianople in August of that same
year.

[204] *Codex Theodosianus* XVI.3.1 (Mommsen II ii.853), dated September of 390 (revoked
a year and a half later, XVI.3.2). Perhaps a response to the success of the Antiochene monks
in averting the imperial wrath following the riot of the statues in 387, cf. Chrysostom, *De
statuis,* 17.1 (PG 49 172D–173B).

[205] Theodoret, *H. rel.,* XIX.2.1–7 (SC 257 60), where a bishop breaks into the cell of an
enclosed ascetic to ordain him and then walls him up again!

[206] Athanasius, *tomus* 9 (PG 26 808A).

[207] Athanasius, *ep. ad monachos,* (PG 26 1188A). Since Athanasius warns against
communicating, associating, or worshipping with the heretics in any way (cf. 1188B–C), it
must be assumed that their campaign was not wholly unsuccessful. In writing to Serapion
of Thmuis about the same time, Athanasius mentions a letter about 'Arianism' written to
the monks (5.2 [Opitz II 180.17–18]) and implies that a lively debate on the heresy is
under way, *Ep. ad Serapion de morte Arii,* 1.2–3, 5.1 (Opitz II 178.8–14, 180.12–14).
There is an extant letter ascribed to one of Pachomius' disciples comforting the monks in

efforts are said to have been made in Syria.[208] None of these efforts seems to have been particularly successful, however, and later reports of 'Arian monks' seem to be based on misunderstandings, deliberate or otherwise.[209] In the end of course it was the Nicenes who 'won', but there was a brief period during which the outcome might have been different. The polemical themes we have been studying are the by-blows of this struggle, one described by Chrysostom as bordering on civil war;[210] one of the weapons of choice in this war was the ancient and honourable distinction between philosopher and rhetor.

Having co-opted the monks doctrinally, the Nicenes hastened to make use of them polemically. In the teeth of the known ascetic orientation of the historical Arius,[211] they turned the heresiarch into a notorious glutton defeated by a fasting saint,[212] and extolled the ability of uneducated ascetics to overcome (in fractured Greek) the

the face of 'Arian' persecution, the *ep. Theodori monachi* in *Bibliothēkē hellēnōn paterōn* 41.126 (= *BHP*), and a cautionary tale about an Arian bishop attempting to pray in a monastic Church against the will of the monks in *V. Pach.* I.138, III.190 (*BHP* 40.185.39–186.6, 41.74.19–29).

[208] Cf. Theodoret *H. rel.,* II 16.1–6 (SC 234 230). The story bears a suspicious resemblance to a similar story told of Antony in Athanasius' *v. Anton.* 69 (PG 26 941A–B) and presumably represents a patriotic effort to claim an equal glory for Syria.

[209] Cf. John of Damascus, *De haer.* 101 (PG 94 765A), where Muhammad is said to have been influenced by an Arian monk. A passage in the *Chronicon ad annum Christi 1234 pertinens,* par. 41 (CSCO 109 [Syr. 56] 177.19–20, translation, 139.23–4) thought to be a reference to 'Arian' monks seems to be a misunderstanding of Socrates' *HE* VII 19 (PG 67 765A–B). Such misunderstandings as were not motivated by malice were made easier by the fact that Melitians could be popularly described in Egypt as *tous ta Areiou phronountas* (Sozomen, *HE* II 19.4 (GCS 50 77.15–16)), and there were undoubtedly Melitian monks until a quite late period, Theodoret, *H. rel.,* I.9.14 (GCS 42.3–8). Another cause of confusion may have been a tendency to link Origenists and 'Arians' during the Origenist controversy, cf. *V. Pach.* III.56, IV. 36 (BHP 41.18.25–8, 101.5–6).

[210] Chrysostom, *Adv. opugn.* I.2 (PG 47 322C).

[211] He is said to have worn the *kolobiōn,* a garment frequently associated with ascetics (Epiphanius, *Panarion haer.* 69.3.1 [GCS III 154.15–16]), and Rufinus describes him as (albeit speciously) 'vir specie et forma . . . religiosus' (*HE* I 1 [PL 21 467A]); he is also said to have had the support of many ascetic women (n. 127 above). According to Alexander of Alexandria, moreover, *ep. Alex.* 41 apud Theodoret *H. rel* 1.4 (GCS 19.15–16), Arius and his followers are said to have described themselves as *monoi sophoi kai aktēmones kai dogmatōn heuretai,* though Opitz, following Jülicher, would conjecture, perhaps correctly, *epistēmones* for *aktēmones* (Urkunde 14, Opitz III 26.11–12).

[212] James of Nisibis, Theodoret, *h. rel.* I 10.40–57 (SC 234 180–82), cf. II 16.1–21.2 (SC 234 230–40); for a very different non–Nicene interpretation of James' role see n. 226 below.

specious arguments of the rhetors.[213] Whatever the effect of such encounters on the believing masses, they were of little avail with the urban elite, and the problem of how to integrate so vast a movement into traditional Graeco-Roman culture remained acute. The problem was no less acute for Christians than for Pagans, for the enthusiasm of a Theodoret or a Sozomen contrasted sharply with the more tempered response of their other contemporaries. Basil experienced considerable difficulty, for instance, in introducing monasticism into his diocese,[214] and in the West Jerome found 'monk' almost a synonym for 'inposter et Graecus'.[215] To be accepted into the wider society monasticism would have to be either modified or rejected, and, if rejected, replaced with an ideal of comparable power. It is by no means accidental, therefore, that in the description of Basil the Great quoted at the beginning of this article,[216] the modest holiness of the retiring philosopher is contrasted with the theatrical individualism of the Cynic Crates, for under the guise of the pagan ascetic we can see a condemnation of the flamboyant individualism of the Syrian countryside. The cultured Basil and the educational parvenu, Eunomius, though divided in all else, were united in a consciousness of the difficulties caused by the new movement. Their solutions, however, were strikingly different. For Basil the answer was the importation and modification of the comparatively moderate coenobitic monasticism of Egypt, with its overtones of a renewed 'philosophy' and its ideal of service to society;[217] for Eunomius it was

---

[213] ibid. VIII 2.1–18 (SC 234 376–8), cf. XXVII 4.2–4 (SC 257 222).

[214] Cf., e.g., Basil, *ep.* 207.2.5–39 (Courtonne II:185–6).

[215] Hieron., *ep.* 38.5, cf. 54.5 (CSEL 54 293.1–4, cf. 470.11–12).

[216] See p. 186 above.

[217] For Basil humanity is a *koinōnikon zōon* and thus neither *monastikon* or *agrion;* service to others is a necessary part of the Christian life, and one inherently impossible for a solitary to fulfill. Thus coenobitic monasticism is inherently superior to eremeticism because a communal dimension is a fundamental part of what it is to be a Christian, Basil, *Regulae fusius tractate* 3.1–2, 7.1–4 (PG 31 917A–D, 928B–933C); cf. *reg. br.* 74 (PG 31 1133C). This emphasis on service to one's neighbour was concretely expressed in Basil's provision for a designated community almoner (*reg. br.* 87, 91, 100, 101 [PG 31 1143B–C, 1145B, 1152B–1153A]), and in the numerous charitable institutions attached to his monastery, Basil, *ep.* 94.25–45 (Courtonne I:205–6). Something similar seems to have been founded or encouraged by Eustathius of Sebaste, but we are not told that it was specifically monastic in character, Epiphanius, *Panarion haer.* 75.1.7 (GCS III 333.22–7). For a description of the *ptōcheion* provided by the monks of Alexandria, see Palladius, *Historia lausiara.* 6.7.47–9.73 (Bartelink 34–6).

the reaffirmation of the traditional spirituality of the urban Churches, and the transformation of the venerable and equally potent figure of the god-touched rhetor.

Whatever Chrysostom's dreams or his opponents' fears there was never any real possibility that monasticism would engulf the classical city; but if the price of its integration was transformation into an elite, that elite was composed in part of those who in earlier centuries had given the city its leaders. Monasticism had provided a significant minority of the city's potential leadership with a compelling vision, but it was a vision which took them outside the city itself. Chrysostom's arguments were aimed not so much at the impoverished masses as at the alarmed and influential parents of these 'dropouts'.[218] If non-Nicenes clung with particular tenacity to the domestic and urban asceticism of earlier centuries, they were as aware as their Nicene counterparts of the need to provide this leadership with a new vision. It was in an effort to do so that they undertook the recreation of one of antiquity's most prestigious public figures, the rhetor. Generations of schoolboys had dreamed of becoming 'a new Cicero or Demosthenes'[219] and even Basil could describe rhetoric as 'the most sought after pursuit of all'.[220] In Philostorgius' description of Eunomius we have already seen hints of the 'lofty brow' and 'winged eye' associated with the late classical rhetor, but the specifically religious dimension was added by consciousness of a divine call. For Aetius this took the form of a waking vision,[221] for Eunomius apparently a dream.[222] In the god-touched figure of Job we have already seen something of the working out of this ideal, but in the wonderworking bishops of Philostorgius we catch a glimpse of the 'divine man' in the flesh. As committed to celibacy (monaulion) as any consecrated virgin,[223] these personages are portrayed as

---

[218] Cf., e.g., Chrysostom, Adv. oppugn. II 2 (PG 47 333B–C).

[219] Juvenal, sat. X.114–117.

[220] Basil, ep. 277.24–6 (Courtonne III:150).

[221] Philostorgius, HE III.15 (GCS 21 46.19–21).

[222] Cf. Eunomius, Apol. apol. I (GNO I 29.25–30.2).

[223] Cf. Philostorgius, HE III 4, (GCS 21 33.18–19, 36–9) for Theophilus, and the v. Luciani in ibid. Anhang VI.2 (GCS 21 185. 1–24) for the austere and celibate life of Lucian of Antioch. The story of Lucian has passed through several Nicene redactions, which makes it difficult to know just what goes back to the non-Nicene original, but in this instance if Lucian is undoubtedly seen through a monastic lens, his characterization is an extension rather than a contradiction of that of Theophilus the Indian and others. We never hear of

consistently active in public life. Aetius, like the martyr Lucian before him,[224] is said to have used his skill in the service of the poor,[225] and James of Nisibis (elsewhere aggressively Nicene) is portrayed as the saviour of his native city.[226] Heralds of an unconquerable faith,[227] non-Nicene stalwarts such as Theophilus the Indian and others were recipients of imperial veneration, and (in words only too reminiscent of Maximus) honoured as the very image of the apostle,[228] *eph' hēmōn Mōsēs,*[229] veritable statues in a shrine.[230] As wonderworkers whose presence could be demanded even by emperors,[231] they were the natural inheritors of the rhetor's magical aura.[232] The fact that almost all of them were associated with the imperial household was no accident;[233] they were heirs of an activist tradition in which participation was a virtue.[234]

a wife for either Aetius or Eunomius and the sexual charges levelled against them never include adultery (see nn. 9, 11 and 12 above); we are told that Eunomius had a married sister and, later, a nephew named Lucian [!] (Philostorgius, *HE* XII. ll [GCS 21 148.1–3]), but never a wife.

[224] Cf. *v. Luciani* in Philostorgius, *HE,* Anhang VI.3 (GCS 21 186.16–19).

[225] Philost., *HE* III.15 (GCS 21 47.10–14).

[226] ibid., III.23, cf. Anhang VII (GCS 21 50.8–12, cf. 211.6–12, 23–6, 31–2). This popular saint, portrayed elsewhere as the very bane of Arius (see n. 212 above), is portrayed by Philostorgius as an intercessor capable of saving a city through his *parrēsia.* Since Philostorgius insists throughout on the necessary link between doctrinal *akribeia* and divine favour (e.g., I.10, III.22 [GCS 21 11.4–8, 49.3–4], etc.), it must be assumed that his intent was to portray James as one of his own.

[227] ibid., III.4ª cf. 15 (GCS 21 34.27–35, cf. 46.16–23): Theophilus the Indian and Aetius.

[228] ibid., III.6ª (GCS 21 36.29–31): Theophilus the Indian.

[229] ibid., II.5 (GCS 21 18.9–12): Wulfila.

[230] ibid., III.6 (GCS 36.1–3): Theophilus the Indian.

[231] ibid., IV.7, cf. II.8, III 4, 6ª, V.2, IX.1 (GCS 21 61.9–16, cf. 20.1–4, 11–14, 34.8–10, 36.31–5, 68.2–5, 116.2–7): Agapetus of Synnada, Theophilus the Indian, Aetius, Eunomius, Leontius, Evagrius, Arrianus, and Florentius.

[232] Cf., e.g., Dio Chrysostom, *or.* 32.39.

[233] Cf., e.g., Philostorgius, *HE* III.5, III.6, 27, IV.1 (GCS 21 18.9–12, 36.1–3, 52.18–53.9, 57.2, 7–11), etc.

[234] It is important to realise in assessing this that Philostorgius did not present a monochrome or purely ecclesiastical ideal. Though seen through 'a Nicene glass darkly' the martyr Artemius presents the corresponding lay ideal (all references are to Philostorgius, *HE,* Anhang i, ii and parallels), though not by any means a professional (i.1, cf. ii.26, 27 [152.7–11, cf. 158.11–159.5, 160.3–4]), Artemius is able to best the apostate Emperor with an impressive display of secular learning (ii.29, cf. 46–7 [160.30–161.18, cf. 163.23–164.15]), and is portrayed as model member of the courts of Constantine and Constantius, truly one of *rōn ep' aretēi kai paideiai lamprynomenōn* and a lover of the Christian faith (i.8 cf. *HE* I.6ª[GCS 21 155. 17–20, cf. 7.19–21]).

Such personages had not rejected asceticism, they had embraced moderation. The moderation of Eunomius, however, was not the moderation of Basil; equally unwilling to countenance the excesses of popular encratite movements, Eunomius was more interested to establish the difference between the use and the abuse of the passions than to condemn their exercise. If the real issue was whether or not to participate in civic life,[235] whether to 'seek the peace of the city' or flee to safety outside it, Eunomius was firmly on the side of the city. The ideal presented to his followers was that of a traditional and moderate Christian asceticism. If widows and consecrated virgins were the temples and altars of the Church,[236] parents were God's fellow-workers, and fruitful sexual union a reflection of the divine fecundity.[237] The asceticism espoused by Eunomius, then, was not that of the monk with his 'sackcloth and hard belt', his 'flesh hanging loose on his sides', 'his ribs like the eaves of a house' so admired even by the moderate Basil;[238] it was the domestic asceticism of traditional urban Christianity, in whose midst even a rhetor might feel at home. It was this incautious espousal of moderation which left him open to the Lucianic brickbats of his opponents. Moderation is rarely popular.

In the war of contending asceticisms represented by these two powerful personalities, Basil was the undoubted victor; the classical city left its moorings and merged with the coenobitic monastery; but the more participatory vision of Eunomius was not without result – and not only in the immense influence of such works as the *Apostolic Constitutions*. His vision became in part the basis on which Medieval Byzantium came to terms with its classical heritage. It is not accidental that Gregory Nazianzen's disgust at the 'court' bishops of Theodosius the Great is expressed in terms so reminiscent of his descriptions of Eunomius. For Gregory these bishops were:

> . . . flatterers of women, disseminators of seductive venom, lions among little folk, craven before the powerful. At every table they make mighty fine parasites . . .; the thresholds worn out by them are not those of the wise, but those of the powerful. [239]

---

[235] Cf. Chrysostom, *Adv. oppugn.* I.7 (PG 47 328B).
[236] See nn. 131, 132, 133 above.
[237] (Ps.–) Ignatius, *Philad.* 4 (Lightfoot II.iii.208.9–10).
[238] Basil, *ep.* 45.1.33–45 (Courtonne I:113–4).
[239] Gregory of Nazianzus, *carm.* I.xii.333–43 (PG 37 1190–91), translation: FC 75.59.

Well, participation has its price; but in Gregory's secularised bishops we can perhaps catch a glimpse of the ecclesiastical luminaries of the Medieval Byzantine court. For though it would doubtless have horrified him to be told it, among the forebears of the Patriarch Photius must surely be placed the heretic Eunomius and all who tried to develop a theology of participation. The city could only be built by those willing to stay within it.

IV
THEOLOGICAL LANGUAGE

Chapter 10

THE BACKGROUND AND USE
OF EUNOMIUS' CAUSAL LANGUAGE

Michel R. Barnes

The Role of Causal Language in Trinitarian Doctrine

If most of those involved in the trinitarian controversies of the fourth century accepted that any doctrine of the Trinity presumed a specific account of Divine causality, what is distinctive to the debate between Eunomius of Cyzicus and Gregory of Nyssa is that they both understood that the Second Person's unity with the First is determined by the unity between the Divine Nature and the Divine causal capacity. Both Eunomius and Gregory attach their understanding of the unity of the Son with the Father to an understanding of the unity of the Divine productive capacity with the Divine nature. My subject in this essay is limited to Eunomius' description of the unity between the Divine productive capacity and the Divine nature, namely his use of *ousia, energeia,* and *ergon* (hereafter translated as *essence, activity,* and *product*). Eunomius' use of essence, activity and product to distinguish stages or levels in a causal sequence has a long and authoritative history in Pagan philosophy and Christian theology.

Essence, activity, and *product* were used as a sequence of terms to describe causal relationships in both theology and philosophy. The sequence usually included another term: *dunamis,* the productive *power.* This traditional causal sequence of *essence, power, activity* and *product* is found in writings by Pagan philosophers such as Galen and Iamblichus, the Christian theologians Clement and Origen, as well as the Pagan theurgist Julian the Emperor. Events in the life of Aetius, Eunomius' mentor, gave him the opportunity to learn of this causal sequence, either from its use in the medical tradition associated with Galen, or from the philosophical traditions associated with Iamblichus, including Julian, a contemporary of Aetius and

Eunomius, as well as from the writings of the Christian theologians of Alexandria. However, given the weight of scholarly accounts that portray Eunomius' theology as barely Christian and the product of a marginal interest, it is best not to rush into picking one precedent as Eunomius' exclusive source. Reductive accounts of Eunomius' theology are not useful. My purpose is to show how Eunomius' language locates him within broad traditions of Christian and Pagan thought. Indeed, Eunomius' causal hierarchy may fairly be characterised as his own distinctive development and application of traditional authoritative causal language.

Essence, Activity, and Product as a Sequence

The terms essence, activity, and product appear in both Eunomius' *Apology (Apologia)* and the *Second Apology (Apologia Apologiae)*. The terseness of Eunomius' statement of doctrine in the Second Apology[1] has led scholars to use the earlier work to elaborate upon Eunomius' summary of his beliefs in the first theological fragment from the *Second Apology*.[2] From the *Apology* we understand that God's essence is wholly identified with *agennetos*,[3] and that the attribution of any other trait not synonymous with *agennetos* contradicts the notion of divine simplicity.[4] Similarly, in the *Apology* Eunomius understands activity to be a cause of temporary duration that produces an effect that is also of temporary duration. The activity produces effects that exist co-extensively in time with it; the effects exist when, and only when, the causal activity exists.[5] This activity is a cause that receives no traits from its associated essence, and transmits or reproduces no essential traits in the product, but instead produces a work that is like the activity in nature, and not like the original essence.[6]

---

[1] At GNO I 71.28 –73.15.

[2] See, for example, 'The Cappadocian Triumph Over Arianism,' Bernard Barmann, diss. Standford 1966, 130–5. L. R. Wickham uses the *Apology* to fill in and explain the theology of Aetius in 'The *Syntagmation* of Aetius the Anomean,' JTS, XIX (1968), 532–69.

[3] *Apology* 7.11.

[4] ibid., 8.16–18.

[5] ibid., 23.13–15.

[6] ibid., 24.3–4.

The product[7] is described in terms which are similar to the activity: it is temporary, existing only so long as its cause exists, and resembling the activity in its nature.[8] For Eunomius, the two most important points of resemblance between the energy and product are *to be caused* and *to be temporal and not eternal.* In the end, Eunomius understands these two traits to be identical. The final descriptive trait of a product worth noting is that it is itself an essence, which possesses its own productive activities.

Eunomius' theology emphasises the causal relationship within the divine life. It is his opinion that causal language most accurately describes the central doctrines of the faith: that the unique status of God is due to His being uniquely unproduced, that is, the only existent who is without prior cause.[9] The Son is related to God by the activity that produced him, and he is similar in nature to this cause. The Son is related to the world by being the creator of everything after him.

In the *Second Apology,* written nearly 18 years after the *Apology,* Eunomius offers a more clearly structured understanding of divine causality. In this later account he gives a more prominent role to the sequence of *ousia, energeia* and *erga.* These terms are important as a sequence in the *Apology,* but in the later *Second Apology* Eunomius makes explicit the theological burden the sequence carries: in the *Apology* the sequence is introduced in the middle of the treatise with no particular emphasis, while in the *Second Apology* the language of causality is presented forthrightly. Eunomius apparently begins the theological part of this later treatise with the following passage:

> The whole statement of our doctrines consists of the highest and supreme essence, and of the one which exists because of that essence, and after that

---

[7] Product *(ergon)* is a term which could be supported by an appeal to Prov. 8:22 – 'The Lord created me as the beginning of His ways unto His *works'* – and its sense in the literature of the era is regularly one of *creature.* Eusebius uses the term to refer to created things, as, for example, when he says in *Demonstration of the Gospel* IV.6, that the sun, the heavens, and the cosmos are *products* of God. Or in *Preparation for the Gospel* VII.18, Eusebius distinguishes between the image and likeness of God and the human body, which he calls a '*work* of God.' Likewise, in Eusebius' extract from Origen's *Commentary on Genesis,* Origen uses *ergon* for the product of an artist's craft, and the products of God's creation *(Preparation for the Gospel* VII.20).

[8] *Apology* 24.10–13.

[9] ibid., 7.3–6 and 26.2–5.

essence has supremacy over all the rest, and of a third which is in no way aligned with them, but subject to the one because of causation and to the other because of the activity by which it exists; the activities which follow from the essences and the names belonging to them being of course treated together for the comprehensive statement of the whole doctrine. But again, since each of these beings both is and is perceived to be absolutely simple and altogether one in its own dignity, and since the activities are defined at the same time as their works, and the works are bounded by the activities of those who effected them, there is surely every necessity both that the activities accompanying each of the essences are lesser and greater, and that some occupy the first and others the second dignity, and in sum that they reach the same degree of difference as their works reach. [10]

This is a terse passage, heavy with jargon, even by the standard of the age. Gregory has great fun plucking out terms such as 'follows' and 'bounded by' and dangling them until they snap.[11] But it is interesting to note that Gregory takes most of the language in this passage seriously, and he seems to recognise most of the key words as accepted terms in theological discourse.[12] Though Gregory rejects Eunomius' particular use of *ousia, energeia,* and *erga,* he has no problem with the terms themselves. Despite the apparently idiosyncratic character of Eunomius' summary of belief, this passage has an important Christian precedent. The structure of Eunomius' summary resembles Eusebius' characteristic theological hierarchies, and some of Eunomius' language repeats Eusebius'. In his *Preparation for the Gospel* Eusebius compares Pagan theism with the religion of

---

[10] *Second Apology,* in Gregory's *Against Eunomius* I, GNO I 71.28 –73.15. Stuart Hall's translation in 'Contra Eunomium I', in *El Contra Eunomium I,* eds. Lucas Mateo-Seco and Juan Bastero (Pamplona: Ediciones Universidad de Navarra, S. A., 1988), 57, slightly modified. Hall translates *symperigraphé* as 'match'; I prefer the Moore and Wilson phrasing 'bounded by', because of, and not despite, its suggestion of a self-conscious way of speaking. *Perigraphé* is used by Origen to indicate the separate reality of the many *dynameis* of God, in particular, the real and separate existence of God's Word, which – unlike the human word inherent in our minds – possesses substance *[hypostasis].* See *Commentary on John* I, 292, which Ronald Heine, *Origen: Commentary on the Gospel According to John Books 1–10* (Washington, D.C.: Catholic University of America Press, 1989), 94, translates as: 'As, therefore, there are many powers of God, each of which has its own individuality *[perigraphé]* . . . so also the Christ . . . will be understood to be the 'Word' – although the reason which is in us has no individuality *[perigraphé]* apart from us – possessing substance *[hypostasis].* . . .' See also SC 120 206.

[11] See GNO I 152.9. 15.

[12] An example of Gregory taking Eunomius' language seriously is Gregory's lengthy reply to Eunomius' statement that 'the same energies produce the same work, and different works indicate different energies', as found in GNO I 140.8 –145.9.

the Hebrews and of Christianity. These comparisons frequently lead Eusebius to describe Hebrew and Christian doctrines in terms of hierarchies. For example, both Eusebius and Eunomius structure their theological hierarchies through the ordering of Divine *beings* or *essences:* there is a First *ousia,* a Second *ousia,* and a Third.[13] This sequence corresponds to a *taxis* among the essences and the respective *axia.* In this kind of sequence the first *ousia* is said to be *anotato,* and is distinguished by being *agen[n]etos.*[14] Both authors emphasise the *simple* or *unmixed* nature of the First Essence, though their specific terms differ. Eusebius uses *amiktos;* Eunomius uses *aplous* and *eilikrines.* There are other incidental doctrinal similarities which are typical of non-Nicene theologies: e.g., the Son is the demiurge of the cosmos, and the role of Holy Spirit is defined by his subjection to the Second Person.

In the passage from the *Second Apology* the sequence of *essence, activity, product* and *name,* as well as the associated distinctions of *simplicity,*[15] *dignity,*[16] and *order,*[17] are explicitly organised as a hierarchy. This hierarchy is fundamentally one of causality where, as Kopecek points out, the essences are arranged in a sequence of space and time.[18] The rank or place of these essences is determined according to their nature as cause. To be specific, the first place in the hierarchy belongs to an essence which is understood to be uncaused, and which is described as the cause of the second and third essences. These two essences are related to the first in so far as they are caused by the first: the second essence exists 'because of that [first] being but after [it] . . .'[19] while the third essence is 'subject to the one [i.e., the first *ousia*] because of causation and to the other [i.e., the *second ousia*] because of the activity by which it exists'.[20] In other words, the Son exists because of God (alone), while the Spirit exists because of God and the Son, and thus follows after them. God, of course, is by

---

[13] *Preparation for the Gospel* VII.12 (SC 215 222–224). Eusebius then moves into his exegesis of Prov. 8:22.

[14] *Preparation for the Gospel* VII.15 (SC 215 238).

[15] GNO I 72.11.

[16] GNO I 72.12.

[17] GNO I 72.18.

[18] Kopecek, *Neo-Arianism,* 453.

[19] GNO I 72.2–3, Hall, 57.

[20] GNO I 72.4–7, Hall, 57.

definition without prior cause, and so He is first in the hierarchy. Thus, Eunomius identifies the productive capacity with the activity; he distinguishes the activity from the essence; and he determines that each activity is uniquely associated with one essence.

Eunomius' 'Aristotelian' Language

One of the more important understandings of Eunomius' use of activity *(energeia)* is that it is somehow 'Aristotelian'.[21] Such a opinion frequently follows the more general judgement that Eunomius' theology is fundamentally Aristotelian in inspiration. The charge that Eunomius is heavily indebted to Aristotle has its origins in Eunomius' own era, for it is a common one among his opponents.[22] Basil characterises Eunomius' logical style as owing to Aristotle and Chrysippus,[23] while both Basil and Gregory speak of the apparent influence of Aristotle's *Categories* in Eunomius' *Apology*.[24] Similar charges against Aetius appear in redactors and historians like Epiphanius and Socrates.[25] Quotations from these authors naturally

---

[21] At the end of the last century there was a split in scholarship on how *dunamis* and *energeia* in Christian writings should be understood. Some scholars like Theodore Zahn, *Marcellus von Ancyra. Ein Beitrag zur Geschichte der Theologie* (Gotha, 1867), 123, tended to see the sense of these terms as Aristotelian. A similar opinion seems to have beeen encouraged in Catholic scholarship by scholastic accounts of the history of doctrine. However, the end of the last century and the beginning of this one saw an attempt by some French Catholic historians of doctrine to lose the scholastic categories: Théodore de Régnon offers his own sense of *energeia* as it is used by the Greek fathers in the later half of the fourth century. 'Ajoutons que les deux mots *energeia* et *dunamis* repondent à des choses de même ordre. Il en résulte que, lorsque nous rencontrerons ces deux mots associés, nous devrons tradire le premier par *action* "efficiente" et le second par *puissance* "efficiente" '. *Études de Théologie positive sur la Sainte Trinité,* four volumes bound as three (Paris: Victor Retaux, 1892/1898), IV:435. (De Régnon's opinion is offered with Petau very much in mind: see his discussion of Petau's *De Deo Uno* V, xx, x–xii, on 431 ff.) Lebreton followed de Régnon in this judgement: 'Chez Aristote, on le sait, le mot *dunameis* signifie fréquemment puissance passive par opposition à *energeia,* acte. Cette signification est sans aucun rapport avec le concept que nous étudions. Dans toute la langue grecque, le même terme à une autre acception beaucoup plus fréquente, celle de puissance active ou de force; c'est en ce sens aussi que la philosophie religieuse l'a employé.' *Histoire du Dogme de la Trinité des origines à Saint Augustin* (Paris: Gabriel Beauchesne, 1910), I:437.

[22] See Wickham's balanced (and brief) accessment in *'Syntagmation',* 561.

[23] In his *Against Eunomius* I.5 (SC 299 173).

[24] Basil says in his *Against Eunomius* I.9 that Eunomius takes the privation language from the *Categories* (SC 299 201). Gregory is traditionally understood to be making a similar comment, if more general in fashion, in his *Against Eunomius* I, but in his edition Jaeger brackets the text reference: see GNO I 41.4–5.

[25] Epiphanius' comments are at *Panarion haer.* 76.2.2. Socrates' are at *HE* IV.7.

serve as the basis for modern scholarly judgements that Eunomius' theology was indeed Aristotelian.

Any claim that Eunomius' use of *energeia* is Aristotelian would seem to require that he would have defined the term in relation to *dunamis,* yet this does not happen. The creed of *Apology* 28 is interesting for the purposes of this discussion, for it contains some of the few Eunomian uses of *dunamis* and *energeia* together.[26] In that creed *dunamis* and *energeia* are used three times as a formula to mean the capacity to act and, probably, the exercise of that capacity.[27] The terms are used together as a recurring formula with two different senses. The first sense of the formula is God's productive capacity as opposed to, and distinct from, His essence. The Son, the creed says, is *generated, created,* and *made* by the *dunamis* and *energeia* only,[28] and is not from the *hypostasis* or *ousia.*[29] Here the terms *dunamis* and *energeia* are synonymous with *boulé.* The second sense of the formula distinguishes the capacity to act from the intention or will initiating and directing that act. This capacity to act is the sense of *dunamis* and *energeia* in the two remaining citations.[30] In both of these passages the author says that the Holy Spirit is made by *exousia* and *prostagma* of God, but by the *dunamis* and *energeia* of the Son. The Spirit is understood to be produced by the Son, in obedience to the sovereign will of God. This hierarchy of causality agrees with the theology of the *Apology.*[31]

[26] Chapter 28 is usually regarded as being *Eunomian,* although not written by Eunomius himself. For example, see Vaggione, 16. Kopecek, on the other hand, assumes that the chapter is *by* Eunomius when he says, 'Because the creed was plainly written by Eunomius, the only question we must face is the question of its date.' *Neo-Arianism,* 402.

[27] *Apology* 28.7.15,26 (Vaggione, 74–75).

[28] The phrase *'generated, created,* and *made'* recalls Arius' early formulations; these parallels are the subject of Vaggione's article, *'Oux os enton gennematon:* Some aspects of Dogmatic Formulae in the Arian Controversy', *Studia Patristica,* XVII (1982), 181–7.

[29] *Apology* 28.6–9, (Vaggione, 74–75): '[F]or he begot and created and made only the Son by his own power and action. He did not, however share out anything of his own substance.'

[30] *Apology* 28.15, '[God made the Holy Spirit] creating him by his own authority and commandment, but by means of the action and power of the Son.' and 28.26, '[the Holy Spirit] made at the command of the Father by the action and power of the Son.' Vaggione, 74–75.

[31] See *Apology* 17.10–12 (Vaggione, 54–5); and 25.22–25 (Vaggione, 68–9).

However, the contrast of *dunamis* and, more importantly, *energeia* with *exousia* and *prostagma* in the creed of chapter 28 does not repeat exactly the thought expressed in the *Apology* itself, for in the latter Eunomius uses *energeia* as a synonym for *boulé* (and *gnomé*),[32] whereas the creed *contrasts energeia* and *dunamis* with *boulé,* or its apparent synonyms, *exousia* and *prostagma*.[33] In the *Apology dunamis* and *exousia* function as synonyms; in chapter 28 they are mutually exclusive terms.[34] There is thus nothing to suggest an Aristotelian understanding of *dunamis* and *energeia,* considered separately or together, in Eunomius' use of these terms.

The most important alternative understanding of *essence* and *activity* (or *energy, energeia*) occurs in the Neo-Palamite scholars, with their emphasis on the 'essence-energy distinction'.[35] A large body of work either produced by Neo-Palamite scholars, or by other scholars who accept at face value Neo-Palamite claims,[36] has focused upon the

[32] *Apology* 24.1 (Vaggione, 64–5).

[33] *Apology* 28.15 (Vaggione, 74–5).

[34] It is tempting to see a formula in the use of these four terms together, so that it would be understood that there was a proportion among them, to the effect that '*exousia: prostagma: dunamis: energeia,*' that is, in both ratios, *capacity* is to *act*. But the scholarly research on associated uses of *exousia* and *prostagma* is lacking.

[35] The beginning of the eastern fascination with *energeia* (to the exclusion of *dunamis*) may be as early as John Damascene. In his review of the evidence for what *energeia* meant in Christian useage, de Régnon refers to Damascene's definition in *On the Orthodox Faith,* II.23. (see Régnon, *Études de théologie,* XXVI, IV:428). De Régnon decides that Damascene's understanding of the relationship between *dunamis* and *energeia* is Aristotelian: 'Je pense que le lecteur a retrouvé ici toute la théorie aristotelicienne de l'act et de la puissance.' I agree with de Régnon.

[36] Some appropriations of Neo-Palamite scholarship are explicit, as in the case of Stead or Hanson. From Stead: 'This theology therefore uses the term *energy* to stand for operations which are distinct from, and even contrasted with, the *substance* or essential nature from which they proceed; and so necessarily conflict with the Aristotelean formulas taken over by many of the medievals . . . the divine energies are regarded as eternal and unvariant manifestations of God's power . . . This distinction between the intelligible divine energies and the inexpressible substance from which they proceed *became an authoritative portion of later Eastern orthodoxy . . .*' *Divine Substance* (Oxford: Clarendon Press, 1977). 279 (emphasis added). From Hanson: '. . . [Eunomius taught that the] Son is in fact like the Father in will and is the image of his will. It is ironic to observe this extreme Arian heretic *welcoming* the distinction between the *ousia* and the *energeia* of God, a distinction which the Cappadocian fathers warmly embraced and *which was to become an integral part of Eastern orthodox theology.*' *The Search,* 267 (emphasis added). Other authors' references are more discreet, as in this quotation from Lionel Wickham, 'Review of *Eunomius: The Extant Works,* by R. P. Vaggione.' *JTS* 39 (1988), 257: 'As Dr. H. Chadwick once remarked to me, how bizarre it is that all the intense discussion about the divine energies should trace its source to Eunomius and Aetius.'

use of essence and energy as a technical phrase. However, this tradition of scholarship finds the first theological use of this distinction to have been by the Cappadocians, who – it is said – built their theology around this distinction. To give but two examples of this judgement, Vladimir Lossky[37] and George Habra both trace the origin of the essence-energy distinction to the Cappadocians, to Basil in particular. Habra says, for example, 'The Eunomians were rather *embarrassed* by *Basil's distinction* between essence and energy . . . and pretended that the essence of God, being simple, everything that was asserted about God was asserted about his essence.'[38] The understanding that Basil introduced *activity* into the debate with Eunomius is untenable. Eunomius' use of the term antedates any appearance of this language in works by Basil or the two Gregories. The appearance of *activity* in polemical works by Eunomius or the Cappadocians cannot support any claim to originating or even introducing such language into the trinitarian debates. Likewise, only an implicit bias in favour of Aristotlianism supports the reading that *energeia* is used in an Aristotelian sense in Eunomius' writings; the same bias probably accounts for reading *activity* in isolation from the other terms in the causal sequence. An entirely different understanding of Eunomius' causal language is reached if one recognises that *activity* is but one term in a sequence of associated terms.

Galen

When Festugière discusses the origin of the sequence *essence, power, activity* and *product* in the *Corpus Hermeticum* he – correctly – finds precedents in Iamblichus, Alexander Aphrodisias and Tertullian, and – incorrectly – Aristotle.[39] But Festugière does not mention the

---

[37] The first mention of 'energy' *(energeia)* that Lossky treats is the famous quotation from Basil's *ep.* 234, *Letter to Amphilocus.* While Lossky does note Eunomius' use of *energeia,* he leaves the impression that the language is primarily Basil's. He says: 'Eunomius also speaks of operations and calls them *energeia.' The Vision Of God* (Leighton Buzzard: the Faith Press, 1973), 65.

[38] 'The Sources of the Doctrine of Gregory Palamas on the Divine Energies.' *The Eastern Churches Quarterly,* 12 (1958), 244–347; here 298–9 (emphasis added).

[39] *La Révélation d' Hermès Trismégiste,* trans. and comm., R. P. Festugière, 4 vols. (1953;rpt. Paris: Société d' Editions Les Belles Lettres, 1983), III:190, n 1.

medical writings associated with the Hippocratic School. The absence of any reference to Galen is especially surprising. The medical tradition takes on particular importance for our study because Aetius is known to have spent some time as a practising physician: he thus represents a link between the Hippocratic tradition and Heterousian theology.[40] Aetius studied medicine in Alexandria early in the decade of the 340s. To study medicine in Alexandria during the mid-fourth century was to study it according to Galen,[41] i.e., to use Galen's own texts, in combination with the philosophical texts of Plato, Aristotle, and of the Stoics.[42]

For the purpose of this study, Galen's clearest statement of the language of the sequence, *power – activity – product,* is in *On the Natural Faculties*. This sequence of terms is central to Galen's thought as presented in this work.[43] With the sequence he offers a systematic account of the relationship between cause and effect in living organisms, and by extension, in the cosmos. For Galen, any cause must be a power, which is the kind of existent that produces (or receives) specific affects. A power is the source of a particular kind of change. An activity is the means of that change or the change in itself. The result of these changes is the product.[44] Following this reasoning, the power is the cause of the activity, but is also indirectly the cause of

---

[40] Galen's early history of influence among certain Christian groups bears noting. Eusebius says in his *HE* V.28.17, that the followers of Natalius in Rome regarded Euclid, Aristotle, Theophrastus and Galen, who was alive at the time, with 'reverence'. He also says that the theology of these late second century Christians was characterised by a devotion to logic and syllogism. In *Galenism* (Ithaca: Cornell University Press, 1971), 55–6, Owsei Temkin adds that it was Galen's 'example of textual criticism of Hippocratic writings that made them apply criticism to the Scripture.' Eusebius thus describes this early Christian use of syllogistic logic in terms that are very close to the description of the Eunomians soon after him.

[41] Temkin, *Galenism,* 70, and A. Z. Iskander, 'An Attempted Reconstruction of the Late Alexandrian Medical Curriculum.' *Medical History,* XX (1976), 235.

[42] Temkin, *Galenism,* 69.

[43] Galen does use essence in his causality, but the essence is understood to be, in itself, unknowable, and thus not to be considered as a cause. Furley comments that '. . . Galen has said that we say the cause of an activity is a faculty [i.e., *dunamis*] as long as we are ignorant of 'the true essence of the cause'; but there is no reason to suppose that any further and unknown cause is supposed by him to underlie the four [reified, primary] qualities, so they should not be called faculties.' *On Respiration and Arteries,* eds., trans. and comm., D. J. Furley and J. S. Wilkie (Princeton: Princeton University Press, 1984), 64, n 14.

[44] *On the Natural Faculties,* I. II. 7, ed. and trans., A. J. Brock, *The Loeb Classical Library* (1916;rpt. Cambridge: Harvard University Press, 1978), 12–13.

products.[45] The traditional medical illustration of these causal distinctions is the baking of bread. The *power* of heat in the fire transforms the dough into the *product* bread through the *activities* of fermentation and baking.[46]

In Galen's writings there is the suggestion that each power can produce multiple activities, but that each activity has only one effect.[47] Activities which might seem to have multiple effects, such as *genesis* (i.e., gestation), *growth,* and *nutrition,* are actually not simple but are compounds with separate, distinct activities.[48] Moreover, each of these activities has only one effect, though several activities are joined together under one name. *Genesis,* as Galen calls *in utero* gestation, consists of the activities of *alteration and shaping.*[49] *Growth,* which for Galen means specifically the body's growth to maturity, consists of the activities of *increase and expansion.*[50] And *nutrition,* which means the maintenance of the body in a mature state, consists of the two activities, *addition* and *assimilation.*[51] Each of these six activities, like all other activities, may be distinguished by their effects.[52]

The causal sequence serves not only to describe the conceptual stages that answer to Plato's adage in the *Sophist* that everything that exists has the power to affect or be affected (itself an adaptation of Hippocratic causal theory). The sequence also serves as a means for knowing what exists. Products are the signs of certain powers, and each product comes from a specific activity. If one knows the product, one can reason to the power.[53] The causal sequence is thus also a epistemological sequence that describes degrees of knowability.[54] For

[45] ibid., I. IV. 9 (Brock, 16–17).
[46] See *On Ancient Medicine,* 13–14.
[47] *On the Natural Faculties,* I. IV. 10 (Brock, 16–17).
[48] ibid., I. IV. 10; Brock, 18–19: 'Genesis, however, is not a simple activity of nature, but is compounded of alteration and of shaping.'
[49] ibid., I. V. 10 (Brock, 16–17), and I, VI, 11 (Brock, 18–19).
[50] ibid., I. V. 10.16–17, and I.VII.16–18 (Brock, 26–29).
[51] ibid., I. VII. 18 to I.VIII.19 (Brock, 28–31).
[52] ibid., I. V. 10; Brock, 16–19: 'The activities corresponding to the three effects mentioned are necessarily three – one to each – namely, Genesis, Growth, and Nutrition.'
[53] ibid., I. IV. 10 (Brock, 16–17).
[54] Because of the biological nature of the objects of knowledge, *knowability* here means accessibility or visibility. In Galen's system *products* are by definition clearly visible or directly observable.

Galen, the power, which causes the activity, is not as available to knowledge as is the activity, but the activity, which causes the product, is not as available to knowledge as the product. An activity, which is the movement or change of state which produces the effect, can be observed through comparison, as well as directly. The power, the source and origin of the activities, is not observable at all, and is said to exist because it is necessary that each activity proceed from an origin, and that this origin exist as a property or body.[55] Since the effect is material, the cause must be material as well, for the reality of the activity cannot be greater than the reality of the cause. This understanding of power as a property or body means that each specific part or organ in the body has an associated power, and conversely, that each power must exist co-extensively with an organ or part, an understanding common to traditional Hippocratic writings, such as *On Ancient Medicine.*

Clement of Alexandria

Eunomius' understanding of God's activity as a temporary cause whose product ceases when the cause ceases is recognizable in Clement's account of the 'Stoic' distinction between synectic and procatarctic causes. The synectic cause, Clement says, '. . . is that which being present, the effect remains, and being removed, the effect is removed.'[56] Clement associates the term *energeia* with this type of cause, as when he says that the synectic cause is also known as the perfect *(autoteles)* cause, because its *energeia* is sufficient in itself to product the effect.[57] On the other hand, Clement repeatedly describes the proctarctic cause with the term *dunamis,* this cause being the one which if removed the effect remains, and which is capable of producing opposite effects.[58] However, in Eunomius'

---

[55] 'Thus we say that there exists in the veins a blood-making faculty, and also a digestive faculty in the stomach, a pulsitile faculty in the heart, and in each of the other parts a special faculty corresponding to the function or activity of that part.' *On the Natural Faculties,* I. IV. 9–10 (Brock, 16–17).

[56] *Miscellanies* VIII. 9. 33. 1, in *Stromata,* (GCS, Clement, III, 101.18). The translation is from that by A. C. Coxe in ANF II:567.

[57] *Miscellanies* VIII. 9. 33. 2–3, (GCS, Clement, III, 101.19–22).

[58] *Miscellanies* VIII. 9. 33. 1, (GCS, Clement, III, 100.22). *Dunamis* occurs at 31.3 and 32.2.

causality, a single cause cannot produce opposite effects: a given energy can only produce a specific product.[59] This set of causal distinctions gives us one tradition of meaning for the term *energeia* as Eunomius uses it.

There are two occasions in Clement's *Miscellanies* where the language of *essence – power – activity* and *product* seems to be used as a sequence. The first is in *Miscellanies* VII.2, where Clement argues that 'the Son is the Ruler and Saviour of all'. Clement is speaking in particular of the Son as the governor of the universe, and he describes this role of the Son in the language of power, activity and product.[60] The chapter continues with Clement speaking of the Son as power and activity with greater detail, including a reference to the Son as Wisdom and Power of God.[61] Because the Son is the Father's Power, Clement says, he existed before the production of all things since, one assumes, the capacity to produce necessarily exists before the products themselves. Clement's emphasis thereafter is on the relationship of the Son to these products. For example, because the Son is an activity of the Father, He can never neglect his work, which is humanity.[62] Or again, because the Son is the Father's power he can do what he wills to do, and is never cut off from any part of the universe, for it is a specific feature of the 'highest Power' to govern every part of the universe.[63]

The second use of the sequence *essence – power – activity* and *product* is more clear and compact than the first. In *Miscellanies* VIII.4 Clement distinguishes the different kinds of knowledge in terms of essence, power, activity and product.[64] The organic application of the sequence in this passage is obvious, and is reminiscent of Galen's account of the sequence, not only in *On the Natural Faculties* but also in a psychological work like *On the Doctrines of Hippocrates and Plato*. Clement's use of the sequence repeatedly turns to distinctions among *living things:* whether the fetus

---

[59] Gregory discusses this aspect of Eunomius' thought at GNO I 72.26–73.3 and 140.3–7.

[60] *Miscellanies* VII.2. 4 (GCS, Clement, III, 5.24–25).

[61] ibid., VII. 7.10–11 (GCS, Clement, III, 7.4).

[62] ibid., 7.20–22, (GCS, Clement, III, 7.7).

[63] ibid., 8.10–12, (GCS, Clement, III, 8.1).

[64] ibid., VIII.4. 9. 1–5 (GCS, Clement, III, 85.3–12).

is an animal, for example, or the different classifications of life among Plato, Aristotle and the Stoics.[65]

The more general application of the sequence in *Miscellanies* VIII.4 (namely, the use of this language to distinguish kinds of knowledge) is similar to the language Eunomius will use to distinguish types of knowledge. At the end of *Miscellanies* VIII.4, Clement summarises the different kinds of questions one can ask: the first question is asked when the essence is known, but one or more of its products is unknown; while the second kind is asked when the *products [erga]* or *properties [pathé]* are known, while the *essence* is not.[66] (Clement's example of such a case is, interestingly, the case of our ignorance of where the *hegemonikon* is in the body, i.e., in what *part* of the body it is.) Eunomius, by contrast, speaks of two ways by which we may discover what we seek: the first is by examining the essences themselves, the second is by examining the effects of the activities.[67] In the *Second Apology* Eunomius re-states the two methods somewhat more directly: in the first method one begins with the essences, by which knowledge of the activities is gained; and in the second method, one begins with the activities in order to gain knowledge of the essences.[68] Clement is stating what we can recognise as the precedent for Eunomius' own methodology, and in so doing shows that this kind of speculation was already in the Christian tradition well before Eunomius.

Origen

The most influential early Christian use of the sequence *power – activity – product* is Origen's. While Clement is an earlier Christian precedent, Origen represents a more authorative and influential source of philosophy and theology for those later Christian authors involved in the trinitarian controversies of the fourth century, especially those with clear ties to his theology, such as Eusebius of Caesarea and Gregory of Nyssa. Origen's writings thus represent a logical occasion for use of the sequence, as well as being both an important witness to the contemporary (particularly Alexandrian) use

[65] ibid., VIII.4. 10. 2–5 (GCS, Clement, III, 85.28–86.6).
[66] ibid., VIII.4. 14. 4 (GCS, Clement, III, 88.26–30).
[67] *Apology* 20.5–11.
[68] GNO I 73 8–13.

of the sequence, and an important source to communicate the technical language (if not the sequence itself) to later authors.

Origen uses power and activity in his exegesis of Wisdom 7:25–26 in *On First Principles* to describe the Son's unity with the Father. The Son is the breath, the power, the emanation, etc., of the Father, and each of these terms describes a form of unity with the Father. Origen considers each of these terms in some detail, and gives particular attention to power. He offers his own definition of *power*, which governs his understanding of its meaning in Wisdom 7. He says:

> Therefore one must understand God's power as that by which he has strength, as that by which he both begins and holds together and governs all things visible and invisible, as that by which he is sufficient for all things, whose providence he wields, in all of which he is present as if united to them. [69]

Origen next focuses on the use of activity in the Wisdom 7:25–26, i.e., 'the *working* of God,' and again offers his own definition.

> Therefore one must understand beforehand the activity of the power, what it is that it is concerned with; which is a certain strength, so to speak, through which the Father works whenever he creates or foresees or judges, or disposes and arranges each individual thing in its own time. [70]

Origen here links activity to power, and gives priority to power by saying 'the activity *of* the power,' though the Wisdom text does not require or even suggest any such relationship between the two terms.

It is possible to see in Origen's definition of *activity* the notion of the associated category, *products* (if not its implicit use). While there is no sign of the term in the definition of activity in the Latin translation, it appears when Origen goes on in the same paragraph to discuss the unity of activity between the Father and the Son, and refers to John 5:19 as a proof-text.[71] Origen seems to be intent on including the notion of products in his discussion. Since Wisdom 7:25 does not provide the term, he turns to John 5:19 where *erga* is used, though *energeia* is not. However, the text does use *poieo*, which is understood to be a synonym for *energei*.[72] *Energeia* does not appear

---

[69] *Peri Archon*, I.2.9, 275–279 (SC 252 130).

[70] ibid., I.2.12, 411–416 (SC 252 138).

[71] ibid., 426, 437. and 439 (SC 252 140).

[72] The free movement from noun to verb (or vice versa) on the basis of the common root (*energeia* to *energei*, *poiema* to *poieo*) is a common interpretive technique for the era.

anywhere in the passage, but Origen can safely assume it to be understood from its synonym *poieo;* the assumption that *energeia* and *poiema* are synonyms can be found in Galen as well, and illustrates the non-Aristotelian understanding of the two terms.[73] Thus, with John 5:19 linked to Wisdom 7:25, the causal series is complete: *dunamis, energeia (poiema),* and *erga.*[74]

The other evidence for an association of activity with products in Origen's text is to be found in his definition of activity. When discussing activity Origen seems to be using the distinction between activity and effect associated with, for example, Galen. In Origen's definition, activity has an instrumental sense: it is that *by which* something is produced or done, i.e., that by which there is an effect. Activity is not an effect: it is not that which is produced or done. Thus, the final category which Origen assumes, but does not name, is product, that which is produced or done.

We should also note Origen's understanding that insofar as God's productive capacity exists, it is productive; and since God was never without this capacity, He was always productive, and thus the eternal existence of the Son is demonstrated. This is, of course, a famous and much commented upon aspect of Origen's thought, to which I only hope to add that Origen and Eunomius thus argue with a similar logic to opposite conclusions. If, as both agree, the productive capacity and the product exist co-extensively in time, then either the capacity and its product are eternal, as Origen concludes, or the capacity and its product are temporary, as Eunomius concludes. Neither acknowledges the possibility that a capacity may exist without a product. Origen's conclusion finds expression in his emphasis on the *power* in describing the source of the Second Person;

---

[73] Galen's understanding of *energeia* and *poiema* as synonyms is noteworthy, for it shows that *energeia* had no particular Aristotelian content to it (or, that Galen was implicitly denying the claim of an Aristotelian content). In *On the Doctrine of Hippocrates and Plato,* VI. 1.24–27, Galen mentions Plato's use of *energeia,* and gives references to this effect, including *Republic* IV, 437b4– c10. In fact, Plato does not use *energeia* in this passage, but *poiema.*

[74] Origen may have been encouraged in this endeavour by the fact that the next association of *dunamis* and *energeia* in Wisdom occurs at 13:4, where the author also uses *ergon* repeatedly, i.e. 13:1, 13:7, 13:10 and 13:12. The continuity is power, working, and works. *Ergon* does appear in Wisdom 7:16 near where there are references to *energeia* (7:17) and *dunamis* (7:20), but there is no strong sense of continuity among the terms in this passage.

Eunomius' conclusion finds expression in his emphasis on the *activity* in describing the source of the Second Person.

Julian's Theology of Essence, Power, Activity and Product

The sequence *essence, power, activity* and *product* is found in the writings of the Emperor Julian, a contemporary of both Eunomius and the Cappadocians, and who seems to have known Aetius.[75] Julian's use of the sequence essence – power – activity – products is a result of his schooling in Iamblichean philosophy.[76] One connnection between Heterousian theology and Iamblichean philosophy is their common centre at Antioch: this city served as a centre of both early and mature Heterousian theology, and, from the time of the 320s, as the home of Iamblichus, and remained, after his death, the site of the school which he founded.[77]

At least three texts by Iamblichus use a causal sequence similar to Eunomius'. In the first text, the *Commentary on the Alcibiades,* Iamblichus remarks that our perception of the demons is through their energies, 'of which the powers are the immediate sources.'[78] Iamblichus adds that '. . . a power is a median between an essence and an activity, put forth from the essence on the one hand, and itself generating the activity on the other.'[79] Iamblichus concludes that the essence of superior beings is extremely difficult for humans to know, and thus that the object of human knowledge is rather the *power* of such beings. The powers themselves are known through the activities.[80] In the second text, the *De Mysteriis,* Iamblichus rebukes Porphyry for failing to distinguish between the essences, powers, and activities of demons.[81] In the third text, the *Commentary on de Anima,*

---

[75] Kopecek, *Neo-Arianism,* 113 and 140. John Rist, however, disagrees. See his 'Basil's 'Neoplatonism': its Background and Nature' originally published in *Basil of Caesarea: Christian, Humanist, Ascetic,* ed. Paul J. Fedwick (Toronto: Pontifical Institute of Mediaeval Studies, 1981), 137–220. The article was later reprinted in Rist's collection *Platonism and its Christian Heritage* (London: Variorum Reprints, 1985), 137–220. In either edition the mention by Rist of Aetius and Julian is on 188.

[76] Julian studied under Eusebius of Pergamum and Maximus of Ephesus who were both students of Aidesius of Pergamum, who was a student of Iamblichus.

[77] *In Platonic Dialogos Commentariorum,* ed., trans. and comm., John M. Dillon, (Leiden: E. J. Brill, 1973), 11.

[78] *In Alcibides,* Fragment 4.84, 13–14, Dillon, 74–5.

[79] ibid., lines 14–16.

[80] ibid., lines 6–13.

[81] ibid., Dillon, 49.

Iamblichus organises his entire discussion of the soul according to the sequence essence, power, activity, and product. In each case, the causal sequence serves an epistemological function: the causal relationship that exists between a power and a product, for example, serves as the foundation for knowledge proceeding from product to power.

For this study, the most interesting of Julian's writings is his *Hymn to King Helios*, written in late 361 or early 362. This date makes it contemporary to the *Apology*, which is dated sometime between late 359 and 365, but usually in the winter of 359/360. *The Hymn* uses the sequence essence, power, activity, and product to describe the Sun God, and thus provides evidence of the Pagan use of these terms in the period contemporary to Eunomius. In the *Hymn* Julian says that one could never investigate or name all the powers of God,[82] but that among the more important ones are: dominion over the intelligible realm; the revelatory power through which the divine essence is manifested in the creation of the immaterial realm;[83] imperishabilty, which is associated with the power of singleness of thought;[84] another power which is the cause of separation in all that exists.[85] Finally, there is the power which holds all existence in harmony.[86] The activities cause beauty, intellect and order to exist in generated entities,[87] while products are the beauty, intelligence, and order that exist in generated entities or are themselves like generated entities. Like Eunomius, Julian often does not separate activity from product in his examples: activity is the production of a quality or type of existence, and products are the works within which this quality of type of existence is found.

Julian focuses most of his attention on the powers of King Helios, and he has less to say about the activities or products (or the essence for that matter). One reason for this emphasis on the power is that Julian believes that there is a continuity or attribution throughout the

---

[82] *Oration IV: Hymn to King Helios*, ed. and trans. W. C. Wright, vol. 1, *The Works of the Emperor Julian*, 4 vols., *The Loeb Classical Library* (1913;rpt. Cambridge: Harvard University Press), 141C:4–7 (384–5).

[83] ibid., 143C: 3–4 (Wright, 390–1).

[84] ibid., 144C: 2–4 (Wright, 392–3).

[85] ibid., 144C: 4–6 (Wright, 392–5).

[86] ibid., 143C: 8–D7 (Wright, 390–1).

[87] ibid., 145A: 8–D6 (Wright, 394–7).

sequence, and this continuity means that what is said of one division is true of them all. That is, whatever characteristic is attributed to the essence exists (in some way) throughout the causal sequence. For example, the essence is said to be intelligent; there is a power of intellect; intellect produces activities; activities produce existents which are intelligent and intelligible.

This unity of attribution throughout the sequence of essence, power, activity, and product is explained by Julian in terms of the efficient movement of a single, simple will.[88] In order to relate the continuity throughout the levels of attribution to the movement of the will, Julian restates each substantive as a verb, which expresses an action of the will. *Ousia, dynamis,* and *energeia* are each restated as verbs: *esti, dynatai,* and *energei.*[89] This restatement makes clear the dependence of each term in the sequence on the generating will. In Julian's view, any lack of continuity of attribution of quality throughout the sequence means that the will is either not simple, or not omnipotent. Neither of these alternatives is acceptable. The simplicity of the will does not require that there be no outward motion, but only that there be but one motion outward, manifesting itself on each of the different levels in the sequence. For Julian that will is 'essential,' while for Eunomius the will cannot be essential. Indeed, the purpose of Eunomius' doctrine of *production by the will* (or activity) is to provide a non-essential productive cause. Here we find a clear difference between Julian's understanding of the causality described by the sequence and Eunomius': for Eunomius attributes of the essence do not apply to the activity and products. Eunomius' causal hierarchy is designed to deny any such continuity of attribution, so as to preserve the unique nature and status of God, the Unbegotten.

Thus, the presence of *power* in the received sequence *essence – power – activity – product* possess several difficulties for Eunomius. First, the sequence tends to be used with the understanding that essence is not entirely or certainly available for direct knowledge; power is regularly used as a mediating category for knowledge of the essence. Second, the causal capacity of the essence is understood to be contained within or by the power. Third, the existence of the power

[88] ibid., 142C: 3–4 (Wright, 388–9).
[89] ibid., 142D: 2–4 (Wright, 388–9).

does not fluctuate, and is not temporary, but is continuous with that of the essence. In short, power, in this sequence, presupposes and describes a causality which is neither optional nor accidental to the essence. Power is the natural expression of the essence, as it must be if it is to serve as the source of knowledge about the essence (as it does for Galen or Gregory of Nyssa).

This kind of causality is directly contrary to Eunomius' theology: he needs a causal sequence which describes an optional causality of temporary duration, with a product of dissimilar nature. Such a product is not burdened with the epistemological task of presenting the essence for knowing; the product need only indicate the dignity of the producer. By dropping the term *power* from the sequence, Eunomius reduces the causal possibilities to one: synectic. At this point Eunomius' doctrine of the kind of unity between God and the Son corresponds exactly with his understanding of the degree of unity between the Divine nature and the Divine causal capacity. Given that Divine causality is extra-natural and does not proceed from a power, any product of that causality will *per force* lack a common nature with its cause. By separating cause from essence, Eunomius' activity-based causality likewise separates the nature of the product from the nature of the original essence. This rather dry sounding insight translates doctrinally into an argument for the dissimilar (indeed, wholly different) natures of God and the 'Son'.

Chapter 11

THEOLOGY AS GRAMMAR: NAZIANZEN AND WITTGENSTEIN

Frederick W. Norris

Studies of philosophical positions in the fathers are at their best when backgrounds to specific arguments form the focus. For example, Raoul Mortley has provided striking new insights into the debate about the meaning of *agennetos* among the Neo-Arians and the Cappadocians, insights gained from philosophical discussions contemporary with those fourth-century debates.[1] What I propose here is the more dangerous type of comparison, that is, how certain philosophical positions within the work of an ancient writer relate to those of a modern figure. The landscape is littered with the bones of such comparisons. They often die because too little attention is paid to the differences between ancient and modern times. In terms of the present concerns it is important to notice that discussions of religious language during the ancient period often considered the existence of

---

[1] Raoul Mortley, *From Word To Silence: The Way of Negation: Christian and Greek,* 'Theophaneia, 31' (Bonn, 1986), Vol. II, 130–9, particularly on the basis of Dexippus (CAG IV. 2, 44), Syrianus (CAG IV, 61) and Alexander of Aphrodisias (CAG I, 327) has added some new and important wrinkles concerning the Eunomian understanding of *agennetos,* 'unbegotten.' In his view, they employed it as an ultimate negation, a way of reaching the 'truest essence of a thing,' not as a privative name referring to the absence of something that already existed (like Aristotle's example of blindness being the privation of sight). Mortley finds these interpretations of Aristotle's *Categories* to be new and interesting. Thus he sees the Neo-Arian position as quite bright and the Cappadocians' interpretation as rather dull, lacking philosophical sophistication.

Mortley's insights do point up the significance of Gregory Nazianzen's unusual rejection of the *via negativa* (*Oration* 28.9), one that is probably a rejection of that Neo-Arian understanding. The Cappadocians appear to use the Ephectic tradition within Scepticism (cf. Diogenes Laertius 9.70) which looks at Aristotle's *Categories* through Plato and Plotinus in such a way that the generation of the Son could occur without beginning and thus the begotten could be co-eternal with the unbegotten. It is the historian Socrates (*HE* 2.35) who apparently read the Cappadocians as operating from that tradition. In that same passage he also talks about the Neo-Arian misunderstanding of Aristotle's *Categories* and thus views the Cappadocian position as properly philosophically sophisticated.

some deity or deities as established although they might be marked by the claim that talk of divine nature had to deal with the inexpressible. In the philosophical circles of postenlightenment modernity the existence of any god has often been denied or at least not taken for granted.[2] Gregory Nazianzen always thought proper religious language referred to God; Ludwig Wittgenstein apparently could concede that God-talk had meaning within certain language games, but he seems to have been less convinced that such words had a referent in reality. Some interpret his advice to be silent when one cannot speak clearly as the most appropriate comment about religion.[3] Yet within limits, comparisons of ancient and modern positions do have merit. My primary interest is in showing that significant views of religious language found in the Theological Orations of the philosophical rhetorician, Gregory Nazianzen, are similar to those of the linguistic analyst, Ludwig Wittgenstein.

Gregory's views of religious or theological language are so intertwined with those of his opponents, the Neo-Arians, that the positions of each must be surveyed in order to understand those of the other. For Nazianzen and the Neo-Arians one of the central issues of the debate is the nature of any language. The Theologian views language as conventional, not natural. Nazianzen follows Aristotle[4] rather than Plato[5] as the Eunomians do. Names of things are contrived, given to them by the humans doing the naming. They have no special connection to the essence of the thing named. We know about animals called dogs and creatures that swim called dogsharks. We have no way of distinguishing which one of these beings best deserves the name 'dog'. There is certainly nothing so

---

[2] See the warning of Frances Young, 'The God of the Greeks and the Nature of Religious Language,' in *Early Christian Literature and the Classical Tradition: In Honorem Robert M. Grant*, 'Théologie historique, 54' (Paris: Éditions Beauchesne, 1979), 45 and 73. Her presentation deals with the problems in the writings of both Gregory of Nazianzus and Gregory of Nyssa. I discovered her article after this essay had been drafted and am most pleased that my efforts turn out to be a variation on the themes she mentions on 72–3.

[3] *The Lectures and Conversations on Aesthetics, Psychology and Religious Belief*, ed. by Cyril Barrett (Oxford: Basil Blackwell, 1966) are taken from student notes that are at times illegible and were never reworked by Wittgenstein. But the two points made here do appear in those student notes (esp. 59–60) and are some of our better leads to Wittgenstein's thought about religion.

[4] Aristotle, *On Interpretation* 16A–B.

[5] Plato, *Cratylus* 430A–431E.

similar about both of them that they should be referred to as dogs or anything so different about them that only one deserves to be named a dog. 'Dog' does not name their shared essence or their differentiated natures.[6]

In a similar view of names, the Theologian concedes that calling God the Father 'unbegotten' is true enough, but only one of a number of appropriate conventional names, not the self-revealed designation of God's specific nature. According to Gregory, the Neo-Arians make a category mistake when they use an alpha privative – and then just one of the many alpha privatives available – to designate the essence of God. Furthermore, no connection is to be made between the names of things and God's revelation because language is not a revelational gift of God,[7] even though Clement of Alexandria and Origen so described it.[8]

It is the pragmata, the facts, that must be looked for, not some kind of magical names that reveal essences or subtle negations that pretend to say something when in fact they say nothing.[9] Theology can gain much from being apophatic, but in the end it cannot operate completely in that mode. It must attempt to say what its subject is. Two times five can be represented as 'not two, not three, not four,' etc., but eventually it is clearer to answer 'ten.' Using a negative word like 'unbegotten' as the name of God says what he is not, not what he is.[10]

Thus Scripture can speak of God as 'theos' or 'the One,' positive answers to the question of who God is.[11] But having those affirmations in the Bible does not mean that names which explain God's essence are present there in Scripture or elsewhere. The real nature of God is incomprehensible. It is not a matter, as it was for Plato,[12] that the nature of deity is inexpressible. A charlatan might claim to know God's essence, but not put it into words that you could

---

[6] Or. 29.14 (PG 36 92B–93A).

[7] Or. 28.9 (PG 36 36C–37B). Or. 29.12 (PG 36 88B–89C).

[8] Clement of Alexandria, Stromata 1.143.6 (GCS II. 89). Origen, Contra Celsum 1.24 (GCS I. 74).

[9] Or. 29.13 (PG 36 92A). Or. 30.20 (PG 36 129A–132A). Or. 31.7, 9, 20–21 (PG 36 140C–141A, 141C–144A, 156A–157A).

[10] Or. 28.9 (PG 36 36C–37B). Or. 29.11 (PG 36 88C).

[11] Or. 30.18 (PG 36 125C).

[12] Plato, Timaeus 28E.

understand. The truth is that God's nature cannot be conceived.[13] The Hebrews even wrote God's name with different letters to mark out how superior his nature was to the ordinary alphabet and common words. A barely visible, always partial conception of God can be gained by looking at his attributes, but his essence remains far beyond our ability to conceive of it. The instruments we use for such a task, our minds, are simply too small for the task.[14]

Yet recognizing the limitations of human thought and language does not mean that ordinary language and its rules are in no way analogous to God-talk, to theology. As noted above, when someone is explaining the kind of language necessary to speak of essence, and insists that a particular name has some magical, revealing connection to that nature, a look at the dog and the dogshark, ordinary words and objects, should straighten that out.[15] Most of the examples given below, ones that show Gregory's reliance on grammar and context, are taken from Scripture and everyday language. Exact talk about God breaks out of the bounds of ordinary language because of his deity. All language about him will be sketchy at best. Indeed the language of Scripture and the language of everyday life must be interpreted in one sense within the terms of everyday usage and in another within the community using the words.

When we read, we look for meanings rather than just the specific words themselves; such meanings come from the immediate context.[16] Yet when the pragmata or the meanings become the focus of attention, theology is not a discipline that is amenable to tightly formed positive propositions; syllogisms do not provide its structure.[17] Seldom is language capable of telling us anything definite, particularly about deity. It can represent faintly so that we can understand each other, but never fully.[18] We should, however, have expected as much because language from ordinary life also is not capable of giving us exact names or the clearest pictures. The strongest objections to a Neo-Arian claim that God's nature can be

---

[13] *Or.* 28.4–5 (PG 36 29C–32C).
[14] *Or.* 30.17 (PG 36 125B–C).
[15] *Or.* 29.14 (PG 36 92B–93A).
[16] *Or.* 31.24 (PG 36 160B–C).
[17] *Or.* 28.7 (PG 36 33B–C). *Or.* 31.7–8 (PG 36 140C–141C).
[18] *Or.* 28.4 (PG 36 29C–32A).

named comes from one who knows that all humans have great difficulty coming to know and naming what human nature is and what the essences are that exist in wider nature. People who insist that they know what the name of God's essence is surely can tell us what the essence of human nature and all nature is. And none of them can.[19]

If this conventional view of language is accepted, then the best theologians will be poets who provide us with better images, even a kind of reasoned truth that will help us see a little more clearly into the mysteries.[20] They will have prepared themselves through study and contemplation in order to deal with their difficult topic. They know that not every speaker on every occasion on any theme before each audience can make any kind of sense. Indeed all educated people should know that set of principles.[21]

We should not infer from this discussion, however, that we can avoid the actual wording of Scripture, or that we have no knowledge of God. But we do not know God's nature as well as God does, a claim that some Eunomians may have made.[22] We know about the divine only what God patiently and carefully reveals to us. Viewed from the standpoint of epistemological concerns, all the core of knowledge about God is at best a probability not to be deduced from the word that names the divine essence or induced from a human search for all the relevant data. Thus a number of the most important tenets of theology must be formed through Aristotle's enthymemes when they deal with arguments not amenable to formal demonstration, when they use a two-fold enthymeme – 'if then' or 'it is so because' – that works with problems that do not fit into deductive, syllogistic systems. A good theology will also notice that inductive argument does not lead to irreformable or irrevisable statements.[23]

A developed sense of the limitations of language and a concern for context and grammar lie behind these views. These principles demand

[19] Or. 28.1–31 (PG 36 25C–72C).
[20] Or. 30.17 (PG 36 125B–C). Or. 28.30 (PG 36 69A).
[21] Or. 27.1–10 (PG 36 12A–25A).
[22] Socrates, HE 4.7. Vaggione, 178–179, considers the fragment to be genuine. Lionel Wickham, 'The Syntagmation of Aetius the Anomean,' JTS, n.s. 19 (1968), 565–6, n. 1, does not.
[23] Or. 28.29 (PG 36 68B–C). Or. 29.10–11 (PG 36 85D–89A).

our attention, and helps us understand, as too few textbooks do, that the fourth-century Arian debate focused greatly, perhaps primarily, on the meaning of Scripture. Eunomius certainly did not avoid Scripture. He apparently wrote a commentary on Romans.[24] In his *Apologia* he either cites or alludes to over seventy passages from the Bible to indicate the scriptural basis of his arguments.[25] In perhaps the strangest reference to the Bible, Aetius in his *Syntagmation* claims that all his arguments, which cite no Scripture, actually come from the mind of Holy Writ.[26] Gregory either quotes or alludes to over seven hundred and fifty biblical passages in his five *Theological Orations*.[27]

The point for this particular comparison of Nazianzen and Wittgenstein is that the exchanges between the Theologian and the Neo-Arians are on the basis of an agreed upon collection of texts and thus to a great degree are concerned with the grammatical analysis of those texts. Although there are certainly different assumptions that the Neo-Arian and 'orthodox' communities brought to the texts, much of the work centres on how those passages are to be understood. In fact, Gregory's arguments are based on his belief that his views can explain not only the texts that are basic to his position but also those that the Neo-Arians find to be central to their arguments. That describes the structure of the arguments in *Orations* 29–31.

Most of Nazianzen's biblical citations or allusions are employed in rhetorical paradoxes that emphasise both the human and divine natures of the Son and the oneness of his person, and also in lists that emphasise the divinity of the Spirit. Gregory notes that some in his circle had drawn up such lists where Scripture spoke of the Holy Spirit. He toys with his opponents' insistence that he is bringing into the discussions a strange and unscriptural God, first by developing a theory of revelation and finally by listing over seventy places within Scripture that lead him to view the Spirit as divine.[28] He had centred

---

[24] Socrates, *HE* 4.7.

[25] See the notes in Vaggione, 34–74

[26] Wickham, 'Syntagmation,' 540 and 545.

[27] See my *Faith Gives Fullness to Reasoning: The Five Theological Orations of Gregory Nazianzen,* introduction and Commentary by Frederick W. Norris, translation by Lionel Wickham and Frederick Williams (Leiden: E. J. Brill, 1990). The translation notes the scriptural citations and allusions.

[28] *Or.* 31.1–33 (PG 36 133B–172A).

his arguments about the Son on clusters of biblical passages taken from either the writings or the public views of his opponents and organised for ease of remembrance into ten points.[29] When his attacks are on target they concern grammatical and contextual principles. The biblical nature of the conflict is most clear in these sections.

He refers to his own circle of theologians as philologists.[30] Gregory himself is best described as a philosophical rhetorician whose studies depended so much on the actual language that he was aware of both its fascination and the importance of context for determining the meaning of words. A group of examples make that clear. The Theologian discusses 1 Corinthians 15:25. That verse claimed that the Son must reign 'until the time of restitution.' Not only Neo-Arians but also Marcellus of Ancyra had seen that as a limitation on the Son. But, Gregory responded, almost in the pedantic but careful sense of a scholar who was putting a dictionary together from slips, that the word 'until' may describe only what happens up to a point and denote or connote nothing about what follows that point. For instance Matthew 28:20 reports Jesus as saying that he will be with the disciples 'until' the end of the age. That certainly does not mean that the Lord will no longer be with them after this age is ended. Thus the meaning of the word 'until' does not always limit what follows. The opponents have missed the sense of the passage because they have cited the wrong context. The Son cannot be placed in a second rank because of the word 'until.' Indeed Paul is just as willing to say that Christ will be all in all as he is to say that God will be all in all.

It is obviously true that as the Almighty King, the Son rules over the willing and the unwilling, producing submission in those who willingly submit. But when they have submitted, there is no longer any need for him to produce submission, so that function ceases. In that sense there is an 'until' which designates cessation. The Son does not cease to be King, but he need not make the faithful obey.[31] The point of Gregory's argument is that the wrong list of word usages has been employed, the wrong context inferred.

[29] *Or.* 30.1–15 (PG 36 104C–124B).
[30] *Or.* 30.16 (PG 36 124C).
[31] *Or.* 30.4 (PG 36 108A–B).

In another section Gregory expands this sense of meaning supplied through context by looking at John 5:19: 'The Son can do nothing of himself, but what he sees the Father do.' The Eunomians had employed this verse as clear evidence that the Son was less than the Father. For Gregory, the debate turned on the meaning of the words 'can' and 'cannot.' He suggested that there were five meanings for the word 'cannot,' ones that any good interpreter should have in mind when looking at the text. First, 'cannot' may refer to strength or time, or imply a specific object. A young child cannot be an athlete, but he may grow to be one. A puppy cannot see and cannot fight, but as he grows stronger, he will see and may become quite aggressive. Second, 'cannot' at times means something that is usually true, but may be negated by a different particular. 'A city set on a hill cannot be hidden,' unless the line of sight is blocked by a higher hill. Third, 'cannot' may refer to something unreasonable, such as the friends of the bridegroom fasting while the bridegroom is with them for the celebration. Fourth, 'cannot' may mean an absence of will as when Jesus could do no mighty works in certain cities because of people's unbelief. He was capable but they were not willing. Gregory suggests that perhaps under this rubric one should also mention the things that seem impossible in nature but are possible to God if he wills them. Fifth, there are things that are absolutely impossible such as God being evil or not existing, or for the nonexistent to exist or two and two to make ten, not four.

John 5:19 fits the last category. It states something that is absolutely impossible. The Son will do nothing without the Father. They have everything in common; their being is of the same essence. As John 16:15, 17:10 and 6:57 indicate, the Son lives by the Father, not in the sense that his life is given to him by the Father, but that he has his being from God before all time and beyond all cause. He doesn't do what he sees the Father do as if he is taught like one who learns to copy pictures or the letters of the alphabet. Wisdom needs no teacher. In context the John 5:19 passage means that the Son has the same authority as the Father. It cannot mean that he who is all Wisdom, he who does all these miracles, could not have done them unless his Father had taught him.[32]

[32] *Or.* 30.10–11 (PG 36 113C–117B).

The later Arians fail in their interpretation of the passage because they do not know what possible contexts are involved, ones both from everyday life and from Scripture. They did not look at the various possibilities for the word 'cannot' and they did not use the wider scriptural context which claims first that the Son is of the same nature as the Father. They would then see that John 5:19 means the Son acts with the same authority as the Father.

Nazianzen employs another principle that is determined by bringing possible contexts to the interpretation of the passage. John 6:38 speaks of the Son as having come down from heaven, not to do his own will, but the will of the one who sent him. Certain Eunomians insisted that this pointed up the difference between the Son and the Father; the Son had a will of his own that conflicted with that of the Father. Gregory says this verse means that divine Son has no will of his own, but that he and the Father have the same will. To attest his point he cites common usage which shows that not every negative can be turned into a positive. John 3.34 says God does not give the Spirit by measure and means precisely that. Any positive restatement of the verse distorts its meaning. In Psalm 59:3 the words 'not my transgression nor my sin' and in Titus 3:5 the words 'not for righteousness we have done' also cannot be turned into positives. They do not mean that the author of the Psalm speaks of sin he had done or that the author of Titus meant we had done righteousness. The later Arians are mistaken. John 6:39 means precisely that the divine Son did not have a will of his own, because his divine will was one with that of the Father.[33]

Gregory makes a similar complaint elsewhere. Eunomians have claimed that Scripture speaks of the Father who begot and the Son who was begotten. They see these words as bringing in the idea of a beginning for the generation of the Son because those verbs are in the past tense. Things in the past have begun and stopped. Nazianzen counters their view, noting that verb tenses cannot be determined by the form of the word alone, for Scripture often interchanges tenses. Psalm 2:1 says 'Why did the heathen rage?' when the context indicates they had not yet raged. Psalm 66:6 says 'They shall cross over the river on foot' when it actually means that they had already

[33] Or. 30.12 (PG 36 117C–120B).

crossed the river. Diligent students of Scripture could create a long list of such differences between the tense in the text and the tense that is actually meant. In each case context determines the meaning. So no one can use the past tense of 'begot' and 'was begotten' to prove that the generation of the Son must have had a beginning.[34] Thus for Nazianzen context determines meaning, not some root meaning behind each word or an essence that word names.

Gregory's sense of context goes even further. In a number of places within the *Theological Orations* he voices his concerns about how the Pagan community will understand the theological conversations and debates of Christians. What will they think when they have a deep commitment to polytheism and hear Christians talking about the birth of a God or the Sonship of Christ and the Fatherhood of God? His concern is heightened by his answer that they will supply the various low and bodily or material conceptions of polytheism as the background for understanding the relationship of Father, Son and Holy Spirit, indeed a travesty.[35] It is possible that they might from that standpoint take up the theological discussions within the Christian community and use them to support their rancid views. It would be much better then for both Eunomians and 'orthodox' to talk of theology, not in the salons of women or in the market places, but among carefully selected audiences where there is a possibility of understanding.[36]

Gregory nowhere says explicitly that context and thus meaning is determined by a community and thus has no talk of anything quite like Wittgenstein's conception of 'language games'. Yet I think it a fair inference to say that he sees the Pagan community as having its own vocabulary, its own context, which will distort the meaning of Christian theology. He does not suggest that each community with its own context and language has an equal claim to truth and reality; rather he attacks Pagan talk about deities as unworthy of rational humans and warns that these Pagans are not to be made judges of what Christians talk about.[37] But he is fully aware that no speaker can

[34] *Or.* 29.5 (PG 36 80A–C).

[35] *Or.* 27.6 (PG 36 17C–20A).

[36] *Or.* 27.2 (PG 36 13A–B).

[37] *Or.* 27.6 (PG 36 17C–D). *Or.* 28.13–15 (PG 36 44B–45C). I wonder if the need for a catechetical tradition in classical Christianity and the various levels of participation in the liturgy could not be described in terms of the recognition that the meaning of language is determined by how a community uses its words. If Gregory (and Wittgenstein) have some

speak about every topic on every occasion to every audience.[38] Perhaps it is his concern for audience, which comes from his rhetorical studies, that forces on him the observation that communities use language differently. He knows that he cannot say everything the same way to every audience, for in that case a series of gross misunderstandings would occur. Furthermore the bulk of his orations are set within the liturgical tradition of his congregations and thus lead again to the strong inference that he knows he is operating confessionally within the context of the Christian community. I think it is no accident that most of his orations are liturgical in orientation, rooting the language of the homily in the worship of the community.

It is also the case that the Theologian has a firm grasp of the need to look for analogies, in fact, the hidden analogy. Part of his criticism of the Neo-Arians involves a critique of the pictures their views either entail or imply. Gregory in a sense knows that his major opponents do not employ bodily language when they talk of God, but he is quite concerned that just behind their discussions lies a picture of God with bodily existence. At least he seems to have heard conversations in Constantinople that rely on that analogy for the puzzles they present to his group.[39] He further rehearses some of the points made by his Neo-Arian opponents about the nature of the Son and warns that the conundrum of the Christ being called the Son does not demand that all the names from our world must be imputed to the Godhead. If that principle or analogy were accepted, then it well might involve the silly claims that God is male because the names *theos* and *pater* are masculine. They might even argue that the Spirit is neuter because *pneuma* is neuter, or that the godhead is female because *theotes* is feminine. Such idiocy would not be far from the gnostic myths of many divine generations.[40] Gregory knows that his opponents make no such claims, but he warns that their arguments about the names 'Father' and 'Son' involving necessary subordination is the wrong understanding of how the image or analogy functions. It indicates

merit on these points, it may be important in the contemporary period for churches to understand that they must teach their participants the rules of the game. Neither evangelism nor edification can do without it.

[38] *Or.* 27.3 (PG 36 13C–D).

[39] *Or.* 28.7–9 (PG 36 33B–37B). *Or.* 29.4, 8, 11 (PG 36 77C–80A, 84A–C, 88B–89A).

[40] *Or.* 31.7 (PG 36 140C–141A).

one truth on one level, not a binding principle that means all aspects
of the human name are to be ascribed to the nature of deity.

Positively, he also searches for analogies to describe the sense of
Trinity. He rejects a number of them and proposes two, one the
relationship of Adam, Eve, and Seth, and the other the relationship of
Father and Son to the sun and its light.[41] He looks at three images he
has heard used as an explanation of the Trinity: a spring, a fountain
and a river; the sun, a ray, and light; a ray striking the water and then
reflected to the wall. Then he analyzes both their strengths and
weaknesses, and rejects them all as inadequate.[42]

Wittgenstein, certainly in his later period, never considered
language as anything but ordinary or conventional. There was no
magical relationship between the name of something and its essence
or nature. Names, indeed all words, followed use; It was how words
were used that determined any meaning they might have.[43] In that
sense the language game of a community, the context in which a
group with similar interests employed words, was the important
aspect for determining what was meant. Sentences and paragraphs
speak, but it is the language game of the community which gives
language its sense. And each of the various language games has its
own rules. Individual words taken out of a particular game with its
rules and stuck in another game with different rules will not only
appear odd; they will be quite odd.[44] It is often the case that analyzing
the grammar of statements for the hidden analogy will more quickly
indicate the problems with that statement than any other method.[45]

Wittgenstein thus regularly unpacks various philosophical
problems by looking at the grammar, the way that the words are used
within a language game by a particular community. He attempts to
get at various difficulties through the comparison of how the
important words are used in ordinary language. In discussing the
meaning of 'I know' he notices that the grammar of the word
resembles that of 'I can', 'I am able,' or 'I understand.' To establish
that connection he gives a series of examples both from learning how

[41] *Or.* 31.11 (PG 36 145A–B). *Or.* 29.3 (PG 36 77B).
[42] *Or.* 31.31–33 (PG 36 169A–172A).
[43] Ludwig Wittgenstein (*Philosophical Investigations,* trans. by G. E. M. Anscombe, 3rd
ed. (Oxford: Basil Blackwell, 1967), #49, 55.
[44] ibid., #7, 24, 136, 179, 195, 656.
[45] ibid., #90–91.

to use numbers and other rather ordinary experiences.[46] Even when he gave lectures on religion, a subject or language game that did not make him particularly comfortable, he tried to treat the game fairly and not allow the rules of other games to determine what must be said by those in religious communities and those trying to respond to them from within other communities. He knew that it was not ordinary language, but he did assume that religious language was 'played' by discernible rules and thus he would have to know more about the fuller context before he could talk about what was meant.[47]

The relationship between Gregory Nazianzen and Ludwig Wittgenstein, between the concerns of philosophical rhetoric and linguistic analysis, is striking. Each is convinced that language is conventional rather than natural. Each sees context as determining meaning and notes that context is formed by a community; each looks for the hidden analogy that tends to distort the meaning of the text; each either has been attacked or discounted as being anti-philosophical. But there are significant differences. Nazianzen prefers to use biblical language and analogies when he develops his theology, but he does not find any harm in using ordinary grammar and contexts to sharpen many of his arguments. To put it in more modern language, he does not see theological language and everyday language as separate language games. In important ways Wittgenstein does.

Perhaps when we again learn what philosophical rhetoricians studied and what they offer, we will have a better appreciation of contemporary linguistic analysis, and vice versa.[48] And when those lines of similarity/dissimilarity are drawn, we may have a stronger sense of what hermeneutics might be and thus how to relate scriptural interpretation, theology and philosophy.

[46] ibid., #143–156.

[47] Wittgenstein, *Lectures and Conversations on Aesthetics (Psychology and Religious Belief: Compiled from Notes taken by Yorick Smythies, Rush Rhees and James Taylor,* ed. by Cyril Barrett (Oxford: Basil Blackwell, 1966), esp. 53–59. Norman Malcolm, *Ludwig Wittgenstein: A Memoir* (London: Oxford University Press, 1958), 72 notes that although Wittgenstein himself did not 'participate' in a religion, he was both 'sympathetic' to and 'greatly interested' in the 'possibility of religion' as one 'form of life' or language game.

[48] A careful reading of Stephen Toulmin's *The Uses of Argument* (Cambridge: Cambridge University Press, 1958), a volume greatly informed by Wittgensteinian analysis, along with a good analysis of Aristotle's *Rhetoric* as in William Grimaldi, *Aristotle, Rhetoric I & II: A Commentary* (New York: Fordham University Press, 1980 and 1988) will point up some of these striking similarities.

INDEX OF NAMES

Only footnote references to Athanasius, Epiphanius, Socrates or Sozomen where specific passages are quoted are included in this index.

Antiquity

Modern and Contemporary

INDEX OF SUBJECTS